# Microsoft® Word Made Easy
## for the Macintosh™

### Second Edition

# Microsoft® Word Made Easy for the Macintosh™

## Second Edition

**Paul Hoffman**

Osborne **McGraw-Hill**
Berkeley, California

Osborne **McGraw-Hill**
2600 Tenth Street
Berkeley, California 94710
U.S.A.

For information on translations and book distributors outside of the
U.S.A., please write to Osborne **McGraw-Hill** at the above address.

A complete list of trademarks appears on page 403.

## Microsoft® Word Made Easy for the Macintosh™
## Second Edition

1234567890    DODO    89876

ISBN 0-07-881269-0

# Contents

## Part 4 Advanced Word Features

**Part 5        Appendixes**

# Introducing Microsoft Word

This book will help you master Microsoft Word. It discusses both the essential and unique features of Word and provides practical suggestions for putting Word to work for you. This book supplements Word's documentation, the Microsoft Word reference manual, by showing you in step-by-step fashion how to use Word.

Even though Word's features appear complex, they are relatively easy to master once you understand the concepts behind them. This book is arranged to teach you these concepts in a natural order, and it reinforces the concepts with many practical examples. The examples demonstrate the numerous word processing functions that are performed in a typical business office, although they are just as useful in any situation that requires advanced word processing capabilities.

Each chapter is divided into lessons, which are fully illustrated with pictures of the computer screen so you will know exactly what to expect as you use the program. There are also review exercises at the end of each chapter.

For those of you who have never used a word processing program before, this book explains basic concepts when they first appear in the text. Even if you have used another word processor, you will find that some of Word's features are unique (for example, it can display several parts of a file simultaneously). These, too, are explained in full, so you can completely understand the power of Word. You only need to know the basics of using the Macintosh to use this book; you do not need to be familiar with MacWrite or any other word processor.

This book also contains information that is not covered in your reference manual. For example, Appendix E thoroughly describes how to set up your computer to use Word; Appendix F covers other applications programs that can work with Word.

This book will be useful to anyone who already has Microsoft Word or to someone who is thinking of buying it. Beginning users will find that the lessons are easy to follow and that succeeding lessons build on concepts learned earlier in the book. Medium-level users will find topics that were mentioned briefly in different parts of the reference manual described fully in one place in this book. Advanced users will appreciate the reference material throughout the book, especially in the appendixes.

If you are using a version of Word earlier than 3, you should upgrade your copy. Version 3 has significant new features and improvements to the user interface. Like every program, Word had bugs in its earlier versions, and most of these have been fixed in version 3. Contact Microsoft to determine how you can upgrade to version 3.

# WHAT IS MICROSOFT WORD?

A *word processor* is a computer program that lets you type and save any sort of text (such as memos, letters, reports, and books). Word processors, such as Microsoft Word, let you easily enter text for a document, revise the text once it has been entered (called *editing*), and print the text out on your printer in a professional form (called *formatting*).

There is a wide variety of word processing software available for many different computers. Some software gives you the bare minimum of capabilities, while other programs, like Word, give you many more useful features to make word processing easier.

Word is useful for all types of word processing, such as writing short memos, business letters, financial statements, articles, books, and long reports. It is generally easy to use, and has many advanced features that you can use or ignore, depending on the type of document you are writing. The more you use Word, the more you will find that it helps free you from thinking about what your text will look like, so that you can spend more time concentrating on what you want to say.

# ADVANTAGES OF USING WORD

If you have compared Word to other word processing packages, you know that it has many features that others don't. Of course, having a plethora of features does not make a word processor good: you have to be able to use these features easily. Since most people need a fair amount of explanation to understand the usefulness of Word's features, they are mentioned briefly below, and described in full in the rest of the book.

 Since it is common to make mistakes when you edit text, Word has an "undo" feature that lets you take out your last change. This means that if you do something that you didn't want, you can tell Word to undo it. This feature can save you a great deal of typing and frustration.

If you are ever unsure of what you are doing in Word, the program can always offer help. This prevents you from having to look up information in the reference manual (or in this book) when you just want to know a small bit of information. The help that Word gives you is often more useful than the help you get from other programs, since it first gives you help on what you are currently doing; if you want different information, it is easy to ask for it.

One problem with many word processing programs is that you can only see a small portion of your document at a time. With Word, you can see many parts of the text at the same time in different windows. This feature is very useful when you are writing a long document, since you can look at what you wrote earlier while you write new text. You can even use Word to look at different files on the screen at the same time, and to move text between files.

# USING WORD IN BUSINESS

You have probably heard of the many advantages that word processing offers over normal typing for a business. Since Word has many more features than most other word processors, it lets you do more work more easily. For example:

- Most businesses have form letters (standard letters for which the computer fills in a different name and address), and many word processing packages let you write simple form letters. Word allows you to integrate other information into your form letters, so that the letters look more personalized. Word can also read the names and addresses from datafiles stored by other programs, such as data management systems, and integrate these names and addresses into letters. This feature is often called *mail merge*.

- Word's advanced formatting lets you make reports that look professionally typeset. With Word, you can design each page to your specifications, and not worry about what it will look like if you change some of the text. You can also use printers that print with proportional spacing, to make your printed output look more like typesetting.

- With Word, newsletters and other bulletins can be printed with many columns on one page, giving your writing a more professional look. You can also use many different type styles (such as boldface or italics) so that your headlines stand out from your text.

- Many of Word's features are especially useful in certain professions. For example, Word's ability to number lines on a page is very helpful for lawyers' pleadings and depositions.

- You can use Word to make an outline, then use that outline to prepare a business document. You can have Word automatically number the headings in your outline, and change those numbers as you move or delete headings.

As you read this book, remember that you can always try out the information that is presented to you. Use the files that the book tells you to type in, or create your own; the more you use Word for your own files, the more quickly you will master Microsoft Word.

## NEW FEATURES IN VERSION 3

Microsoft Word version 3 has many features that did not appear in previous versions. These features make Word easier to use and allow you to prepare business documents in a more natural way.

- There are now *style sheets* that make formatting your text much easier and more consistent than previously.

- Version 3 has a sophisticated outline processor that lets you collect your thoughts into easy-to-manage outlines. You can use these outlines directly in preparing documents. You can even number the headings in the outline automatically.

- Word now makes it easy to generate tables of contents and indexes. Using *hidden text,* you can specify any part of your document for inclusion in the table of contents or index.

- Rearranging tables is significantly easier because you can make selections based on columns.

- Parts of your document can be sorted in alphabetical order. For example, if you have a long list of items, you can select that list and sort it easily.

- You can use Word as a minicalculator to perform simple mathematical functions, such as adding a column of numbers.

- Word now allows you to create side-by-side paragraphs. With this function you can format two-column business documents, placing headings on the left and text on the right, for example.

# Getting Started

This chapter explains the few steps you need to follow before you can begin to use Word for your Macintosh and shows you how to start up the program. After following the installation instructions, you can immediately start to edit and format documents; in fact, you will start using Word in Chapter 1 to enter a business letter that will be utilized throughout the next six chapters and in many other sections of the book as well.

If you have no word processing experience, the following section will give you a quick overview of many of the terms you will find in this book. If you are familiar with another word processor, you can probably skim the section.

## WORD PROCESSING TERMS

Word processing programs give you two major capabilities: editing and formatting. *Editing* is the ability to enter text into the program, make corrections, save the text on disk, and later change the text. *Formatting* is the ability to specify how the text will look when you print it out. For example, formatting allows you to add special features to the printout, such as page numbers on each page, and to specify the width of the left and right margins.

In order to make a word processing program work, you give it *commands*, instructions that tell the program what you want to do. In Word, you can give commands by using the mouse or by pressing the *command key* (marked with the ⌘ symbol) and another key at the same time.

When you write a document, you *insert* text into a file. This is done simply by typing the text as you would on a typewriter.

1

Once this has been done, you can use editing commands to correct mistakes or to rearrange the text. While you are editing, you can move around in the text so you can edit different parts. When you want to see text that is not on the screen, the word processing program will *scroll*, or move, the screen to the desired location. When you are done with a file, you can *save* it on disk; when you want to use the file later, you tell the word processing program to *load* it from disk.

If you have entered text that you no longer want in the file, you can *delete* it. Word allows you to delete groups of words or lines easily; for instance, if you want to delete a paragraph, you *select* the paragraph (with a selection command) and then delete it all at once. If, instead, you want to move the paragraph to some other location in the document, you can *cut and paste* the text as if you were using scissors and tape, inserting the paragraph in a new location.

When you write longer documents, you may want to find a specific part of the text so you can edit it. The easiest way to do this is to *search* for a particular word that is in the area you want to edit. Word, like most word processing programs, can also search your entire document and automatically change one set of words to another; this is called *global search and replace*. For instance, if you use one person's name throughout a file and want to change it to another name, you only have to give one search-and-replace command. When you are editing in Word, you normally edit just one file. However, you can edit more than one file at a time by opening a *window*; this is like splitting your screen into two smaller screens.

A word processing program with many formatting features can give you finished copy that looks professionally produced. When you use a typewriter, you often do a great deal of formatting, such as *indenting* the first lines of paragraphs (usually the first five spaces from the left margin) and putting the page number on each page. Word processing programs can do many formatting tasks for you automatically. For instance, if you want to insert a standard line of text at the top or bottom of each page (called a *header* or *footer*), you can tell the program to do that for you.

Like some other word processors, Word lets you use many different styles of characters (or *fonts*) in your text. For example, you can print in *italics*, the font used for introducing terms in this book. Other fonts that you can use in Word are **boldface** and SMALL CAPS. You can also choose any of the fonts available on your Macintosh.

The way you format paragraphs can make a big difference in the appearance of the text. Word allows you to choose *ragged-right* or *justified* margins. Ragged-right text does not line up exactly; justified text lines up at the right margin, like the text in many books and magazines. In addition, any line you want can be *centered* between the margins. This is useful for titles and headings.

When you reach the bottom of a page, you may not want the remainder of a paragraph to appear on the next page; you might prefer to leave extra white space at the bottom and put the full paragraph on the next page. Word allows you to *keep* a paragraph together to make the text more readable, although the pages may have uneven lengths. For aesthetics, it is usually sufficient to prevent *widows* and *orphans*, and Word automatically does this for you. When the last line of a paragraph is typed at the top of a new page, it is called a widow; an orphan is the first line of a paragraph typed at the bottom of a page with the rest of the paragraph typed on the next page.

## PREPARING FOR WORD

The Word program comes on a disk containing the programs and special files needed for running Word; this is called the *Master Disk*. Follow the directions titled "Personalizing Your Master Disk" at the beginning of the Word manual, which tell you how to put your name on the Master Disk and on all copies that you make. If your copy of Word is owned by your company, you may want to use your company's name instead of your own.

Next, copy the Master Disk and label the copy *Program Disk*. You will use the Program Disk instead of the Master Disk to start Word. Since you cannot know when a disaster may strike, put the Master Disk in a safe place, preferably far away from the computer; if there is a fire or your Program Disk is stolen, you can use the Master Disk. You may also need the Master Disk if you accidentally erase some important files from your Program Disk, since you cannot write-protect it.

You should have a few initialized diskettes for storing the text that you enter. If you have a hard disk, you do not need these diskettes, since you can keep everything on the hard disk.

## STARTING THE WORD PROGRAM

You start Word in much the same way you start other Macintosh application programs. Boot your Macintosh from the Program Disk; to start editing a new file, simply double-click the Word icon, as in Figure GS-1. To edit a Word file that is on the disk, such as the Inventory file, double-click that file's icon. Remember to start Word from your Program Disk, not from the Master Disk.

## GIVING WORD COMMANDS

As soon as Word is loaded, it is ready for you to start entering text. Near the upper-left corner, the blinking vertical bar is where the first letters you type will appear. This bar is called the *insertion point*, just as it is in the Finder. Figure GS-2 is a quick reminder of what the parts of the screen are called; most of it will already be familiar to you.

When you first start Word, your screen may look slightly different than the one shown in Figure GS-2. If you only see one

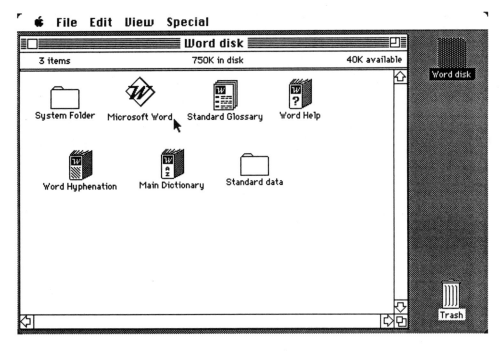

**Figure GS-1** *Starting Word*

rectangle in the lower left of the screen and no split bar in the upper right part, it is because you are using a feature called *short menus.*

Microsoft included short menus in order to allow Word to look like Apple's MacWrite, which has many fewer features than Word. Although short menus have clear, simple screens, they offer fewer choices and have limited usefulness.

To switch from short menus to full menus, give the Full Menus command from the Edit menu. In case you are unfamiliar with how to give commands on the Macintosh, this procedure is covered in the next section. After you choose full menus, Word will start up with full menus the next time you run it.

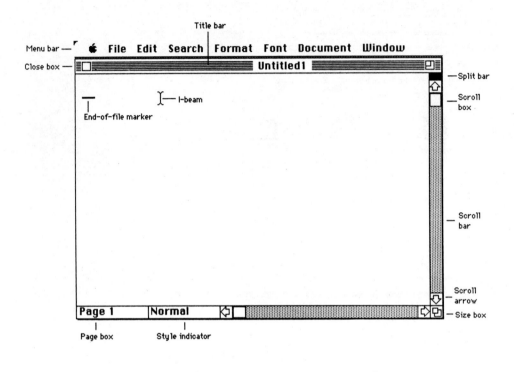

**Figure GS-2**    *The parts of the screen*

Word may also show you a character that is not in Figure GS-2. The top part of your screen may look like Figure GS-3. The character to the right of the insertion point is a paragraph marker, described later in this chapter. Like short menus, it is not often useful. To clear it from the screen, give the Hide ¶ command in the Edit menu. Word will also remember this setting the next time you start it.

You can type just as you would on a typewriter. To start experimenting, type the following words: **This is just like a**

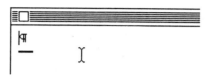

**Figure GS-3**   *The paragraph marker*

**typewriter.** If you make a mistake as you type, you can use the BACKSPACE key to erase the letter (or letters) you just typed.

It is important to understand the difference between the arrow pointer, the I-beam, and the insertion point. The arrow pointer and the I-beam are both mouse pointers; as you move from a command or window control area to the text area, the pointer changes. When you click the I-beam, Word puts the insertion point in the place where you clicked; however, the insertion point does not move as you move the mouse around your desktop. The insertion point simply tells you where the next letter you type will appear in your text.

Now move the I-beam to different parts of the text and experiment with clicking and dragging. Notice that the darkened rectangle moves to the left and right. The rectangle is the *selection indicator*, which is described in detail later in this chapter. The thick underline is a marker that shows you the end of the text and is sometimes called the *end-of-file marker*.

So far, you have only entered text, not edited it. To edit the text, you have to give Word commands. There are two ways to give commands: with the mouse and with the keyboard. As you learn Word, you will usually give commands with the mouse, not the keyboard. Later, you will probably use a mixture of mouse and keyboard commands.

## Giving Commands With the Mouse

The mouse is a simple tool used for pointing at parts of the screen. As you have seen in other Macintosh programs, moving the mouse around on your desk moves the pointer; but this never executes a command. To tell Word that you want to do something with a piece of information, you must point the mouse at the information and click, double-click, or drag the pointer.

Microsoft designed Word so that you can use it without a mouse if you have an extended keyboard, such as the one on the Macintosh Plus. However, the method you must use to do this is so convoluted that it is unlikely you will want to. If you are interested in using Word without a mouse, see the Keyboard section of the Word manual.

It may take some practice to get used to pointing with the mouse; a common mistake is to click the button so hard that you move the mouse, with the result that the pointer is no longer exactly where you want it on the screen. When you point at information on the screen, it is the tip of the arrow or the middle of the I-beam, not the whole pointer, that Word uses to determine what you are pointing at. If you slowly move the pointer to the left border of the screen, you will see the shape change to an arrow pointing up and to the right.

As you use the mouse, you will find that your coordination will quickly get better. As practice, first move the mouse on your desktop so that the I-bar is between the letters "j" and "u" in the word "just" that you typed (as in Figure GS-4).

If you see an arrow instead of an I-beam, you are pointing above the letters. When you see the I-beam, click the button on the mouse and drag the pointer to the right. The selection indicator (shown by the highlight) now covers the letter "u" and the insertion point disappears. This is shown in Figure GS-5.

You have now given a selection command; that is, you have selected a portion of text. Whenever you give Word commands that have an effect on text in your file, the effect is only on the

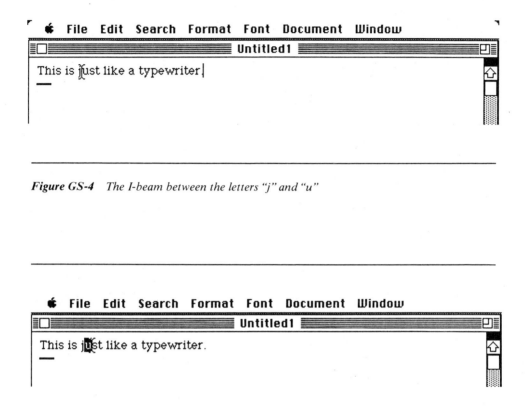

**Figure GS-4**   *The I-beam between the letters "j" and "u"*

**Figure GS-5**   *The letter "u" selected*

selected text. You can have anywhere from one character to the whole document selected at any time. The text that is highlighted is the text that is currently selected (in this case, the "u").

You have just seen how to select a single character with the mouse. Now, without moving the mouse, double-click on the word "just" (as shown in Figure GS-6). The selection indicator

**&#xF8FF;   File   Edit   Search   Format   Font   Document   Window**

Untitled1

This is ▓just▓ like a typewriter.

*Figure GS-6*   *The word "just" selected*

stretches to show that you have selected the whole word. Now press the COMMAND key while you click once, and the whole sentence is highlighted, indicating that it has been selected (see Figure GS-7).

You cannot move the mouse pointer completely off the screen. A bit of the pointer will always show on the screen, even if it is near the edge of the screen. You can move the pointer to the middle of the screen again by simply moving the mouse around your desktop.

Remember that Word never executes a mouse command until you click the button. In different parts of the screen, clicking and double-clicking the button have different meanings (as summarized in Appendix C).

Once you have selected some text, you can move the I-beam and the text will remain selected. Word will not change anything until you click the button on the mouse. You change the selection by moving to some new text and clicking; this removes the previous selection and sets the insertion point. You can make only one selection or have only one insertion point at a time.

The Word menus are listed at the top of the screen. To see the submenus you point at the names, just as you do with other

Macintosh software. Move to the letter "u" in "just" again and double-click the mouse so that the word "just" is selected. Now move to the word "Edit" in the menu bar and drag down to the word "Cut." Release the button, and the word "just" will disappear from the text (see Figure GS-8).

You have now executed the Cut command on the selected text. This is the most common way you will execute Word commands.

**Figure GS-7**   *The whole sentence selected*

**Figure GS-8**   *Removing the word "just"*

To see how Word inserts text, type the word "not" followed by a space. Word moves all the text after the insertion point to the right of your new characters. You always insert text at the insertion point, as shown in Figure GS-9.

## Giving Commands From the Keyboard

In Word you use the COMMAND-key combination to give commands in much the same way as you do with other word processing programs for the Macintosh. Note that Word does not use a cursor to identify text; there are no cursor control keys. However, you will often use other special keys, such as the TAB key, the RETURN key, the ENTER key, the OPTION keys, and the BACKSPACE key. The keys used for giving commands are shown in Figure GS-10. If you have one of the newer keyboards with the numeric keypad and direction keys, your keyboard layout is slightly different (see Figure GS-11).

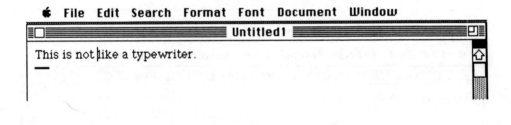

*File Edit Search Format Font Document Window*

Untitled1

This is not like a typewriter.

**Figure GS-9**  *The word "not" inserted*

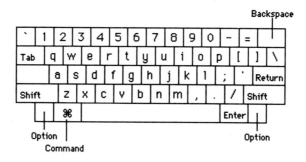

**Figure GS-10**   *Special keys on the small Macintosh keyboard*

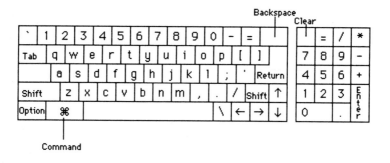

**Figure GS-11**   *Special keys on the Macintosh extended keyboard*

It is to your advantage to learn how to use both the mouse and the keyboard. You will find that using the keyboard is faster than using the mouse for some commands (such as Paste and Cut).

## ENTERING NORMAL TEXT

As you have seen, Word lets you enter text in a fairly normal fashion. When you type in text, you can correct typing mistakes by pressing the BACKSPACE key to erase the character to the left of the selection. If you later move the selection indicator to an error in the text you did not catch immediately, you can also use the Cut command to delete the selected characters.

Word treats all characters in your document, whether they are letters, numbers, or symbols, the same. The following sections discuss special symbols (for paragraphs and spaces) that Word treats as characters. Like normal text, you can insert them when you enter new text or when you edit.

### Making Paragraphs in Word

In your text, each set of lines that is grouped as a unit is called a *paragraph*. This is, unfortunately, easy to confuse with the definition of a paragraph that you learned in grammar school, which is a group of sentences developing an idea. In Word, a paragraph is really just a line or group of lines that appear visually to be an independent unit. For instance, in a business letter, the line with the date, the lines that show the recipient's address, and the line with the salutation are all paragraphs, as is each group of sentences in the letter. When you see the word "paragraph" in this book and the Microsoft Word reference manual, it will refer to Word's definition.

Word identifies the end of a paragraph by a special mark that it puts in your text when you press the RETURN key. For this reason, you do not use the RETURN key at the end of each line inside a paragraph. One of Word's features that makes typing much easier is automatic *wordwrap*, which eliminates the need to decide where to end each line. As you type in a paragraph, Word automatically figures out where to start a new line. You only press RETURN at the end of the paragraph.

If you want to force Word to start a new line within a paragraph (but not start a new paragraph), hold down the SHIFT key while you press the RETURN key. This key combination is called NEWLINE, and it lets you make lines of different lengths within a paragraph that are not like the lines of a paragraph made with wordwrap. The reason that you would use NEWLINE instead of starting a new paragraph is that many of Word's formatting commands pertain to the whole paragraph. If you signal a paragraph with RETURN, you have to format it; if you use NEWLINE, you only need to format the whole paragraph once.

A good example of using NEWLINE is in typing the recipient's address in a letter. You will learn in Chapter 13 how to see the difference between the end of a paragraph and NEWLINE; for now, it is not important.

## Nonbreaking Spaces

A nonbreaking space acts like a piece of glue between two words and prevents wordwrap from placing them on different lines. For example, it is common typing practice not to leave a short abbreviation at the end of a line. Instead of having text look like this —

> Please be sure that all of the samples are sent to Ms. Price as soon as possible.

—you would want to move the abbreviation to the second line:

> Please be sure that all of the samples are sent to Ms. Price as soon as possible.

This is, of course, easy when you are typing on a typewriter. However, remember that Word will wrap words for you automatically, sometimes splitting an abbreviation from what follows.

If you want to be sure that a space between words is never broken, use a nonbreaking space, which is simply typed in as COMMAND-SPACEBAR (press COMMAND and then SPACEBAR). The space will look identical to a normal space on your screen, but Word will know never to use that word break as a line break.

## CHOOSING PREFERENCES

Word lets you adjust certain aspects of the program, such as the way it displays text. After you make some such changes, the program remembers the new settings and starts with them each time. You saw examples of this earlier in the chapter with the Full Menus and Hide Paragraph Marker commands in the Edit menu.

There is another set of preferences available in the Preferences command in the Edit menu. If you prefer to work in metric units rather than inches, you can select centimeters under the Measure choice. Other choices in the Preferences command are described elsewhere in this book.

Word also lets you choose different type styles. Up to now, all the text you have typed in has been in New York, but many Macintosh users prefer to use the Geneva font. If you want to use Geneva as Word's default, follow these instructions. (If you don't know how to make choices in the Macintosh's dialog boxes, see the lesson on this in Chapter 1.)

To make Geneva the normal text used:

1. Give the Define Styles command in the Format menu. Word shows the dialog box in Figure GS-12.

2. Select the style called "Normal" in the list at the upper left of this dialog box.

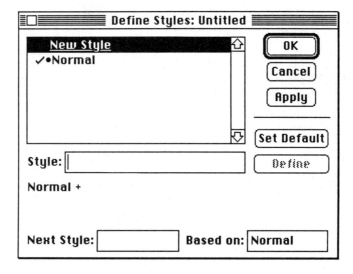

**Figure GS-12**   *Define Styles dialog box*

3. Now, while this dialog box is still open, pull down the Format menu again and give the Character command. The Character dialog box is shown in Figure GS-13.

4. Scroll through the list under "Font name" (in the lower left of the dialog box) until you find Geneva and select it. Click the OK button in the Character dialog box.

5. Now click the Set Default button in the Define Styles dialog box. Word asks if you are sure that you want to change the default. Click "Yes". Finally, click the OK button.

You will find out more about these steps in Chapter 10. For

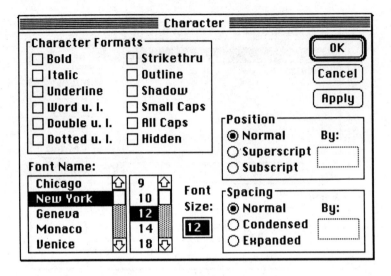

**Figure GS-13**    *Character dialog box*

now, rest assured that they will change the default font used. The examples in the rest of this book use the Geneva font.

## GETTING HELP

Word's Help command is a quick way to get information about a command or to figure out what is happening in the program. The Help command has a menu of choices that you can use to get information about any command and all of its subcommands and choices.

You can start the Help command by pointing with the mouse at the apple on the menu bar and dragging down to "About Microsoft Word." After clicking the Help button in the dialog box, you can select the topic you want help on from the list box shown in Figure GS-14. When you are finished, click the Cancel button to continue with Word.

You can also get help on specific Word commands. To do this, press COMMAND-?. (You do not need to use the SHIFT key for this.) The arrow pointer becomes a question mark, which you can use to select the command you want help with. For instance, to find out how to open files, press COMMAND-?, then pull down the File menu and select the Open command.

You can also get help on particular dialog boxes by pressing COMMAND-? when the dialog box is on the screen.

## LEAVING WORD

Since you have only entered practice text, it is unlikely that you want to save it in a file (don't worry; the real text comes at the beginning of the next chapter). When you leave Word, the program checks to see if you have saved your text in a file before it returns you to the Finder. It is easy, however, to tell Word not to bother.

When you want to exit from Word and return to the Finder, give the Quit command from the File menu. If there is text that

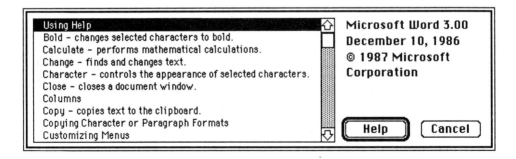

**Figure GS-14**   *List box for the Help command*

you have not saved on disk (you will learn how to do this in the next chapter), Word will show the prompt in Figure GS-15.

If you want to save your text, click the Yes button in the box. In this case, however, you can click the No button, since the material is just for practice. If you realize that you want to do more editing, click the Cancel button. You can also quit from Word with the COMMAND-Q key.

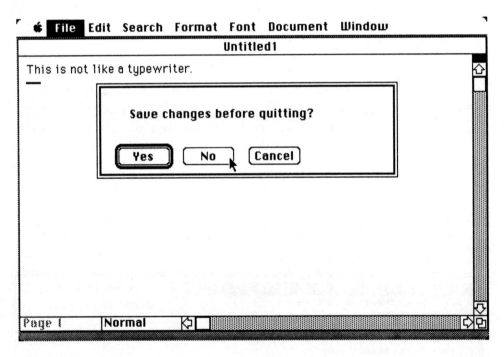

***Figure GS-15***   *Quitting Word*

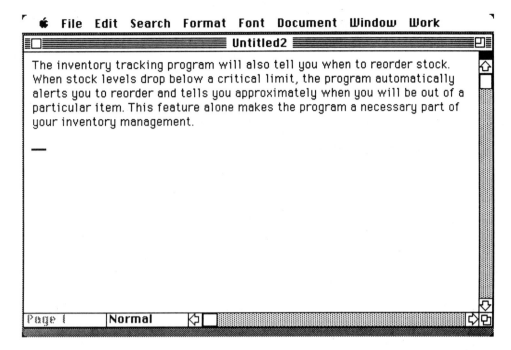

The inventory tracking program will also tell you when to reorder stock. When stock levels drop below a critical limit, the program automatically alerts you to reorder and tells you approximately when you will be out of a particular item. This feature alone makes the program a necessary part of your inventory management.

*Figure GS-16    Sample paragraph*

# REVIEW

*1. Running Word from the Finder*

How do you tell Word that you want to start editing a file called "Timeclock"?

*2. Using the selection*

Enter the paragraph in Figure GS-16. What is the easiest way to select the words "the program automatically alerts you"?

3. *Deleting text (Cut)*

What is the easiest way to delete the last sentence from the text shown in question 2?

4. *Paragraphs*

Give an example of using NEWLINE in a business letter.

5. *Nonbreaking spaces*

Which key combination do you use to make a nonbreaking space? In the following sentence, mark the spaces that should be nonbreaking:

Later in the conversation, Ms. Sharon Neilsen referred to "1 or 2 other issues" that she had raised earlier.

# Part 1

## Using Word
## To Edit

# Chapter 1

## Basic Editing With Word

This and the next six chapters show you how to enter and edit a variety of documents, from short memos to long reports. The lessons in this chapter use the sample business letter that you will type in the next section.

## LESSON 1    Typing In Your First File

Now that you know how to start Word, how to enter text, and a bit about giving Word commands, you are ready to type your first exercise, a business letter. Type it in using the rules you have learned so far; if you make mistakes, correct them with the BACKSPACE key or the Cut command. As you have moved the insertion point around with the mouse, you have probably noticed already that when you type new text into Word, it always appears just to the left of the insertion point. Thus, whenever you want to add text to the middle of text that you have already entered, simply move the I-beam to the desired location, click the mouse button, and type. (By the way, you should erase your practice sentence before you type in the letter.)

As you type the letter from Figure 1-1 into Word, remember to press the RETURN key only at the end of each paragraph. Use the NEWLINE key (the SHIFT-RETURN combination) in the two addresses, and let Word form the other paragraphs with word-wrap. Don't be surprised if this feels a bit strange at first; you will find it more natural as you continue to use Word. Press RETURN twice to leave a blank line between the paragraphs (you will learn a better way in Chapter 8 and an even better way in Chapter 10).

The next section explains how to save the letter you have just typed in a file on disk. This file will be used in many of the chapters in this book.

## LESSON 2    Saving Your Text in a File

Now that you have text that you want to keep, you need to know how to tell Word to save it in a file. To do this, you use the Save

```
   ☾   File   Edit   Search   Format   Font   Document   Window
▤□▦▦▦▦▦▦▦▦▦▦▦▦▦▦▦▦▦▦▦ Sample 1 ▦▦▦▦▦▦▦▦▦▦▦▦▦▦◩
```

January 11, 1987

Chris Richford, Vice President
Manufacturer's Bank of the Northeast
1000 First Avenue
Millerton, CT  06492

Dear Ms. Richford:

I am pleased to send you the latest update on the results of our expanded
product line. The enclosed summary documents our increased profit margin
(7%) for the fourth quarter of 1986, which is largely due to the successful
introduction of our new model, the DC50. In 1987 we expect to continue
increasing our profitable inroads into this new area.

As you can see, we are well within the projections we outlined to you when
you helped us obtain short-term financing. Thank you again for all your
assistance. If you have any questions regarding this information, please feel
free to call me.

Sincerely,


Thomas Mead, Controller
National Generators
1275 Oak Glen Industrial Park
Oak Glen, CT  06410


—

**Figure 1-1**   *Text of the first letter*

command. First, select the File menu from the menu bar (shown
in Figure 1-2). Now drag down to the Save As command and
release the button. Word displays the dialog box in Figure 1-3.
Type in **Sample 1** and press RETURN (or type in **Sample 1** and
click the Save button). Word saves the file on disk. You can

continue to edit the file if you wish, or you can leave Word with the Quit command.

You have other choices in the Save As command that you will not use yet, but that you should know about. Click the File Format button if you want to use one of Word's other file formats; these are described in Chapter 12. Clicking the Make Backup button tells Word to keep a copy of your file without any changes since the last time you saved it. Since this is a new file, this is not useful here.

If you want to save the file on a different disk, click the Eject

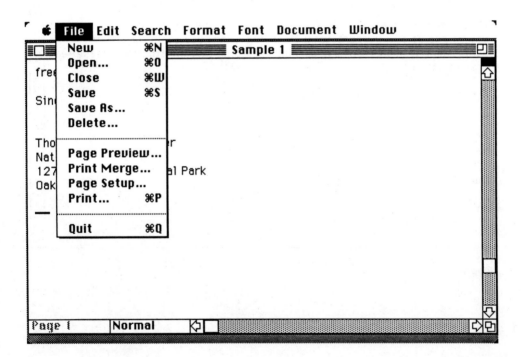

*Figure 1-2*   *The File menu*

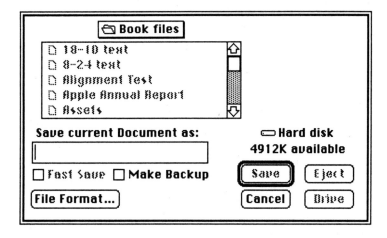

**Figure 1-3**   *Dialog box for Save As command*

button and insert the new disk. If you have more than one disk drive and want to save the file on the other disk, click the Drive button.

If you later want to edit this file again (which you will, since it is used for examples throughout the book), you will open it with the Open command. If you make editing changes in a file and you do not want to save those changes (for example, if you are experimenting with some of Word's commands and do not want to change the file on disk), use the Quit command; when the command prompt asks if you want to save your changes, click the No button.

# LESSON 3   Moving Around and Inserting Text

Word gives you many ways to move around in a file when you are editing. You can select any part of a file by using the mouse. You can always tell where you are in a file by noting where the selection or insertion point is.

To start this lesson, move to the beginning of the Sample 1 file. If you have closed the file or quit from Word since saving the file, open it with the Open command. Move to the beginning of the text by dragging the scroll box (on the right side of the screen) to the top of the scroll bar. Your screen should now look like Figure 1-4.

To see different parts of your text, use the scroll bars on the right and bottom borders of the window (you will rarely use the one on the bottom border). These act just like the scroll bars in the Finder.

For example, to scroll the screen down one line, click the arrow that is pointing down at the bottom of the screen. If you point at this arrow and continue to hold down the button, the screen will continue to scroll.

To jump to a particular place in your text, you can drag the scroll box up and down the scroll bar. This is sometimes called thumbing, since it is like thumbing through a book. To get to the end of a file, simply drag the box to the bottom of the bar; drag it to the top to get to the beginning of the file.

# LESSON 4   Making a Selection

As you saw in the last chapter, the Cut command always deletes the entire selection. There are other commands that edit and format the selection; these commands are covered throughout

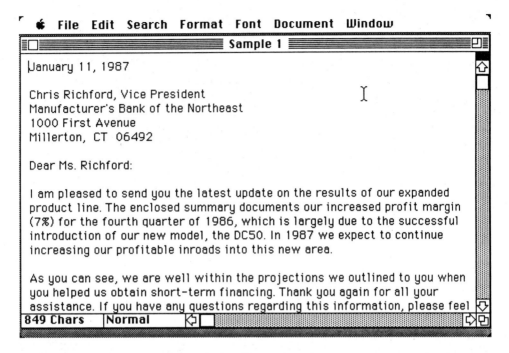

**Figure 1-4**    *The beginning of the Sample 1 file*

the book. Word gives you a number of ways to make selections with the mouse so you can edit or format the text.

You can choose from six different kinds of selections of fixed lengths:  a character, a word, a sentence, a line, a paragraph, and the entire document. If you want to select a portion of text that is not included in the six choices (several words but not a sentence, several sentences but not a paragraph, several paragraphs but not an entire document), you can also make selections of varying lengths.

You already saw in the last chapter how to select a character, a word, and a sentence by dragging, double-clicking, and clicking with the COMMAND key, respectively. To review the steps, point at any letter in the word "update" in the first sentence. Click the button to set the insertion point, double-click to select the entire word, and press both the COMMAND key and the button together to select the entire sentence (see Figure 1-5).

To select larger areas of text, move the mouse pointer into the *selection bar*, the blank column between the left window border and the text. When you point to the selection bar, the arrow changes and points up and to the right. For example, point to the selection bar on the third line, which begins with "(7%)", as in Figure 1-6. Clicking now has a different function. Single-clicking selects the entire line, double-clicking selects the entire paragraph, and pressing both the COMMAND key and the button together selects the entire document. Typing COMMAND-OPTION-M also selects the entire document. Experiment with each of these choices.

**⊆ File  Edit  Search  Format  Font  Document  Window**

**☰☐════════════════ Sample 1 ════════════════☐**

January 11, 1987

Chris Richford, Vice President
Manufacturer's Bank of the Northeast
1000 First Avenue
Millerton, CT  06492

Dear Ms. Richford:

I am pleased to send you the latest update on the results of our expanded product line. The enclosed summary documents our increased profit margin (7%) for the fourth quarter of 1986, which is largely due to the successful introduction of our new model, the DC50. In 1987 we expect to continue increasing our profitable inroads into this new area.

As you can see, we are well within the projections we outlined to you when you helped us obtain short-term financing. Thank you again for all your assistance. If you have any questions regarding this information, please feel

**Page 1     Normal**

*Figure 1-5   Selecting the first sentence*

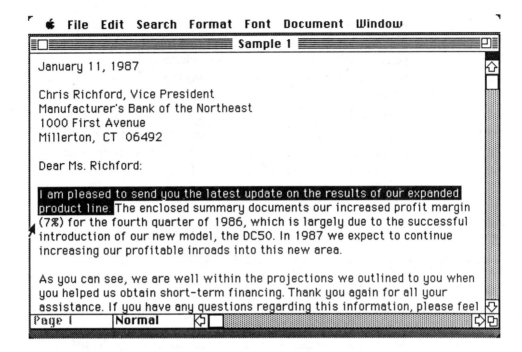

**Figure 1-6**   *Pointing in the selection bar*

In some instances, none of these choices may be exactly what you want. However, you can select a variable amount of text with the mouse, just as you can in the Finder. You can select any text on the screen with this method, provided that the text is a connected group of words. To select text on the line that precedes or follows the line you started on, simply move the mouse up or down, always holding down the left button. Again, this may take a bit of practice, since you sometimes move the mouse farther than you want. If so, you can simply move back to your intended position and try again.

If the text that you want to select is not completely on the screen, you can extend the selection by scrolling the screen. To do this, start your selection and briefly bring the pointer into the upper or lower screen border. Word then scrolls the screen, and you can continue to extend your selection. Sometimes Word scrolls more than you expect, so using this method may be a bit tricky.

Spend some time experimenting with different methods of selecting different amounts of text. Remember that you can always select a portion of text by starting at either end and moving the mouse to cover the whole portion.

## LESSON 5  Moving and Deleting with the Keyboard

Most people prefer to use the mouse for moving the insertion point and selecting text. This is because using the mouse makes a very visual connection to the document and you don't have to remember which keys to use.

Microsoft has, however, added keyboard commands to allow you to move the insertion point and to delete characters and words. If you use computers other than the Macintosh, such as the IBM PC, you have already memorized keyboard commands to do simple things like moving the insertion point and will feel right at home with Word's keyboard movement commands.

If you have an old-style keyboard, all the commands require that you hold down the OPTION and COMMAND keys. If you have one of the newer keyboards with a numeric keypad and direction keys, you can use some of those keys by themselves or in combination with the COMMAND key. To use the numeric keypad to move the insertion point, you have to enable it by pressing the CLEAR key.

The numeric keypad can be used in two ways: to enter

numbers (as you would expect), and to enter Word commands. If you see an "N" at the right of the menu bar, the keypad will enter numbers; if there is no "N," it will enter cursor movement commands.

You will probably find that using the numeric keypad to move the insertion point is just as confusing as trying to remember the COMMAND-OPTION sequences.

Table 1-1 shows the keyboard commands that you can use to move the insertion point and to delete characters on both keyboards. Table 1-2 shows the keyboard commands that you can use on extended keyboards. Figure 1-7 shows the location of some of these commands so that you can see Microsoft's logic for their placement.

**Table 1-1**   *Insertion Point Movement and Delete Keys*

| Key | Action |
|---|---|
| COMMAND-OPTION-L | Move character right |
| COMMAND-OPTION-K | Move character left |
| COMMAND-OPTION-O | Move line up |
| COMMAND-OPTION-, | Move line down |
| COMMAND-OPTION-; | Move word right |
| COMMAND-OPTION-J | Move word left |
| COMMAND-OPTION-Y | Move paragraph up |
| COMMAND-OPTION-B | Move paragraph down |
| COMMAND-OPTION-P | Move screen up |
| COMMAND-OPTION-. | Move screen down |
| COMMAND-OPTION-[ | Scroll line up (don't move) |
| COMMAND-OPTION-/ | Scroll line down (don't move) |
| COMMAND-OPTION-Z | Jump to last insertion place |
| COMMAND-OPTION-F | Delete character to the right |
| COMMAND-OPTION-G | Delete word to the right |
| COMMAND-OPTION-BACKSPACE | Delete word to the left |

*Table 1-2*   *Insertion Point Movement with the Extended Keyboard*

In this table, NUMERIC indicates the number on the numeric keypad.

| Key | Action |
| --- | --- |
| → | Move character right |
| ← | Move character left |
| ↑ | Move line up |
| ↓ | Move line down |
| NUMERIC-1 | Move to end of line |
| NUMERIC-2 | Move line down |
| NUMERIC-3 | Move page down |
| NUMERIC-4 | Move character left |
| NUMERIC-5 | No action |
| NUMERIC-6 | Move character right |
| NUMERIC-7 | Move to beginning of line |
| NUMERIC-8 | Move line up |
| NUMERIC-9 | Move page up |
| COMMAND-NUMERIC-1 | Move to end of sentence |
| COMMAND-NUMERIC-2 | Move paragraph up |
| COMMAND-NUMERIC-3 | Move to end of document |
| COMMAND-NUMERIC-4 | Move word left |
| COMMAND-NUMERIC-5 | No action |
| COMMAND-NUMERIC-6 | Move word right |
| COMMAND-NUMERIC-7 | Move to beginning of sentence |
| COMMAND-NUMERIC-8 | Move paragraph down |
| COMMAND-NUMERIC-9 | Move to beginning of document |

# LESSON 6   Giving the Undo Command

Now that you know how to select any text you want, you can experiment with the Cut command by selecting different amounts of text. With most word processors, when you delete

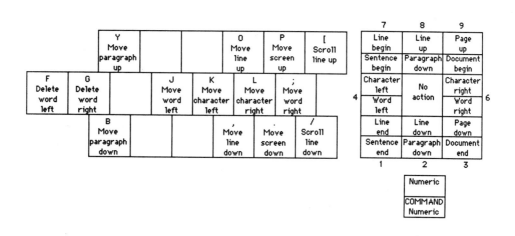

**Figure 1-7**   *Placement of the keys to move insertion point*

information it is gone forever. With Word, however, you can use the Undo command to restore text that you deleted with the BACKSPACE key or the Cut command.

The Undo command restores your text to the way it was before your last edit. For example, if you select a paragraph of text and then delete it, you can use the Undo command (in the Edit menu, or use COMMAND-Z) to bring the paragraph back, even if you have moved to a new selection. The Undo command only works to restore the last editing command that you have given (such as giving the Cut or Copy commands or pressing BACKSPACE a few times) and cannot restore earlier edits.

The Undo command can also undo your Undo command. This may seem strange, but it is useful if you are not sure that you want to restore an edit you have made. For example, if you delete a sentence but are not sure that you deleted the correct sentence, you can undo the deletion, and if it turns out that you did delete the correct sentence, simply give the Undo command again.

To experiment with the Undo command, delete the date from the letter (see Figure 1-8). Now give the Undo command and the date is restored, as in Figure 1-9.

As you will see in later chapters, you can use the Undo command to reverse a number of different editing commands. You may well find it to be a safety net at a critical moment. Remember, however, that Undo can only restore your last edit; anything done before that cannot be undone.

**🍎 File  Edit  Search  Format  Font  Document  Window**

Sample 1

Chris Richford, Vice President
Manufacturer's Bank of the Northeast
1000 First Avenue
Millerton, CT 06492

Dear Ms. Richford:

I am pleased to send you the latest update on the results of our expanded product line. The enclosed summary documents our increased profit margin (7%) for the fourth quarter of 1986, which is largely due to the successful introduction of our new model, the DC50. In 1987 we expect to continue increasing our profitable inroads into this new area.

As you can see, we are well within the projections we outlined to you when you helped us obtain short-term financing. Thank you again for all your assistance. If you have any questions regarding this information, please feel free to call me.

Page 1        Normal

*Figure 1-8    Deleting the date*

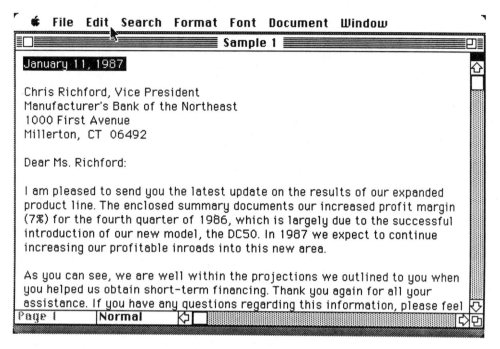

**Figure 1-9**  *After the Undo command*

# LESSON 7   Making Choices in the Dialog Boxes

All of the Word commands introduced so far have been quite simple. When you give some commands, however, you are offered a dialog box of items from which you can choose. This lesson is a quick refresher on how to use the mouse and the keyboard to make dialog box choices.

The Character command in the Format menu is a good example of a command that has a dialog box. When you give the command, Word presents you with the dialog box in Figure 1-10. Most of the dialog boxes that you see in the Finder have only one or two buttons, such as OK or Cancel. Here, you see four sets of buttons, as well as two lists with scroll bars. One of the sets of buttons includes the familiar OK and Cancel.

The choices under Character Formats allow you to set the type style for the selected characters, just as in MacWrite and MacPaint. If you click on one of the buttons (such as Bold), an "X" appears in the box (see Figure 1-11). This indicates that the style is selected. A list of square boxes indicates that you can

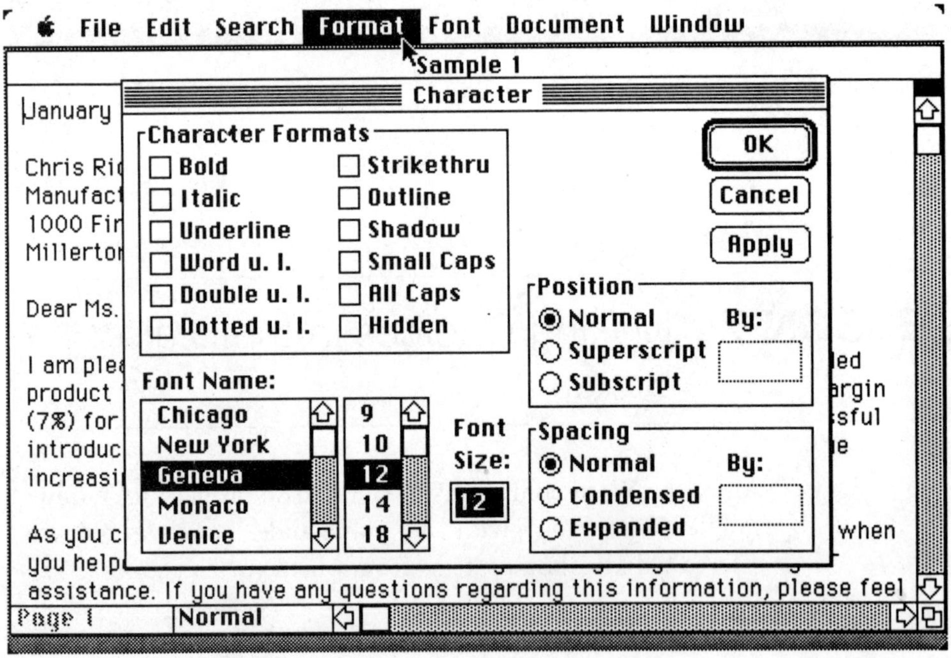

**Figure 1-10**   *The Character dialog box*

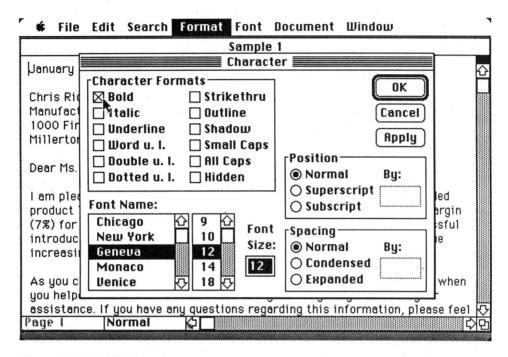

**Figure 1-11**    *"Bold" selected*

select more than one of the boxes at once, as in Figure 1-12.

The buttons under Position are round, which indicates that only one of the choices can be selected at a time. For instance, if you click the Subscript button, the Normal choice is unselected (see Figure 1-13).

Selecting fonts from the list is similar to selecting items in the Finder. You can select from the list simply by clicking on the name. If the scroll bar is dark, as in the list of sizes for the fonts, you can scroll through the list in the normal fashion.

Some dialog boxes allow you to type in text or numbers; you have already seen this in the Save As command. In the window here, you can either choose a font size from the list or enter one in the box in the lower right-hand corner.

# LESSON 8   Printing Text

Normally, the primary purpose of word processing is to obtain a finished printed document. At this point you have learned the basics of using Word to input and edit a document. Now that you have edited your text, it is likely that you want to see it on a printed page.

To print the file that you are editing, you use the Print command in the File menu. When you give this command, you

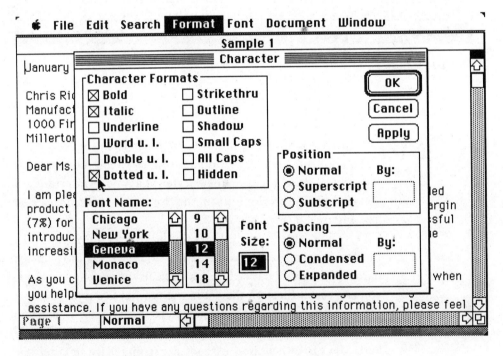

***Figure 1-12***   *More than one style selected*

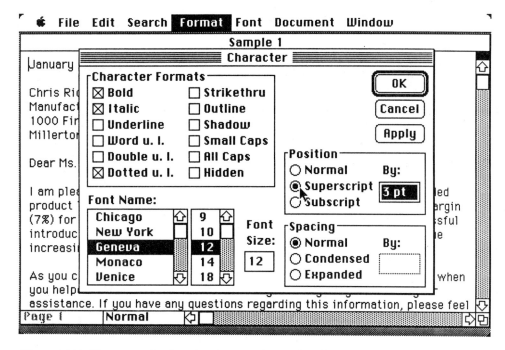

**Figure 1-13**  *"Superscript" selected and "Normal" unselected*

will see the dialog box in Figure 1-14. These choices are explained in detail in Chapter 11. If you are using an Imagewriter printer, simply click the OK button to begin printing. If you are using a different printer, you should wait until Chapter 11 to try printing (you can, if you wish, read that chapter now so you can print). You will also see in Chapter 11 how to use the Page Setup and Printer Setup commands.

Before printing, be sure that your printer is turned on and that it is properly connected to your Macintosh. If you want to stop the printer, press COMMAND-PERIOD. It may take a while for the printer to stop printing.

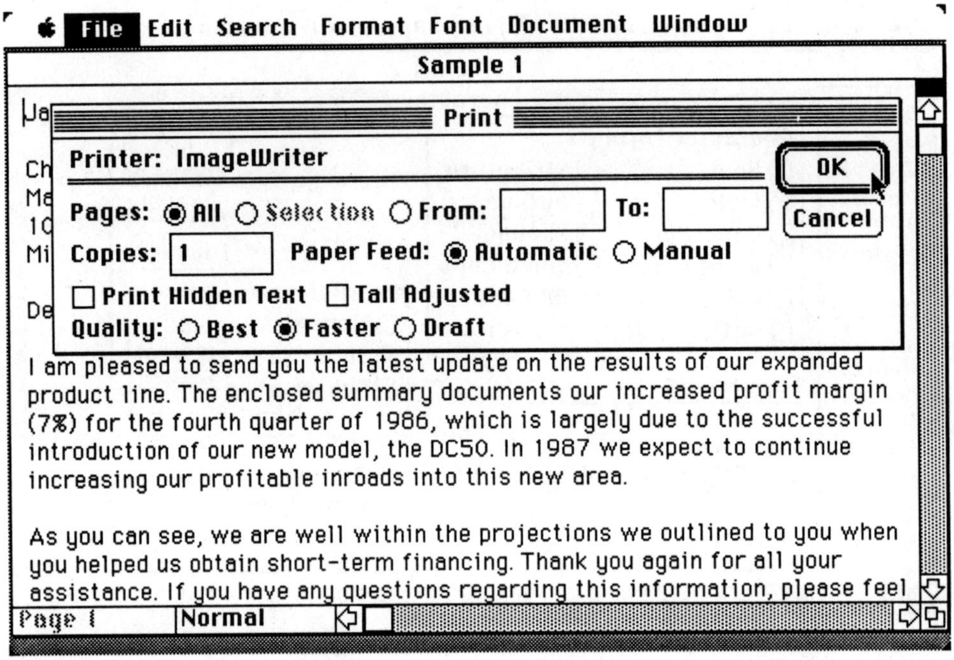

**Figure 1-14**   *Print dialog box*

# REVIEW

1. *Loading your text in a file (Open)*

   Name the steps for executing the Open command to load a file called Orders.

2. *Moving and making selections*

   What are the types of selections you can make with the mouse, and how do you make them?

3. *Using the scroll box*

   How do you go directly to the beginning of a file? To the end? To the middle?

4. *Recovering text (Undo)*

   Which of the following actions can be reversed with the Undo command?
   - *a.* going to the end of the file
   - *b.* deleting a phrase
   - *c.* changing a letter from lower- to uppercase
   - *d.* selecting a sentence

5. *Simple printing*

   What should you do before giving the Print command?

# Chapter 2

## Moving and Copying Text

So far you have learned how to enter text, how to move the insertion point and selection, and how to use the Cut command to remove text from a document. This chapter explains how to use the Cut and Paste commands to move text from one part of a file to another, and how to make many copies of a piece of text in your file with the Copy command.

The ability to move sections of text is one of the most useful features of word processing. For instance, after writing a report you may decide that you want to change the order of paragraphs or sentences. Since you can rearrange your ideas after seeing them on paper or on the screen, you will find that your finished writing will be much better organized. In the next lesson, you will see that moving text is easy to do with Word.

# LESSON 9    Moving Text Within a Document

To delete selected text, you use the Cut command from the Edit menu, which can also be given as the COMMAND-X key. This deletes the selected text to the Clipboard. You can see the contents of the Clipboard with the Show Clipboard command in the Window menu.

For example, select the word "latest" in the first paragraph of the Sample 1 letter and delete it with the Cut command. Give the Show Clipboard command, and Word now shows the Clipboard window in Figure 2-1. The Clipboard in Word acts just as it does in the Finder and other applications. Thus, if you now select another word in the file and delete it, the Clipboard no longer contains the word "latest." When the text is no longer in the Clipboard, you cannot use the Undo command to restore it.

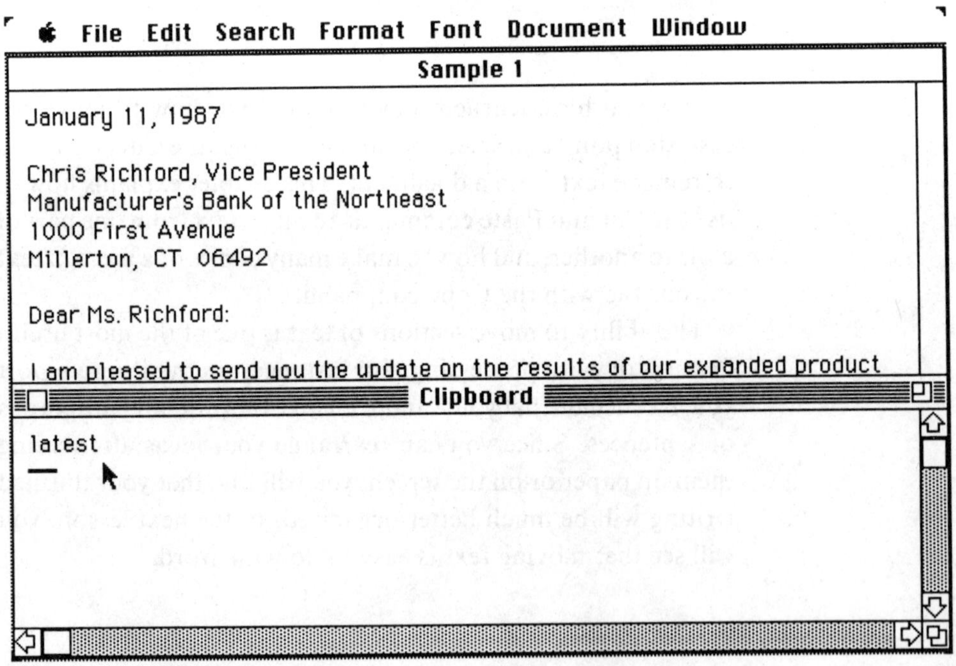

**&#x20AC; File   Edit   Search   Format   Font   Document   Window**

| Sample 1 |
|---|
| January 11, 1987 |
| |
| Chris Richford, Vice President |
| Manufacturer's Bank of the Northeast |
| 1000 First Avenue |
| Millerton, CT  06492 |
| |
| Dear Ms. Richford: |
| |
| I am pleased to send you the update on the results of our expanded product |

| ≡≡≡≡≡≡ Clipboard ≡≡≡≡≡≡ |
|---|
| latest |
| — |

*Figure 2-1*    *The Clipboard window*

Note that deleting characters with the BACKSPACE key does not put the characters into the Clipboard; only the Cut command and the Copy command (described later) put text in the Clipboard. However, you can still use the Undo command to restore text erased with the BACKSPACE key.

The Paste command copies the contents of the Clipboard to the position of the insertion point or selection. The quickest way to give the Paste command is from the keyboard: you simply press the COMMAND-V key.

You may be able to guess how you can move text from one part of a file to another; first select the text you want to move, delete it, move the insertion point to the position where you want to move the text, and use the Paste command. For instance, try switching the second and third sentences of the second paragraph. To do this, first select the third sentence: point at a character in the sentence, hold down the COMMAND key, and click. Then delete the sentence, as in Figure 2-2.

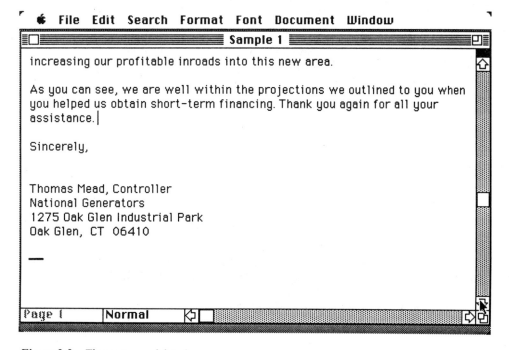

*Figure 2-2*   *The sentence deleted*

Now set the insertion point at the beginning of the second sentence and give the Paste command. Press the SPACEBAR to separate the two sentences, as in Figure 2-3. Notice that Word automatically reformats the paragraph for you.

This is the way that you most often use the Clipboard. Since it can hold any amount of information (depending only on the amount of room on your disk), you can use it to move large portions of your text. This is also a convenient method for moving phrases around in a sentence to see different effects on sound and meaning. Practice moving text around in your file using the Clipboard and the Cut and Paste commands.

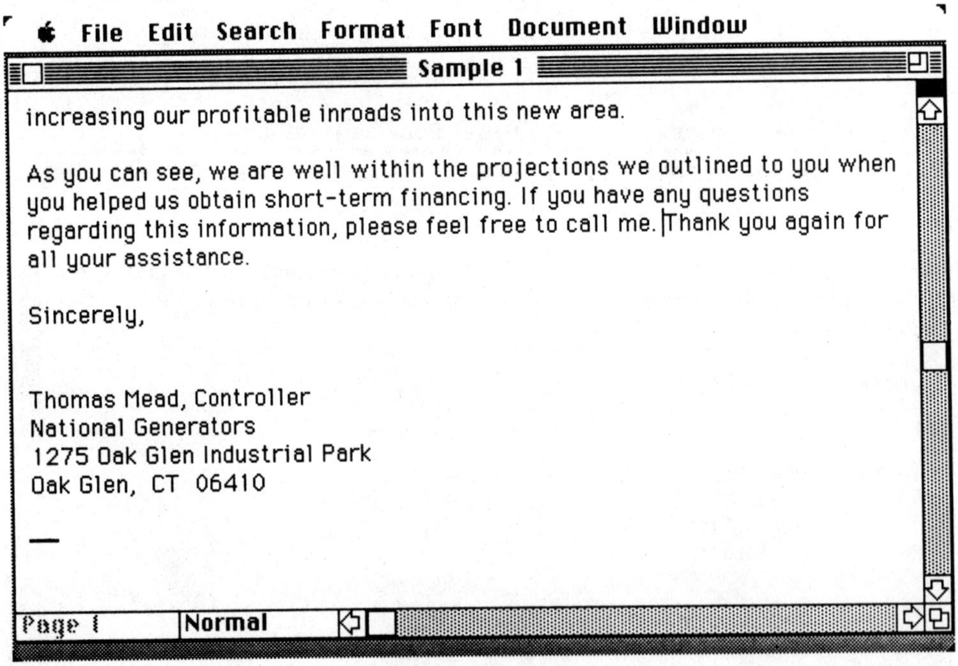

**&#xF8FF; File  Edit  Search  Format  Font  Document  Window**

**Sample 1**

increasing our profitable inroads into this new area.

As you can see, we are well within the projections we outlined to you when you helped us obtain short-term financing. If you have any questions regarding this information, please feel free to call me. Thank you again for all your assistance.

Sincerely,


Thomas Mead, Controller
National Generators
1275 Oak Glen Industrial Park
Oak Glen, CT  06410

Page 1          Normal

*Figure 2-3*   *The sentence pasted from the Clipboard*

## **LESSON 10**   Copying Text Within a Document

The Clipboard is also useful for making copies of parts of your text. Although copying text is not as common as moving text, you may find that a sentence or a line of text is used over and over in your document. If you copy the text, you will not have to retype it each time it is used.

To copy text you use the Copy command, which puts the contents of the selection in the Clipboard. The original text remains in your document, and a copy of it is placed in the Clipboard.

Before beginning the following example, you should stop editing the Sample 1 file and start a new file. To do this, close the window by clicking in the close box in the upper left-hand corner of the window (see Figure 2-4). Word will ask if you want to save your previous edits, which you do not, since you were just experimenting. Click the No button. Word clears the screen. Now give the New command from the File menu, or press COMMAND-N, and you get a fresh work space.

Now you can begin the copy operation. First type in five asterisks (*****), press RETURN, and then select the asterisks (excluding the paragraph marker) as in Figure 2-5. Use the Copy command to copy these to the Clipboard, then give the Insert command five times (you can use COMMAND-V to do this). You have quickly made a line of 30 asterisks. Now select the whole line, copy it to the Clipboard, and give the Insert command five times again. As you can see, this is much easier than typing 180 asterisks.

As mentioned earlier, it isn't often that you will need to copy text from one part of a document to another. You might find it useful, however, in transcribing a song with repeated lyrics in a chorus, and in similar instances. You will also see its use in Chapter 4, where you will copy text from one file to another.

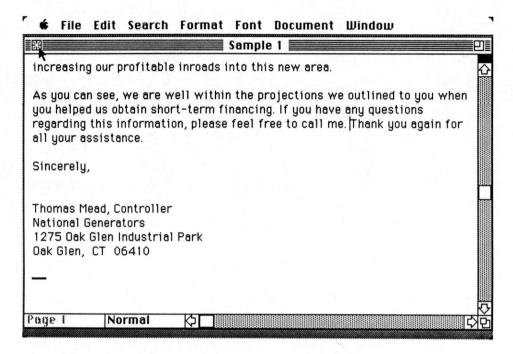

**Figure 2-4** *Close box of the text window*

# LESSON 11 Moving and Copying Without the Clipboard

The previous lessons showed you how convenient it is to use the Clipboard to move and copy text. However, there are times when you want to move or copy text without using the Clipboard. For example, you may have something on the Clipboard that you do not want to lose, but do not want to bother to copy to the Scrapbook.

To move text without using the Clipboard, you can use the COMMAND-OPTION-X key. It is best to see the steps with real text, such as the Sample 1 file. The steps are

1. Select the text that you want to move.

2. Press COMMAND-OPTION-X. When you do this, notice that the page box in the lower left corner of the window now says "Move to," as shown in Figure 2-6.

3. Now move the insertion point to the place where you want the text, and click. Notice that the insertion point is a dotted line instead of a solid one, as shown in Figure 2-7.

4. Now press RETURN. Word moves the text to the new position.

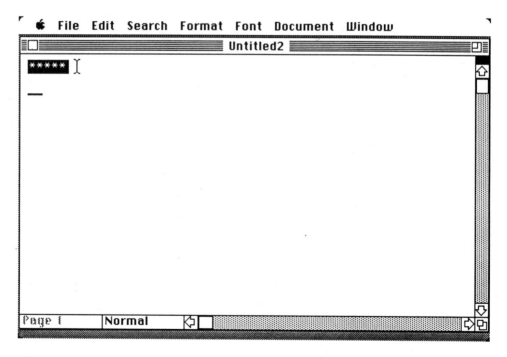

**Figure 2-5** *Five asterisks*

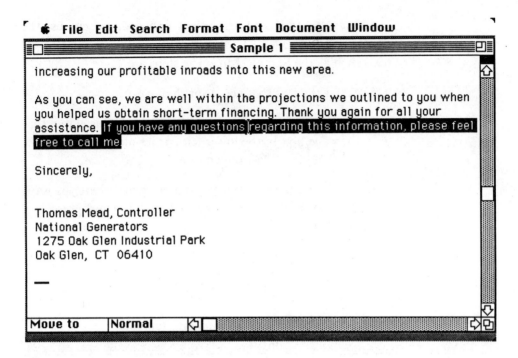

**Figure 2-6**   *The "Move to" message*

If you change your mind after pressing COMMAND-OPTION-X, you can press COMMAND-PERIOD instead to cancel the operation.

Copying text is similar to moving it. Follow the above steps, but instead of pressing COMMAND-OPTION-X to move the text, press COMMAND-OPTION-C to copy it.

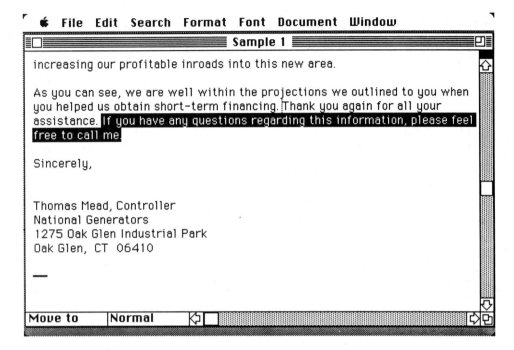

**Figure 2-7**   *The dotted insertion point*

# REVIEW

*1. The Clipboard*

How do you show the contents of the Clipboard on the screen? What commands put text into the Clipboard?

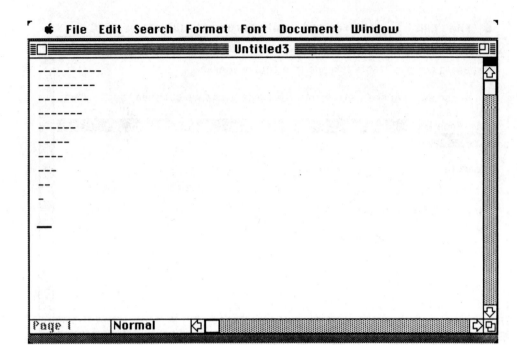

**Figure 2-8**    *Copying text exercise*

2. *Moving text*

State the steps needed to move the first three words from the beginning to the end of the following sentence:

Over the years, she became less tolerant of noisy neighbors.

3. *Copying text*

Describe a fast way to make the picture in Figure 2-8.

# Chapter 3

## Searching and Replacing

**LESSON 12** Searching for Text
**LESSON 13** Replacing Text
**LESSON 14** Using Special Characters in Find and Change

As you have seen, you can easily move the selection around the screen and change the selection. If you know where you want to go (for example, "about 20 lines down" or "to the end of the file"), you can quickly scroll through your text. However, you will often want to select a specific word or phrase. Instead of searching visually for the phrase, you can move to its exact position with the Find command.

Searching has many uses other than simply moving to a certain word or phrase. For instance, you can find the first occurrence of a particular word by moving to the beginning of a document and then searching for the word. You can review your text to see whether you defined new terms when they first appeared. Since you can also search for groups of words, you can easily check for phrases that you may have overused.

# LESSON 12   Searching for Text

The Find command quickly moves the selection to the first instance of a word or phrase. The movement is always relative to your current position in a file; for example, if you are in the middle of a file and search for the word "invoice", Word will find the next occurrence of "invoice" that appears in the text. If it does not find the word when it reaches the end of the file, it searches from the beginning.

Move to the beginning of the Sample 1 file and give the Find command (from the Search menu) or press COMMAND-F. Word brings up the Find window shown in Figure 3-1. The blinking insertion point in the "Find What:" box indicates that you should fill in the word or phrase that you want to search for. Enter the word **please** and press the RETURN key (or click the Start Search button); as before, you can correct errors with the BACKSPACE key. The selection indicator will jump to the first instance of the word "please" in the letter, which in this case is in the word "pleased".

If you want to search for the same word or phrase again, you do not need to retype it. Simply click the Find Next button, and Word searches again. When you are finished searching, click the Find window's close box or the Cancel button. You can drag the Find window around by its title bar, like most of the windows in Word. If you close the Find window and want to repeat the search, press COMMAND-OPTION-A to repeat the Find command.

The Find command's other choices are easy to understand.

- Choosing "Whole Word" indicates that you want Word to restrict your search to whole words. If you click the button, for example, and the text you are searching for is "the", Word will not stop if it finds "they". Thus, if you don't click the button, Word will stop even if the text you are searching for is part of another word.

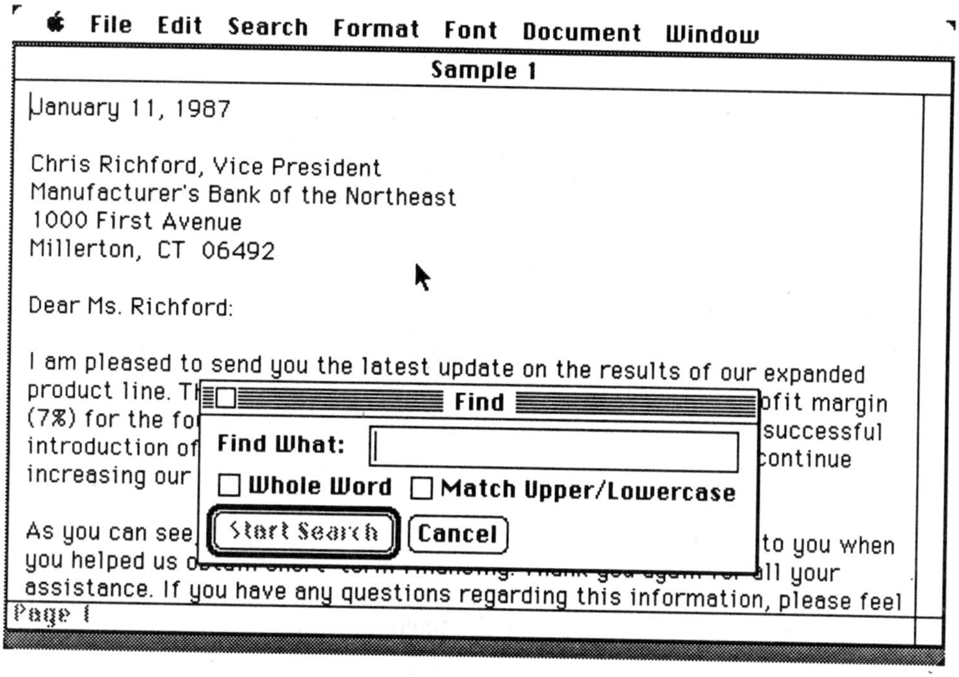

```
 🍎  File  Edit  Search  Format  Font  Document  Window
```

**Sample 1**

January 11, 1987

Chris Richford, Vice President
Manufacturer's Bank of the Northeast
1000 First Avenue
Millerton, CT 06492

Dear Ms. Richford:

I am pleased to send you the latest update on the results of our expanded
product line. Th... ▯▯▯▯▯▯▯▯▯▯▯▯ **Find** ▯▯▯▯▯▯▯▯▯▯▯▯ ...fit margin
(7%) for the fo...                                           successful
introduction of   **Find What:** [_____]        continue
increasing our    ☐ **Whole Word**  ☐ **Match Upper/Lowercase**

As you can see,   [ **Start Search** ]  [ **Cancel** ]      to you when
you helped us o...                                          ll your
assistance. If you have any questions regarding this information, please feel

Page 1

*Figure 3-1*    *The Find window*

- For "Match Upper/Lowercase", you must decide if Word should pay attention to whether the letters in the text are upper- or lowercase. If you do not click the button, Word will ignore case, meaning that Word will not notice the difference between upper- and lowercase letters as it searches the text. Clicking the button is more restrictive: the text must be an exact match of the word or phrase you are searching for, including capital letters. Thus, if you click the box for the case choice and you are searching for "the", Word will not stop when it finds "The".

Word remembers the last setting for each of these choices whenever you use the Find command. For example, if you change the setting of the case choice to check for case, the next time you give the Find command it will still be selected.

To see how to use the choices, move the insertion point to the beginning of the first full paragraph of the Sample 1 file and give the Find command. Enter the word **As** (with a capital "A") and click the case button (as shown in Figure 3-2).

When you execute the command, the word "As" at the beginning of the second paragraph is selected; if you had not chosen to search for the matching case, the lowercase "as" in the word "pleased" in the first paragraph would have been found first.

To see the effect of the whole word option, move the insertion point to the beginning of the file and give the Find command again. Change "Find What" to **as**, click the Whole Word button, and click the Match Upper/Lowercase button to unselect it.

**   File  Edit  Search  Format  Font  Document  Window**

**Sample 1**

January 11, 1987

Chris Richford, Vice President
Manufacturer's Bank of the Northeast
1000 First Avenue
Millerton, CT 06492

Dear Ms. Richford:

I am pleased to send you the latest update on the results of our expanded product line. Th[...]ofit margin
(7%) for the fo[...]successful
introduction of[...]continue
increasing our

**Find**

**Find What:** | As

☐ **Whole Word**   ☒ **Match Upper/Lowercase**

[ **Start Search** ]   [ Cancel ]

As you can see[...]to you when
you helped us o[...]ll your
assistance. If you have any questions regarding this information, please feel

Page 1

***Figure 3-2***   *Selecting the "Match Upper/Lowercase" button*

Now, even though the search is not restricted to an uppercase "A", it is restricted to "as" only when it is a separate word. Thus, Word will skip over the "as" in "pleased" (and in "increased" and "increasing"), going directly to "As" in the second paragraph.

The text that you search for can be as many as 255 characters long. It can also include special characters, which are discussed at the end of this chapter. If Word finds the text, the entire word or phrase is selected. If the text does not appear in the file, Word displays an alert box with "Search text not found" and does not move the selection indicator. If you began the search at any location other than the beginning of the file, Word stops at the end and prompts "Continue search from the beginning of the document?" Click the No button to stop the search. You can also cancel a Search by pressing COMMAND-PERIOD.

## LESSON 13   Replacing Text

It is common to replace every instance of a particular word or phrase in a document with some other word or phrase. For example, you may want to change "pleased" to "happy" throughout a letter. Or you may need to change many (but not all) instances of a person's name to another name. You may also want to replace a wordy phrase with a more concise one throughout a document.

The Change command found in Word's Search menu (or COMMAND-H) lets you change all instances of one word or phrase to another. You can also have Word show you each instance of the phrase you want to change so you can choose whether or not to change it based on its context. Changes can be undone with the Undo command.

The Change command's choices are similar to those of the Find command. For instance, go back to the top of the file, give the Change command, and enter the words **pleased** and **happy** for "Find What:" and "Change To:". This window is shown in Figure 3-3.

The menu has buttons labeled Start Search, Change, Change All, and Cancel. If you click the Change All button, Word simply replaces each occurrence of the specified word or phrase throughout your document without asking for confirmation. If you click the Start Search button, Word stops at the first word to be replaced. You now have two choices: No Change and Change. Clicking the Change button indicates that you want to make the replacement for the current selection, while clicking the No Change button indicates that you do not. If you are finished replacing words, close the window or click Cancel.

As you might guess, the Change command can ease the job of changing many items in a long file. For instance, if one person is mentioned repeatedly throughout a long memo, and that person changes jobs within the company, you may have to change many

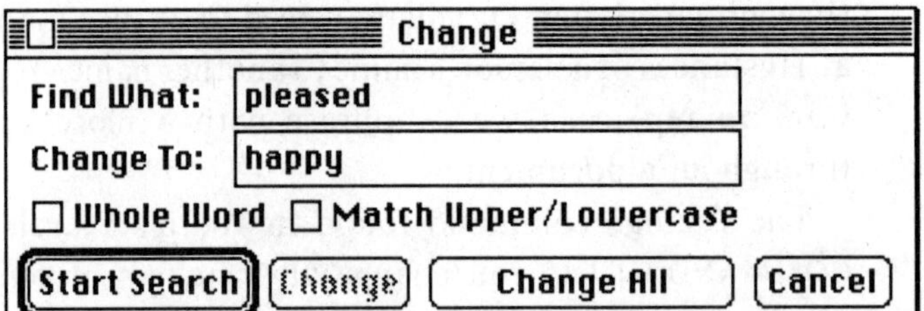

*Figure 3-3*   *The Change window*

instances of the person's name. The Change command allows you to do this with just one command. If the person's name needs to be changed in many, but not all, instances, the confirmation choices let you look through the file easily. Like Find, you can drag the Change window around the screen.

If you do not choose to match the case when replacing text, Word will intelligently choose how to replace the letters. For instance, if you choose to change "airplane" to "boat" with no case requirement and Word finds the word "Airplane," it will replace it with "Boat," since this is most likely what you would want. Word's rule is that words with initial- or all-capital letters (Airplane or AIRPLANE) are replaced with corresponding capital letters (Boat or BOAT).

## LESSON 14   Using Special Characters in Find And Change

Word searches for the exact text you specify in the Find and Change commands. However, there are times when you will want Word to search for less specifically defined words. The Find and Change commands allow you to include a question mark in order to make your search more broad.

If Word sees a question mark in the text you tell it to search for, it will assume that any character can match it. (If you are familiar with "wild-card" characters in file names on other computers, this is identical to the question mark used there.) For example, if you search for "f?r", Word will stop when it finds "far", "for", "fur", and so on. The question mark indicates that any character at all (even numbers and punctuation marks) can be in the position you indicate.

Move to the beginning of the first paragraph and give the

Find command. Enter **e?s** for the "Find What" text, then press the RETURN key. Word selects the "eas" in "pleased" (shown in Figure 3-4). Now click the Find Next button and Word selects the "eas" in "increased", shown in Figure 3-5. Clicking the Find Next button again selects the "e s" in "the successful", and so on.

You may also want to search for characters that are special to Word but that you cannot normally enter in the Find or Change commands. For instance, you may want to find the word "The" preceded by a TAB character. Since you can't normally enter a TAB character as text to search for (Word will think you want to move to the next choice for the Find command), you need a way to indicate that you want to search for the TAB character. This is done with a caret character.

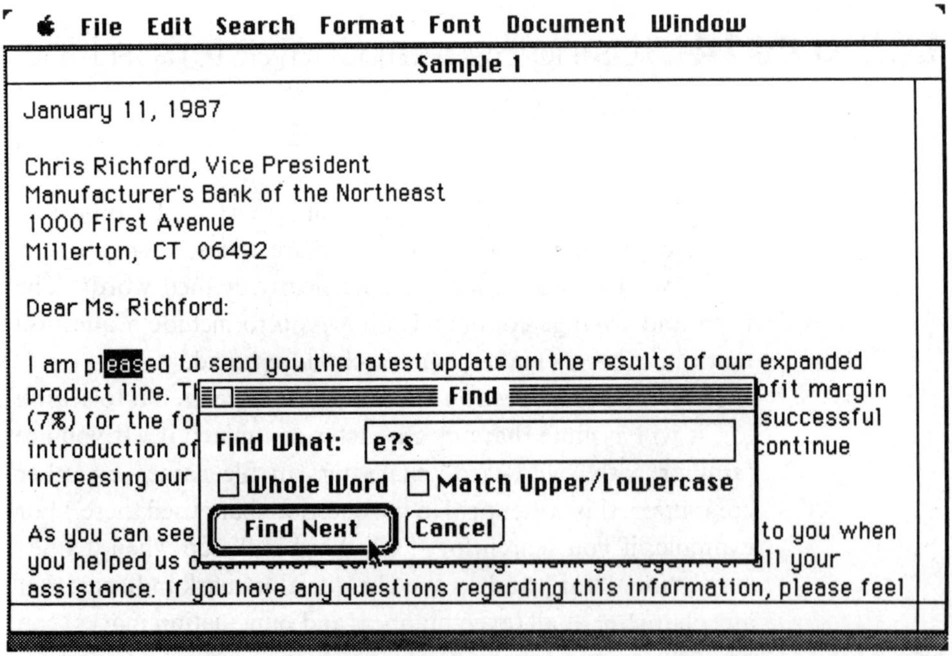

 File   Edit   Search   Format   Font   Document   Window

**Sample 1**

January 11, 1987

Chris Richford, Vice President
Manufacturer's Bank of the Northeast
1000 First Avenue
Millerton, CT  06492

Dear Ms. Richford:

I am pleased to send you the latest update on the results of our expanded
product line. T                           Find                    ofit margin
(7%) for the fo                                              successful
introduction of   Find What:   e?s                           continue
increasing our      ☐ Whole Word  ☐ Match Upper/Lowercase

As you can see   [ Find Next ]  [ Cancel ]                   to you when
you helped us o                                      all your
assistance. If you have any questions regarding this information, please feel

***Figure 3-4***   *First "eas" selected*

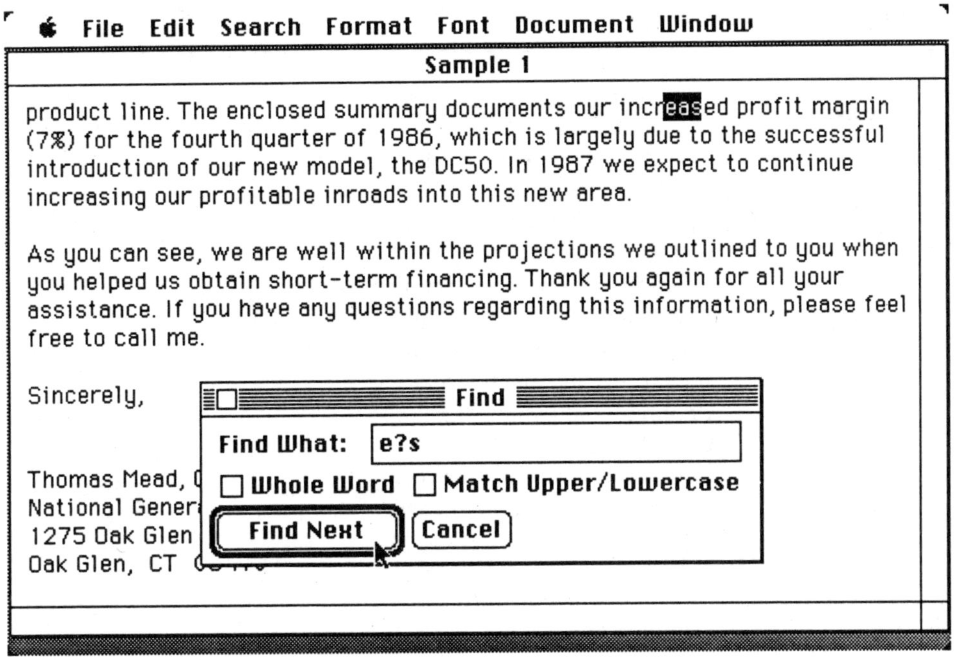

 File  Edit  Search  Format  Font  Document  Window

Sample 1

product line. The enclosed summary documents our incr█ased profit margin
(7%) for the fourth quarter of 1986, which is largely due to the successful
introduction of our new model, the DC50. In 1987 we expect to continue
increasing our profitable inroads into this new area.

As you can see, we are well within the projections we outlined to you when
you helped us obtain short-term financing. Thank you again for all your
assistance. If you have any questions regarding this information, please feel
free to call me.

Sincerely,

Find

Find What:  e?s

☐ Whole Word  ☐ Match Upper/Lowercase

Thomas Mead,
National Gener
1275 Oak Glen
Oak Glen, CT

Find Next   Cancel

*Figure 3-5*  *Second "eas" selected*

Caret characters are special characters that you precede with
a caret mark ($^\wedge$). The caret characters are shown in Table 3-1.
Note that you use two characters, the caret and the character
indicated. A caret character is not a control character.

To search for the word "me", followed by a paragraph marker
and the word "Now", the search text would be that shown in
Figure 3-6.

In the Change command, you can enter any of the listed
special characters in the blank for "Change to" except the
question mark, "$^\wedge$?", and "$^\wedge$w". If you use a question mark, it is
actually inserted there; if you use a "$^\wedge$w", it is replaced with a
"w".

*Table 3-1*    *The Caret Characters*

| Character | Meaning |
|-----------|---------|
| $^\wedge$s | A nonbreaking space |
| $^\wedge$t | A TAB character |
| $^\wedge$p | A paragraph marker |
| $^\wedge$n | A NEWLINE character |
| $^\wedge$d | A section marker (described in Chapter 7) |
| $^\wedge$w | White space; this is any number of spaces, tabs, paragraph marks, NEWLINE characters, division markers, and page-break characters |
| $^\wedge$- | A nonrequired hyphen |
| $^\wedge$ $^\wedge$ | A caret character ($^\wedge$) |
| $^\wedge$? | A question mark character (?) |
| $^\wedge$nnn | A graphics character that represents a number (described in Chapter 7) |

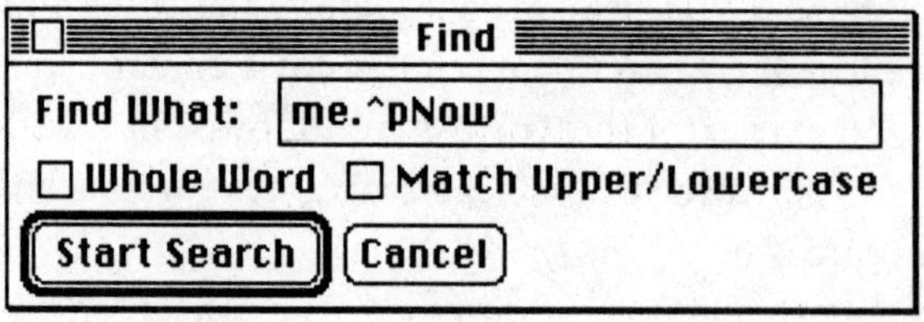

*Figure 3-6*    *Searching for the paragraph marker*

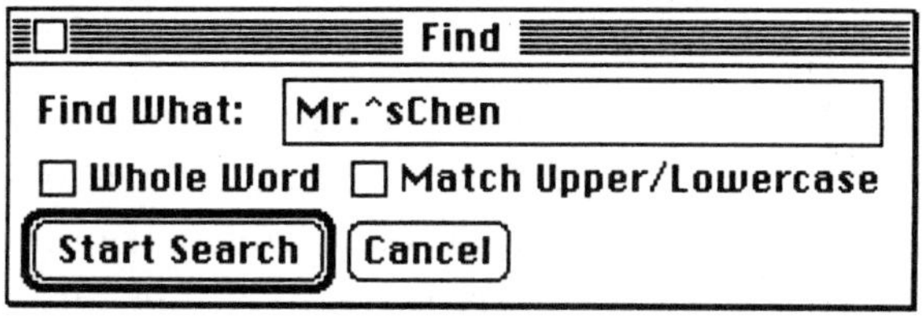

```
┌─────────────────────────────────────────────┐
│ ▣ ▤▤▤▤▤▤▤▤▤▤▤▤ Find ▤▤▤▤▤▤▤▤▤▤▤▤ │
│  Find What:  │Mr.^sChen                    │ │
│     □ Whole Word  □ Match Upper/Lowercase   │
│   [ Start Search ] [Cancel]                 │
└─────────────────────────────────────────────┘
```

***Figure 3-7***    *Searching for white space*

For instance, if your text contains the words "Mr. Chen" with a nonbreaking space and you want to replace it with a normal space, you would give the string shown in Figure 3-7.

In the Change command you can also indicate that you want the contents of the Clipboard inserted in place of the text found. To do this, use "^c" in the "Change to" text instead of giving the actual text, as in Figure 3-8.

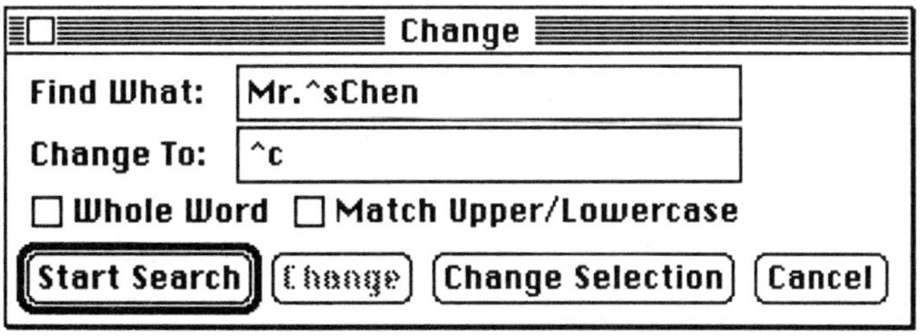

```
┌───────────────────────────────────────────────────────┐
│ ▣ ▤▤▤▤▤▤▤▤▤▤▤▤▤ Change ▤▤▤▤▤▤▤▤▤▤▤▤ │
│  Find What:   │Mr.^sChen                            │  │
│  Change To:   │^c                                   │  │
│     □ Whole Word  □ Match Upper/Lowercase             │
│  [ Start Search ] [Change] [Change Selection] [Cancel]│
└───────────────────────────────────────────────────────┘
```

***Figure 3-8***    *Replacing from the Clipboard*

## REVIEW

1. *Finding text*

   Assume that you are in the middle of a long report. How would you find the second occurrence of the phrase "not profitable" following your current position? How would you find the next occurrence of the phrase "From the preceding" at the beginning of a sentence?

2. *Changing phrases throughout a file*

   You have decided to change all instances of the word "buy-out" to "takeover" in a memo. What should you consider before using the Change command?

3. *Searching with special characters*

   You are sure that you used the word "fundamentally" somewhere in a long memo, but the Find command does not find it. What should you try next?

# Chapter 4

## Using Word's Windows

Word's use of windows will probably save you more time than any of its other editing features. Up to now you have used only one window in Word. You can easily split the large window into two smaller ones. You can also have many separate windows in different files open at once. At first this may seem like a feature that only advanced users would want; however, it is likely that you can now start using windows in your everyday editing and find a number of different uses that meet your particular needs.

For instance, if you are editing the top of a letter and want to look at some information near the bottom, you do not need to take your attention away from either part if you split your window into two. If you are writing a memo and need to look at a report you wrote earlier, you can use one window for the memo and another window for the report.

# LESSON 15    Splitting a Window in One File

To see how two windows can greatly help editing, start Word normally with one window on the Sample 1 file. You can now split the window horizontally to get two views of the file. When you are looking at two parts of one file, it is common to make a split about halfway down the screen.

The one feature of the Word window that you may have noticed was different from those you see in the Finder is the black bar near the top of the scroll bar, above the up scroll arrow. This is called the *split bar* because you use it to split a window.

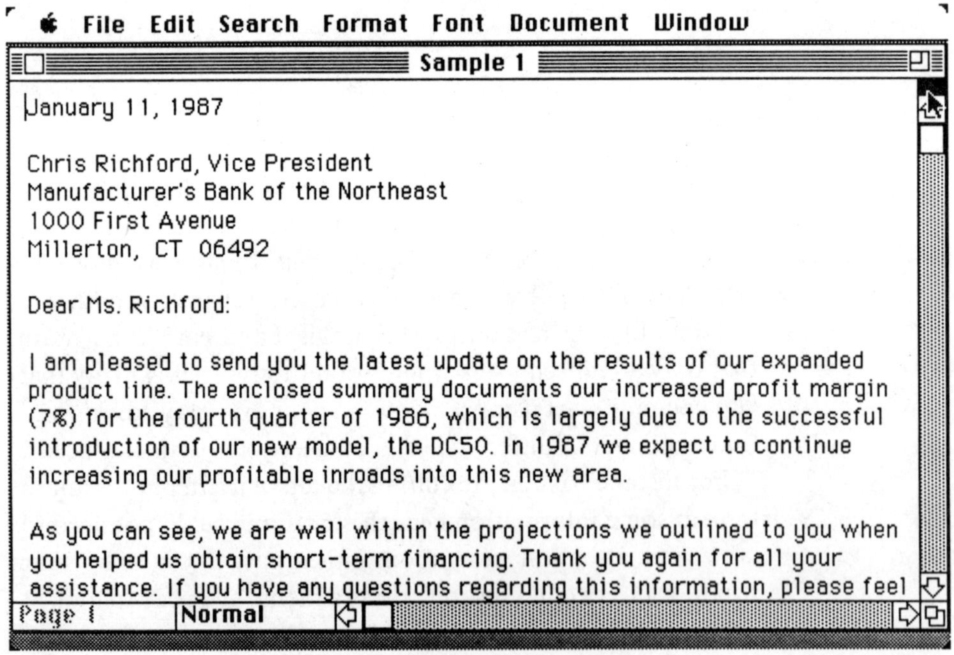

*Figure 4-1*    *Pointing at the split bar*

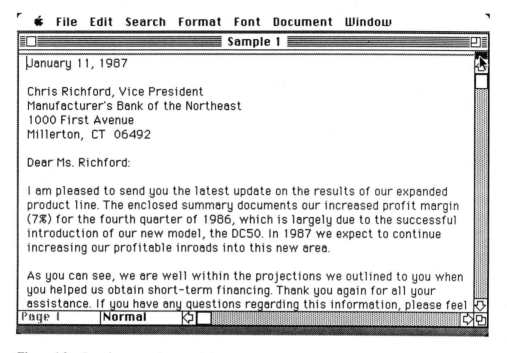

**Figure 4-2**   *Gray bar near the top of the window*

Splitting a window is simple. Point at the split bar, hold down
the mouse button, and drag the split bar down to where you
want to divide the window; when you release the button, the
window is split. To see this, point to the split bar (see Figure 4-1).
When you press the button, notice that Word draws a gray bar
across the screen. It may be hard to see the bar at first; it is right
below the title bar in Figure 4-2. Now drag the split bar down
until the gray bar is below the line that begins "I am pleased..."
(as in Figure 4-3). When you release the button, Word creates
the two halves of the window, each with their own separate
vertical scroll bars, shown in Figure 4-4. You also can split a

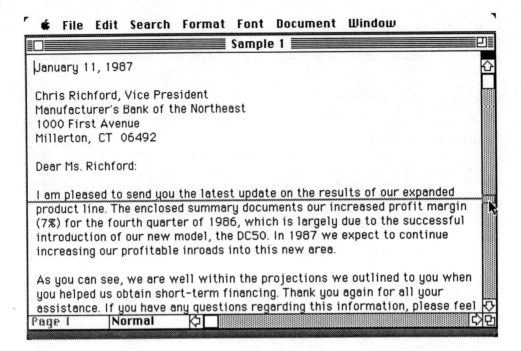

**Figure 4-3**   *Dragging the split bar*

window by pressing COMMAND-OPTION-S.

You can change the position of the split at any time by dragging the split bar to a new location. Go back to a single window by dragging the split bar all the way to the top or bottom of the window.

Once you have split a window, simply point to either part when you want to move the selection from part to part. The text that you view in each part of a window can be moved independently. For example, split the window again (if you closed it) and move the selection to the bottom half. Scroll to the end of the file

```
 ⌐   ⚫  File  Edit  Search  Format  Font  Document  Window      ¬
┌─────────────────────────────────────────────────────────────────┐
│ ▣□══════════════════════ Sample 1 ══════════════════════ ▣▣ │
├─────────────────────────────────────────────────────────────────┤
│ January 11, 1987                                              ⬆ │
│                                                               ▓ │
│ Chris Richford, Vice President                                ▓ │
│ Manufacturer's Bank of the Northeast                          ▓ │
│ 1000 First Avenue                                             ▓ │
│ Millerton, CT  06492                                          ▓ │
│                                                               ▓ │
│ Dear Ms. Richford:                                            ▓ │
│                                                               ▓ │
│ I am pleased to send you the latest update on the results of our expanded ⬇ │
├─────────────────────────────────────────────────────────────────┤
│ product line. The enclosed summary documents our increased profit margin ⬆ │
│ (7%) for the fourth quarter of 1986, which is largely due to the successful │
│ introduction of our new model, the DC50. In 1987 we expect to continue │
│ increasing our profitable inroads into this new area.         ▓ │
│                                                               ▓ │
│ As you can see, we are well within the projections we outlined to you when │
│ you helped us obtain short-term financing. Thank you again for all your ⬇ │
│ Page 1      Normal      ◁□                                   ▷▣ │
└─────────────────────────────────────────────────────────────────┘
```

**Figure 4-4**   *After releasing the button*

(notice that each half of the window has its own scroll bar). The lower half now shows the end of the file (see Figure 4-5).

Now move the insertion point to the beginning of the file in the lower half, so both windows show the same text. After the line "1000 First Avenue" in the top half, add the line **Suite 120** and notice that the second window is updated almost simultaneously.

Each half of a window can be used independently. You can also use the Find command to find specific information in one part of the window without losing your place in the other.

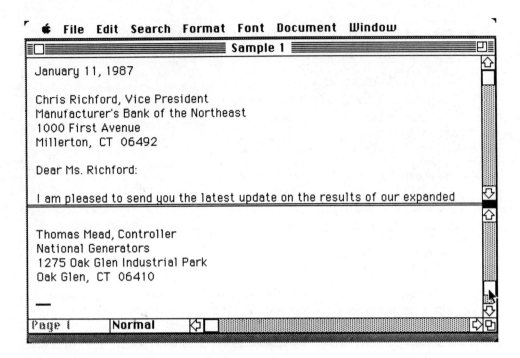

**Figure 4-5**    *Scrolling the bottom half of the window*

The Copy, Cut, and Paste commands become even more powerful when they are used with split windows, since you can use the Clipboard to move text from one part of the window to the other without losing your place in either part of the file. This lets you instantly see the results of moving text as you perform the commands.

For instance, you might want to see the effect of adding "From" and the sender's name to the top of the letter. You can do this easily by showing the beginning of the letter in the top part and the end of the letter in the bottom.

With the window split into two halves, position the text as shown in Figure 4-6. Type the word **From:** before the salutation on the line above Chris Richford's name, press the RETURN key, and move to the lower half. Select the line with Thomas Mead's name; then give the Copy command. Now move to the top window and use the Paste command to place the line under the "From:". Add another line after the name by pressing the RETURN key.

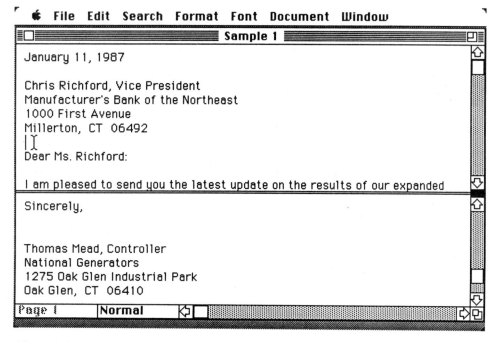

**Figure 4-6**  *Preparing to copy text*

# LESSON 16 Using Two Windows in Two Files

You may have already guessed the next step in using windows: using one window to look at one file and a second window to look at a different file. To look at two different files, you simply use the Open command to open a window for a new file. You can have many windows open at a time, including the Find, Change, and Show Clipboard windows.

To see how useful multiple windows are, close the Sample 1 window by clicking the close button to clear your experimental modifications out of Word's memory. Give the New command, and enter in the short report shown in Figure 4-7. (Use the TAB

```
 File  Edit  Search  Format  Font  Document  Window
═══════════════════════════ Untitled2 ═══════════════════════════

From: Sandra Phillips
To:    Thom Mead
Re:    Summary of annual figures
Date: January 4, 1987

Here are some preliminary figures on the company; I'll have complete totals
early next week.

Total income:          $17,500,000
Total costs:           $14,250,000
Inventory on hand:     $1,250,000

Let me know if you need more details before then.

Page 1        Normal
```

*Figure 4-7*   *Short report*

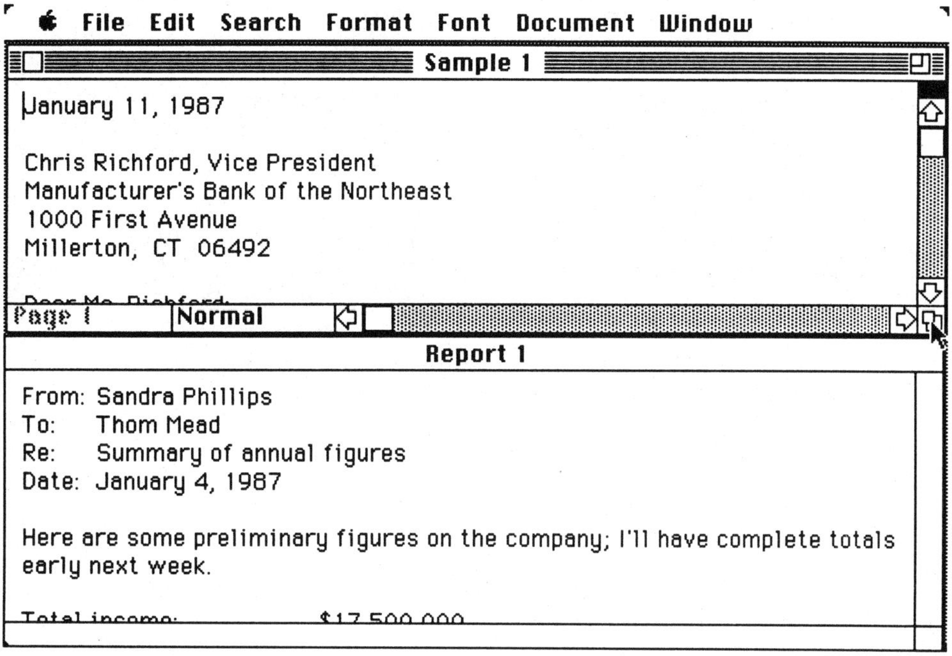

**⚫ File  Edit  Search  Format  Font  Document  Window**

▭▭▭▭▭▭▭▭▭▭ **Sample 1** ▭▭▭▭▭▭▭▭▭▭

January 11, 1987

Chris Richford, Vice President
Manufacturer's Bank of the Northeast
1000 First Avenue
Millerton, CT  06492

Page 1        Normal

**Report 1**

From: Sandra Phillips
To:     Thom Mead
Re:     Summary of annual figures
Date: January 4, 1987

Here are some preliminary figures on the company; I'll have complete totals
early next week.

Total income:              $17,500,000

*Figure 4-8*    *Two windows*

key to line up the figures.) Save this on disk with the name
Report 1.

Use the Open command to open a window with the Sample 1
file. Shrink both windows to be about half the size of the screen,
and drag the Sample 1 window to the top of the screen and the
Report 1 window to the bottom. Your screen should look like
Figure 4-8.

As you are editing Sample 1, you may need some of the
information in Report 1 — for instance, if you wanted to include
some round numbers. You could see those numbers by scrolling
through Report 1, and you could even copy the whole table to
Sample 1 with the Copy and Paste commands. To do this, add
text between the paragraphs of Sample 1, as in Figure 4-9. Now

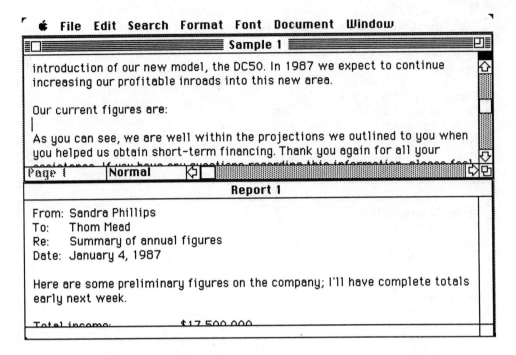

**Figure 4-9**   *New text ("Our current figures are:")*

move to the bottom window and select the figures, as in Figure 4-10. Use the Copy command to copy these to the Clipboard, switch to the top window, and use the Paste command to copy the text from the Clipboard after the new text, as in Figure 4-11. You can also switch windows with COMMAND-OPTION-W.

Of course, if you have more than two windows active, you can have that many files open at the same time. If you have edited the text in a window, remember to save it with the Save or Save As commands before closing the window. If you don't, Word will remind you that the window has been edited and ask whether you want to save the edits.

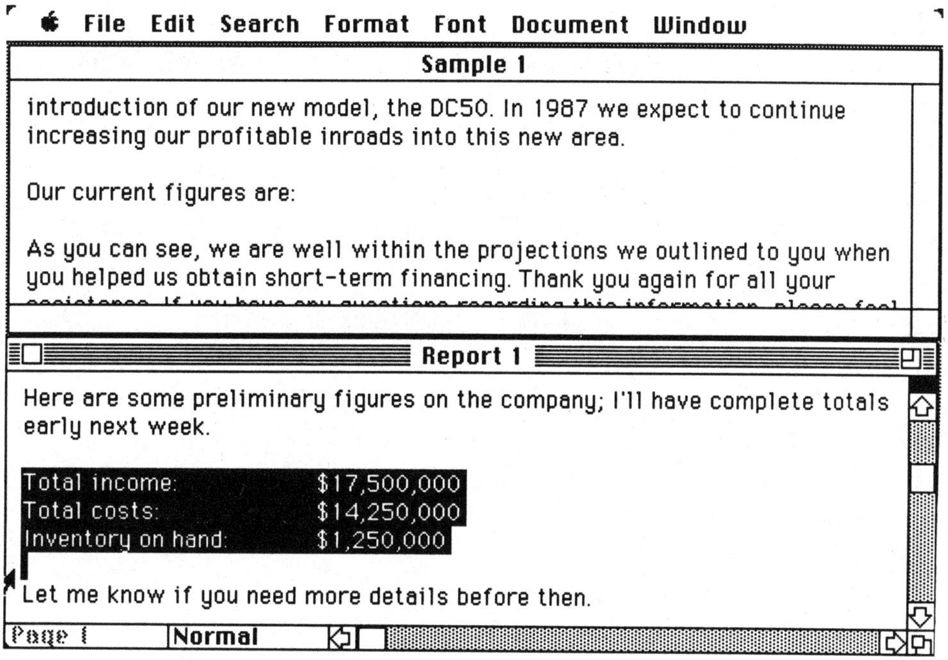

```
  ┌                                                                          ┐
       🍎  File  Edit  Search  Format  Font  Document  Window
    ┌──────────────────────────────────────────────────────────────────┐
    │░░░░░░░░░░░░░░░░░░░░░░░░░░░Sample 1░░░░░░░░░░░░░░░░░░░░░░░░░░░░░░░░░░░│
    ├──────────────────────────────────────────────────────────────────┤
    │ introduction of our new model, the DC50. In 1987 we expect to continue │
    │ increasing our profitable inroads into this new area.              │
    │                                                                    │
    │ Our current figures are:                                           │
    │                                                                    │
    │ As you can see, we are well within the projections we outlined to you when │
    │ you helped us obtain short-term financing. Thank you again for all your │
```

Here are some preliminary figures on the company; I'll have complete totals
early next week.

Total income:        $17,500,000
Total costs:         $14,250,000
Inventory on hand:   $1,250,000

Let me know if you need more details before then.

Page 1     Normal

**Figure 4-10**   *Selecting the figures to be moved*

# LESSON 17   Moving Windows

When you open a new window, you can change the size and shape with its size box and move it by dragging it around the screen. For instance, you may want to enlarge the first window of the previous example so that you will have more area on the screen for editing the Sample 1 file (this, of course, reduces the amount of text you see in Report 1).

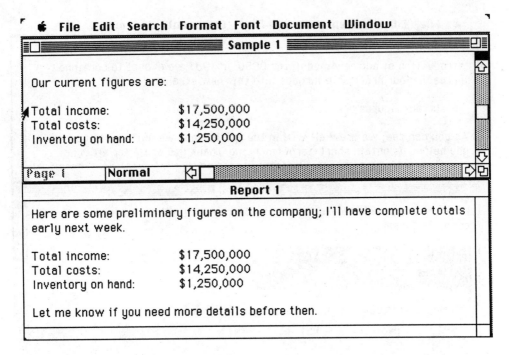

**Figure 4-11**   *Pasting the figures*

To see this, first shrink the Report 1 window as small as you can, as in Figure 4-12. Drag it down, then select the Sample 1 window and enlarge it (see Figure 4-13).

You also can change the size of Word windows using the *zoom box* in the right side of the title bar. Clicking this box causes the window to grow to the full size of the screen or, if it is already enlarged, to shrink to its previous size. This is handy if you have many windows that you open only occasionally. After you close these less-used windows, instead of having to drag down the size box of your main window, you can simply click its zoom box (or use COMMAND-OPTION-]).

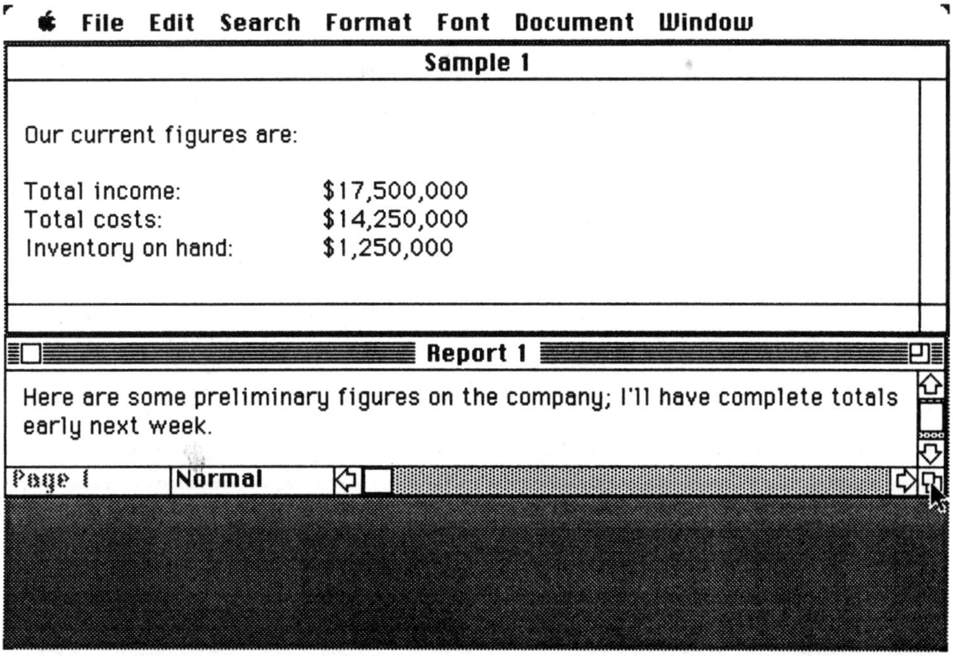

```
 ┌  ⬣ File  Edit  Search  Format  Font  Document  Window        ┐
 ╔═══════════════════════════ Sample 1 ═══════════════════════════╗
 ║                                                                ║
 ║ Our current figures are:                                       ║
 ║                                                                ║
 ║ Total income:          $17,500,000                             ║
 ║ Total costs:           $14,250,000                             ║
 ║ Inventory on hand:     $1,250,000                              ║
 ║                                                                ║
 ║                                                                ║
 ╟─────────────────────────── Report 1 ───────────────────────────╢
 ║ Here are some preliminary figures on the company; I'll have complete totals ║
 ║ early next week.                                               ║
 ║ Page 1      │Normal    │                                        ║
 ╚════════════════════════════════════════════════════════════════╝
```

**Figure 4-12**   *The Report 1 window shrunk*

For example, close the Report 1 window (first save the results). Your screen now looks like Figure 4-14. Click the zoom box to enlarge Sample 1 to full screen, the size it was before you opened Report 1. You can click the zoom box again to reduce it.

The zoom box remembers the shape of the window that you last used. If you change the window, zoom to full screen, then zoom back, your window will be the same size and shape and in the same location as it was before you zoomed to full screen. For example, use the size box to shrink the Sample 1 window to the middle of the screen, as in Figure 4-15. Now click the zoom box a few times to see how zoom remembers the last window.

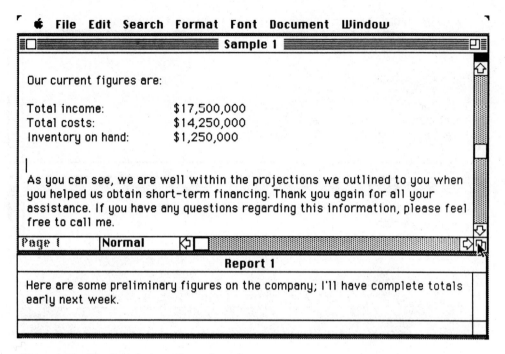

**Figure 4-13**   *The Sample 1 window enlarged*

# REVIEW

1. *Creating windows*

   Describe how you would open three files with two approximately square windows and one wide window, as in Figure 4-16.

2. *Using windows for multiple views of a file*

   In which of the following situations would two views of one file be useful?

   *a.* Moving a sentence from the beginning of a memo to the end

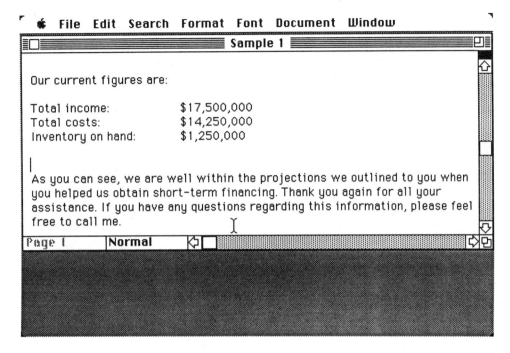

**Figure 4-14**   *The Sample 1 window by itself*

    *b.* Moving a sentence from the beginning of a paragraph to the end

    *c.* Changing all instances of one word to another

    *d.* Comparing two tables in a long report

*3. Using windows with multiple files*

Describe a situation in which you would want to have three windows open, each looking at a different file.

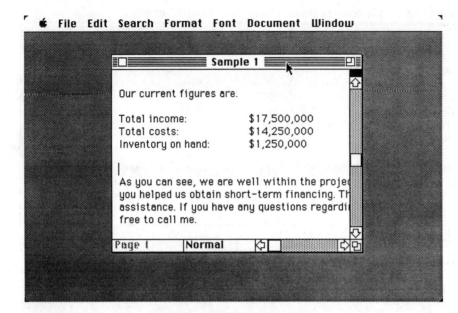

**Figure 4-15**   *The Sample 1 window made smaller*

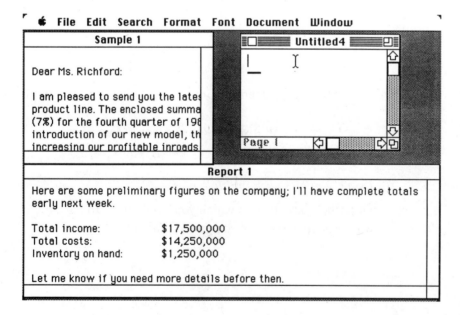

**Figure 4-16**   *Three windows*

# Chapter 5

## Merging Text and Pictures

**LESSON 18**  Merging Non-Word Files
**LESSON 19**  Using Art in Your Text

In Chapter 2 you learned how to use the Clipboard to copy and move text in a file. Often, however, you will want to incorporate a copy of an entire file into a file that you are editing. For instance, you may keep important charts in separate files so you can include them in a variety of memos.

You can merge two files by selecting the entire contents of one file, copying it to the Clipboard with the Copy command, opening the second file, and adding the Clipboard to the second file with the Paste command. However, there are a few situations where this method is not desirable. For example, if you have text in the Clipboard, you may not want to lose it when you merge the files. In this case, use the Scrapbook to store the text you don't want to lose. The file you are merging may be very large, so you could possibly run out of memory or disk space (however, Word will warn you before this happens).

# LESSON 18   Merging Non-Word Files

Word can merge any text whether or not you entered it with Word if you use the Clipboard. Text produced by an applications program (such as an accounting program or a report manager) can be moved from the Clipboard into a Word file with the Paste command. After you merge the text into a Word file, you can use Word commands to format the file.

You will probably want to edit the non-Word text that you transfer because its format may not match your other Word documents. It is also likely that Word will treat each line in the non-Word file as a paragraph; you may want to avoid this result (possibly by inserting NEWLINE characters where necessary).

You should be careful when transferring text from other applications programs, since some programs may use special formatting codes in the text in the Clipboard. Word does not recognize the codes inserted by other programs, so you may have problems incorporating text from other programs unless they store items to the Clipboard or Scrapbook without the codes.

Word can also read text files written by MacWrite and other programs. In fact, if you have MacWrite files on your disk, they will appear in the list box of the Open command. When you save these files, they will be stored in Word format. Word will convert as much of the MacWrite formatting as it can to Word formatting; however, you should check that the document looks the way you expect.

Word also lets you save files in different formats. This is useful for transferring formatted information to other word processing programs. To see which formats you can use, give the Save As command. Clicking on the File Format button gives you the list of formats that Word can save; these are shown in Figure 5-1.

The interchange format (RTF) at the end of the list was

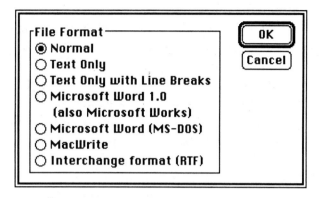

**Figure 5-1** *File formats that Word can save*

designed by Microsoft to transfer formatted text between programs from different manufacturers. Other programs also use
RTF, so you can transfer Word files back and forth between
programs by saving in RTF format.

# LESSON 19   Using Art in Your Text

There are many times when you might want to include art in
your text. Word allows you to use drawings from programs such
as MacPaint in your text by pasting them from the Clipboard
with the Paste command. Word also can read the visual images

from most other Macintosh programs. Check the manual for the program to be sure.

After you have included one of these images in your text, you can use Word to change its shape and size. All art images are stored as characters. You can treat the graphics just like other characters, including formatting them. Using character formatting for graphics is covered in Chapter 7.

There are two main purposes for including art in your text:  to show something that is being written about, and to provide decoration. Informational images are useful if you are talking about a product or a location where there are some salient features to the image that are best described with a picture. Decorative art often makes an otherwise boring report more interesting to read.

If you want many pieces of art in your Word document, store them in the Scrapbook, then cut them to the Clipboard. If you use this method you will not have to switch constantly between your drawing program and Word. Using MacPaint images that are selected with the lasso is easier than using those selected with the rectangle, since the lasso leaves no white space around the image. You cannot "edit" an image once it is pasted in your Word document other than by moving it around and stretching the entire image.

For example, suppose that you want to include a product shot in the Sample 1 file. First draw it in MacPaint (as in Figure 5-2), and then copy it to the Clipboard. Quit from MacPaint, run Word, and add a new sentence to the Sample 1 letter:  **Here is a picture of the DC50.** (See Figure 5-3.) Now give the Paste command, and Word puts the picture in the letter, as shown in Figure 5-4. Word now treats the image as if it were a character. If

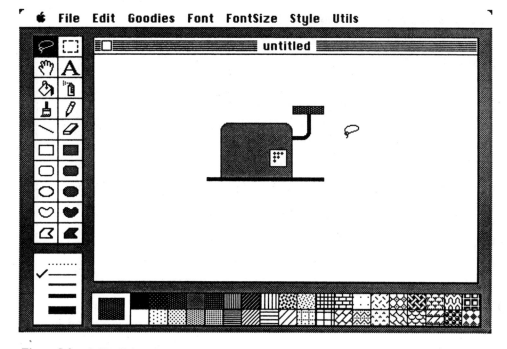

**Figure 5-2**  *A MacPaint picture*

you click anywhere in the picture, Word selects the picture by
surrounding it in a border with boxes on the bottom and right
edges of the border, as in Figure 5-5. This border does not
appear in the printout and disappears when you select any other
text.

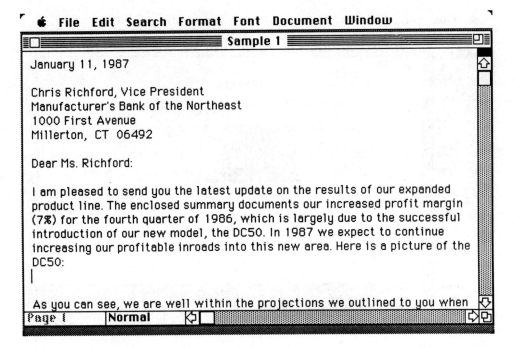

**Figure 5-3**    *New sentence added to Sample 1*

You can resize the picture frame by dragging on one of the squares. As Figure 5-6 illustrates, the box on the bottom edge stretches the bottom border vertically to show you how much length will be added to the picture. The right box allows you to stretch the picture frame horizontally. If you want to stretch the picture frame to the left and down by the same dimensions, drag the box in the corner until you create the space you want the enlarged picture to fill. If you want to stretch the graphic image

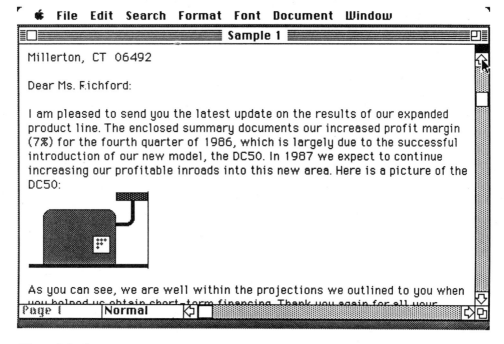

**Figure 5-4** *Picture pasted into letter*

itself, instead of just its frame, hold down the SHIFT key while you drag one of the boxes. This resizes the image.

Word centers the image within the stretched frame. The page box shows the length of the frame if you drag the left or bottom handles, or the percent change if you drag the corner. To shrink the frame to the smallest size that fits around the graphic, double-click the selected graphic.

Notice, however, that stretching the image (not just the box) usually makes patterns look strange. When you release the

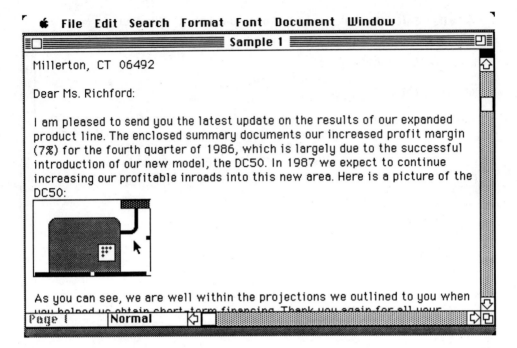

**Figure 5-5**   *Picture selected*

mouse, any text you have covered up moves to accommodate the new image. Of course, you can also move the images around your document just as you would any other paragraph by using the Cut, Copy, and Paste commands.

Word lets you add text to a graphic in an interesting fashion that is described in Chapter 8. For now, you can assume that if you have a heading that you want next to a graphic, or some text that you want to overlay on the graphic, you will be able to do that.

Word also allows you to save formatted text as a picture. This might be useful to you if your drawing program (such as Mac-Paint) does not give you as many choices about how to handle

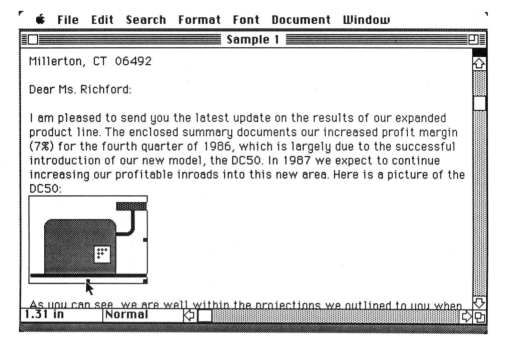

**Figure 5-6**   *The bottom border stretched vertically*

text as Word does. To save formatted text as a picture, select the text and press COMMAND-OPTION-D. This copies the text as a picture to the Clipboard.

# REVIEW

*1. Including non-Word files in Word*

How do you load text into Word from MacWrite? From other programs?

*2. Using art in Word files*

How does Word handle graphics?

# Chapter 6

## Using Glossaries

As you work more with a word processor, you will probably find that particular phrases or blocks of text are used over and over, such as the name of a company or a long product name. Typing this text many times in a report or memo is tedious, and copying it from another file each time can take almost as long as typing it.

Word eliminates this problem with *glossaries*. A glossary is a set of abbreviations that, together with the longer phrase, corresponds to each entry. Instead of repeatedly typing in the longer phrase, you simply type COMMAND-BACKSPACE followed by the abbreviation. Any phrase or block of text may be abbreviated. An abbreviation can consist of as many as 64 letters or numbers—for example, "gemcol". One active glossary is available when you run Word, although you can store many separate glossaries on disk.

For instance, in the Sample 1 file, Thomas Mead's name and address could be saved as an abbreviation in the glossary for those occasions when he types his address at the bottom of a letter. Chris Richford's name and address and the name "National Generators" could also be saved. Table 6-1 shows the suggested entries for this glossary.

Glossaries can be great timesavers since they eliminate the necessity of having to type sections of text that you often use. They also prevent typing mistakes in commonly used terms and names (it could be very embarrassing to misspell a client's company name in a letter). You can also store graphics in the glossary.

The rest of this chapter explains how to set up glossaries and how to use the entries in them. Although glossaries are an advanced feature available in only a few word processing programs, it is likely that you will find many uses for them after reading this chapter.

***Table 6-1***   *Glossary Entries for Sample 1*

| Abbreviation | Expanded Text |
| --- | --- |
| ng | National Generators |
| thomaddr | Thomas Mead, Controller<br>National Generators<br>1275 Oak Glen Industrial Park<br>Oak Glen, CT 06410 |
| richford | Chris Richford, Vice President<br>Manufacturer's Bank of the Northeast<br>1000 First Avenue<br>Millerton, CT 06492 |

# LESSON 20 Creating a Glossary

You can create a glossary entry (an abbreviation and its associated text) with the Glossary command in the Edit menu. While editing a file, select a phrase or block of text for which you want to have an abbreviation. Then give the Glossary command, enter the abbreviation, and click Define. This creates the entry.

Now use the Sample 1 letter to see how to save entries. To save Chris Richford's name and address under the abbreviation "richford", select the text. Now give the Glossary command to open the Glossary window; Figure 6-1 shows the Glossary window

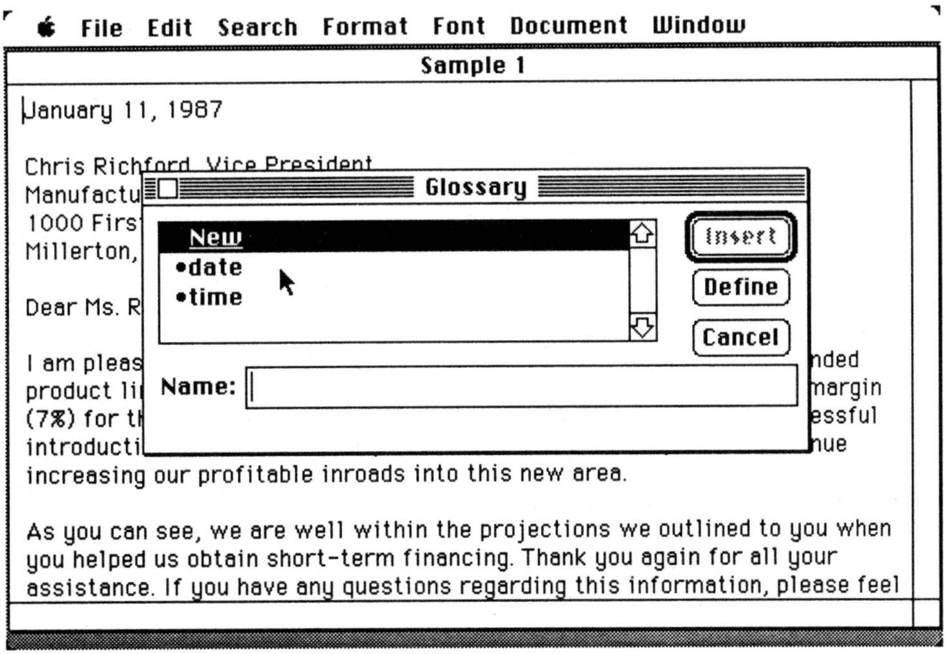

***Figure 6-1*** *Glossary window*

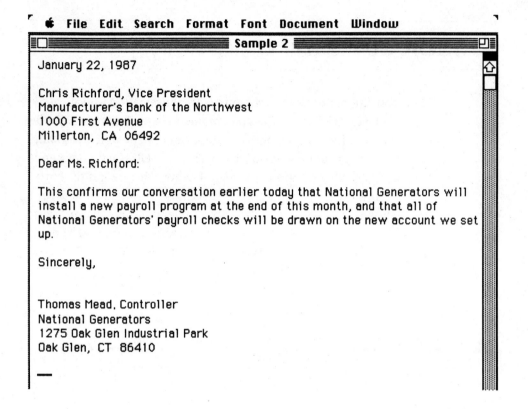

**Figure 6-2**   *Text of the second letter*

open on the Sample 1 file. Note that "New" is selected in the list box. In the Name box, type **richford**. Click the Define button. The text you selected now appears in the lower left corner of the box.

Also notice that the name is now in the list of abbreviations. To see what an abbreviation stands for, simply select it from the list. You will notice two items already in the list, "time" and "date", that you did not create. These are described later in the chapter.

When you want to expand an abbreviation, you simply press COMMAND-BACKSPACE, type the abbreviation, and press RETURN. To practice expanding abbreviations, save the three entries in Table 6-1 to the glossary (you have already saved "richford"). Close the Glossary window and the Sample 1 window, and give the New command to start a new letter. Your finished text will look like Figure 6-2, but you will use the abbreviations in the glossary instead of typing the names and addresses or the company name in the body of the text.

Start by typing the date. Next, press COMMAND-BACKSPACE and type **richford**, as in Figure 6-3. Now simply press RETURN. As Figure 6-4 illustrates, the abbreviation is expanded into the complete name and address. Continue the letter, using the abbreviations when you can. You can also insert text by giving

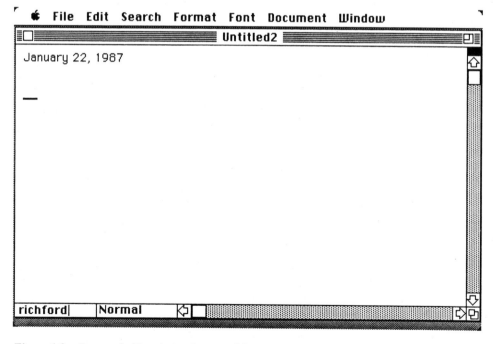

**Figure 6-3**   *Date and abbreviation in second letter*

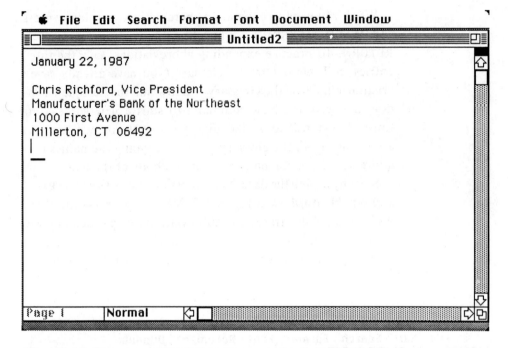

**Figure 6-4** *Abbreviation expanded*

the Glossary command, selecting the name of the abbreviation, and pressing the Insert button.

If you want to remove some of the entries in the glossary, give the Glossary command, select the entries, and give the Cut command. To replace a glossary entry, type the new text that you want for the abbreviation and select it. Give the Glossary command, select the abbreviation, and click Define.

# LESSON 21   Storing, Retrieving, and Printing Glossaries

To save the new glossary entries, give the Save As command from the File menu while the Glossary window is open. The dialog box shown in Figure 6-5 will appear. Notice that Word

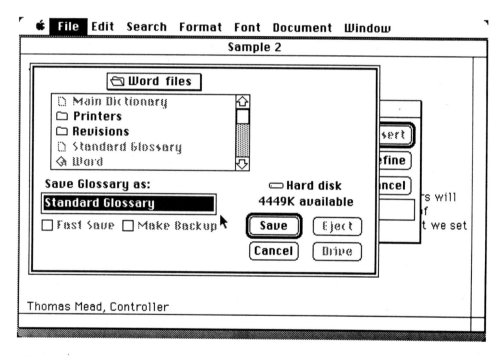

***Figure 6-5***   *Saving glossary entries*

fills in the name of the current glossary in "Save Current Glossary as". In this case, click the Save button to save the glossary with the name Standard Glossary, which is the glossary that Word loads automatically when you start it. If you quit from Word without saving new glossary entries, Word will ask if you want to save them.

If you want to use a glossary other than the standard one, give the Open command while you have the Glossary window open. You will see a list of the other glossaries, as shown in the dialog box in Figure 6-6. Select the name of the glossary you want to use. However, you will find that you most often will use the glossary that Word automatically reads, Standard Glossary. Having many glossaries is useful only if you have abbreviations that have the same name, but this is rarely the case.

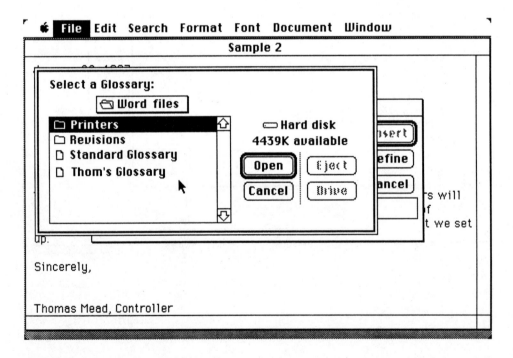

*Figure 6-6*   *Choosing another glossary*

As your glossary gets large, you may forget what is in it. To print out your glossary, give the Glossary command, and while the Glossary window is open, give the Print command.

# LESSON 22    Special Glossary Entries

Word has two predefined glossary names: "date" and "time." These entries are replaced with the current date and time when you use the Glossary command. It is likely, however, that you will want to put not the current date and time on your memo, but the date and time when it is printed. You can do this by adding two other glossary entries.

As you will see in Chapter 9, the date and time in headings are updated every time you print your document. You can add these special date and time entries to your glossary and use them in your text. To add these to your glossary:

1. Give the Open Header command from the Document menu. Word opens up a window with icons at the bottom of the screen, as shown in Figure 6-7.

2. Click on the clock icon. Word types the current time in the Header window. Select this time and give the Glossary command. Type in the name **timeprint** (or whatever name you want) and click Define. Word puts a rectangle in the lower left corner, as shown in Figure 6-8.

3. Next, click on the calendar icon. Word types the current date in the Header window. Select this date and click the Glossary window. Type in the name **dateprint** (or whatever name you want) and click Define. Word again puts a rectangle in the lower left corner. Now close the Glossary window.

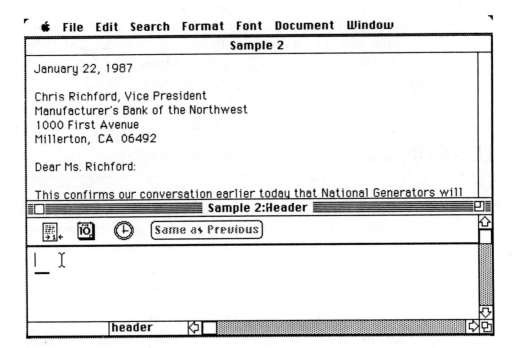

**Figure 6-7**    *The Header window*

4. Select all the text in the Header window and delete it. Click the Header window's close box, and when Word asks you if you want to save the header, click the No button.

Now you can use these new glossary entries in your documents. You also can add the page number icon from the header to the glossary.

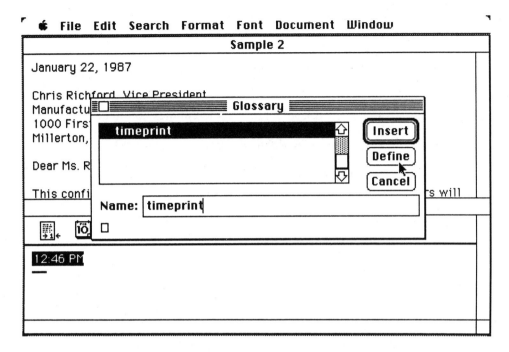

**Figure 6-8**    *The Glossary window with timeprint*

---

# LESSON 23    Finding Other Uses
## For Glossaries

---

Glossaries can reduce typing and increase accuracy in many
different applications. The following list should give you some
ideas for using glossaries in your daily word processing, and

Table 6-2 shows examples of some of these uses.

- Complex scientific phrases, such as the names of chemicals, long theory names, process names, and the names of reactions

- Standard legal citations, case names, and legal jargon

- Long, nearly identical names, such as model numbers

- Phrases that are heavily used in a document

# REVIEW

*1. Using glossaries to reduce typing and mistakes*

Suggest how you can use different abbreviations to distinguish the following pairs:
- *a.* Microsoft Word, *Microsoft Word*
- *b.* The New York Times, New York Times
- *c.* automatic error recovery, automated error recovery

**Table 6-2**    *Suggested Uses for Glossaries*

| Abbreviation | Contents |
| --- | --- |
| 13cb | anhydrous 1,3-dichlorobenzene, U.S.P. |
| rsae | Rivest-Shamir-Abel encryption |
| mcatcom | methyl-selenium catalytic combustion |
| yrox | Youngblood-Roberts oxidation |
| fiduc | 34 N.E. 2d 68, 70 |
| rw | Roe v. Wade |
| eqpro | equal protection of the laws |
| cl12 | Colonial 12-422 Model S |
| cc | press the COMMAND-C key |

2.  *Using the glossary window*

    How can you get a list of all the currently defined abbreviations? How do you remove glossary entries?

3.  *Saving and restoring glossaries*

    Which glossary is automatically loaded when you start Word?

# Part 2

## Using Word
## To Format

# Chapter 7

## Basic Formatting With Word

As part of the editing process, you will want to alter the way your text looks so your reader will more readily understand your meaning and so the information is presented in an interesting form. Word's formatting capabilities let you choose exactly how your text will look when it is printed out.

In order to make formatting easier, Word stores a great deal of information with your text. You do not see the special formatting codes that Word stores in your text; instead, the screen displays the properly formatted text, which is the result of the special codes.

Adding a formatting characteristic to text is called *direct formatting*. The concept of direct formatting is easy to grasp, since it is so similar to what you normally do when typing text. For instance, when you make changes on a first draft, you might decide to underline a phrase, change a font, or indent paragraphs. In doing this you are adding characteristics directly to text.

# LESSON 24   Introducing Formatting

The basic concept behind Word's formatting is that all text has certain characteristics associated with it. After you have specified the characteristics (such as underlining and indenting), Word automatically displays the text with those attributes. If you move the text to some other place in your document, the characteristics move with it.

You can enter an entire document without worrying about its formatting and then move to the beginning of the text and format the document. Or, if you wish, you can format your text as you enter it. Each time you add a characteristic, you see it instantly. Thus you can experiment with different formats, seeing which one best fits the meaning of the text.

Word gives you three "units" of formatting: characters, paragraphs, and sections. At the level of the smallest unit, Word lets you change the format of each character. For example, you can underline, boldface, or italicize characters, as well as change type fonts, with different formatting commands. Character formatting is most often used to make certain words stand out in your text. Figure 7-1 shows some character formats.

You have already learned to use the RETURN key to make paragraphs in Word; paragraphs are the second formatting unit. The paragraph is important to Word because Word stores formatting information for each paragraph when you press RETURN. In fact, all of the characteristics of a paragraph are stored in a bit of white space that is placed at the end of the paragraph (this is actually a paragraph mark).

For instance, many people like to indent every paragraph five spaces. Most word processors require you to press the TAB key (or press the SPACEBAR five times) at the beginning of each paragraph; Word, however, remembers this format once you have specified it and inserts the spaces for you in succeeding paragraphs unless you tell it otherwise. Other paragraph

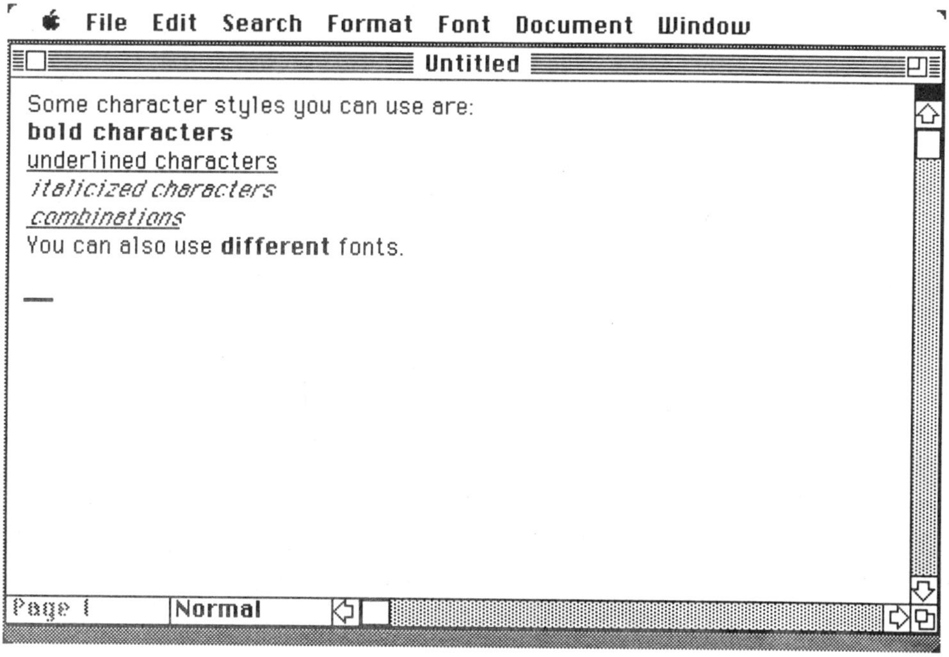

```
 ⌘  File  Edit  Search  Format  Font  Document  Window
╔══════════════════════ Untitled ══════════════════════╗
│ Some character styles you can use are:                │
│ bold characters                                       │
│ underlined characters                                 │
│ italicized characters                                 │
│ combinations                                          │
│ You can also use different fonts.                     │
│                                                       │
│ ___                                                   │
│                                                       │
│                                                       │
│ Page 1      Normal                                    │
╚═══════════════════════════════════════════════════════╝
```

*Figure 7-1*   *Character formats*

formats that you can specify include the indentation of the entire paragraph and alignment with the margin.

You will often want to set different formatting characteristics for a particular paragraph. For example, when you include a long quotation in text, you usually indent the whole quotation a few spaces from the margin. Tables, which are treated as paragraphs in Word, are also formatted differently from normal text paragraphs.

Since Word stores paragraph formatting characteristics in the paragraph mark, you can use the Copy and Paste commands to set the special formatting characteristics of one paragraph again for another paragraph. Simply copy the paragraph mark that you want to the Clipboard, move to the insertion point after the paragraph mark that you want to replace, press BACKSPACE, and then give the Paste command. All of the formatting characteristics are then applied to the new paragraph.

Word lets you set up different characteristics for each section, which is the third formatting unit. These are usually characteristics that do not change from paragraph to paragraph (for example, page headings and margin size). Since sections correspond to chapters of a book, you can, for example, format the introductory material differently from the chapters. You do not see section formatting on the screen; instead, it appears when you print your text.

It is important to remember that each element of your text, whether it is a character, a paragraph, or a section, has a set of formatting instructions attached to it. The end result is that formatting your documents is much easier with Word, since you can copy the specifications of one element from one formatting unit to another.

You may be wondering what all of these "characteristics" are. They will be discussed in this chapter and in Chapters 8 and 9, and are listed in Appendix B. For now, think of a direct formatting characteristic as a description of how the text looks or its position on the page.

## LESSON 25    Entering Formatting Commands

You can enter formatting commands in Word from the Format menu or with special key combinations. The formatting commands are much like the editing commands that you have already learned. You do not need to use the menus to enter every formatting command. Some character and paragraph formatting commands can be entered by pressing the COMMAND and SHIFT keys and a letter at the same time, such as COMMAND-SHIFT-B to boldface characters. These key sequences are described in this chapter and in Chapter 8.

The most common type of formatting you use is character formatting. For instance, book and magazine publishers commonly use italics for emphasis, foreign words, and book titles; they use underlining and boldface in different kinds of headings. The rest of this chapter discusses character formatting, Chapter 8 discusses paragraph formatting, and Chapter 9 discusses section formatting.

## LESSON 26    Using Common Character Styles

The purpose of using character styles is to make the reader notice a group of characters or words. This is often useful for emphasis, but common publishing practices also require it; for instance, book titles should generally be shown in italics.

Type in the text shown in Figure 7-2, which will be used to experiment with character formatting. Save this on disk with the name Character Test.

If you want to change the style of a group of characters, you

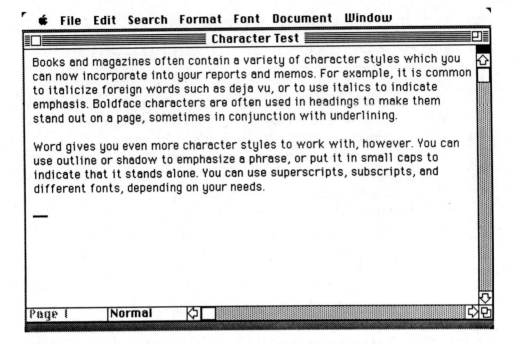

**Figure 7-2**   *Character Test*

will first select the group and then use the Character command in the Format menu (or COMMAND-D). The dialog box shown in Figure 7-3 appears.

You can change any of the toggles to indicate the styles you want. In fact, you can choose more than one style for your text. For example, you might want a title on a report to be both underlined and boldfaced. You can also set the toggles from the Format menu by dragging down to the item you want to set and releasing the button. When a toggle is set to "on," a checkmark appears next to it in the Format menu. If you are giving some text more than one format (such as both underlining and italics), you have to give separate commands.

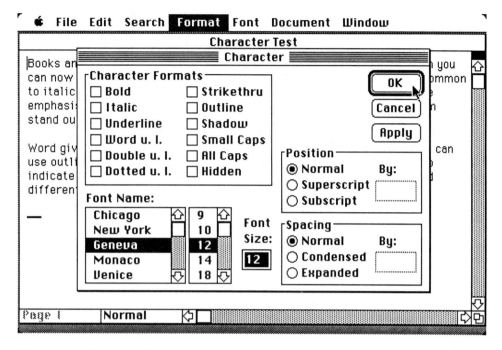

**Figure 7-3**  *Dialog box for character formats*

The styles that most people use in their writing are plain (no emphasis), italics, boldface, and underlining. Now, as an experiment, select the words "deja vu" in the text and give the Character command in the Format menu. Position the pointer as it is in Figure 7-4. Click the Italic button and then "OK". When the dialog box disappears, the words "deja vu" become italic, as in Figure 7-5. Move the selection away from the words so you can see them better.

Choosing boldface and underlining is similar to choosing italics. Select the words "stand out" and then boldface them by dragging down the Format menu to "Bold" and releasing the button; select the word "underlining" and give the Underline

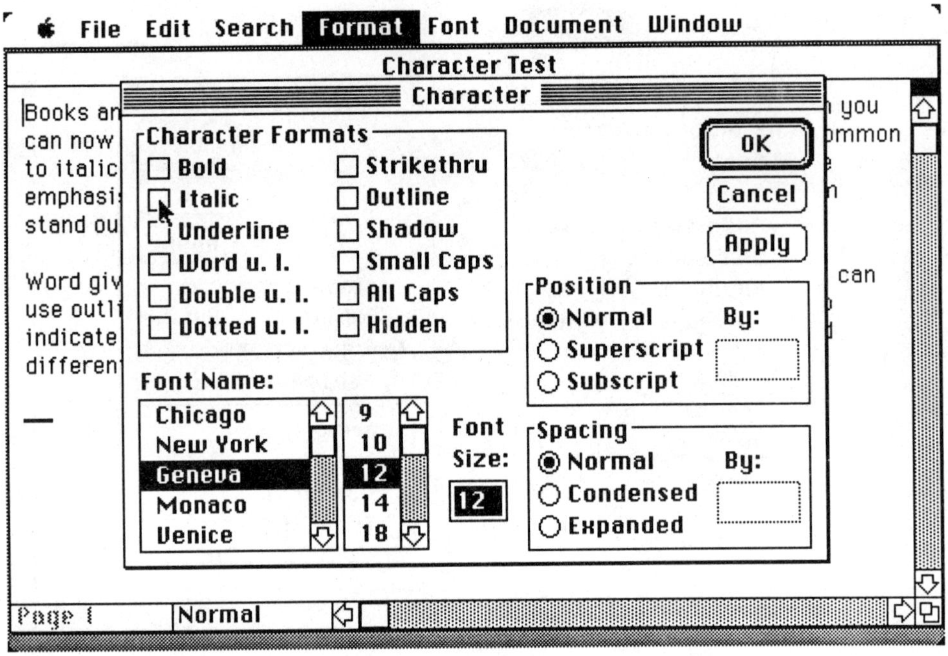

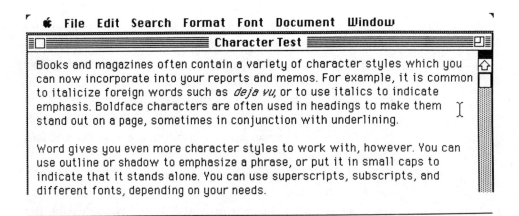

**Figure 7-4**   *Choosing italic style*

**Figure 7-5**   *Italics in text*

command (if you wish, you can also underline the period after it). The results are shown in Figure 7-6.

As mentioned before, you can apply more than one style to a section of text. To see this, select "in conjunction" and give the Character command. Now click both the Bold and Italic buttons, then click the OK button. Figure 7-7 shows how the text will look.

When you format characters, Word first checks the current formatting. For example, if you select the word "underlining" again and pull down the Format menu, the Underline option is already checked, as in Figure 7-8.

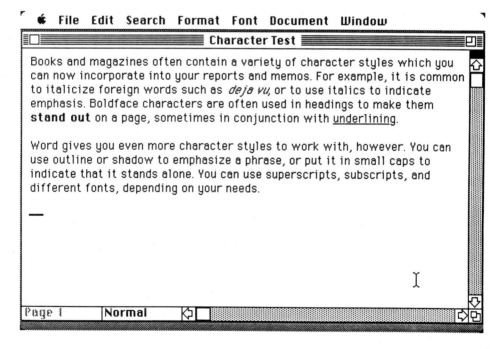

**Figure 7-6**  *Bold and underline in separate text*

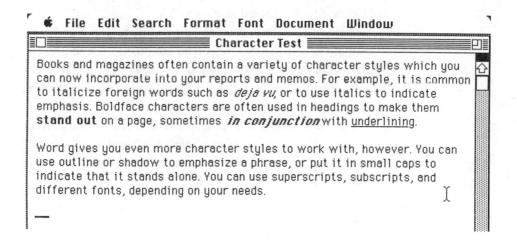

**Figure 7-7**   *Bold and italic together*

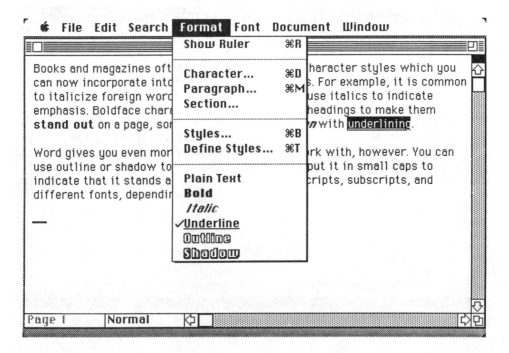

**Figure 7-8**   *Character menu set for Underline*

# LESSON 27    Using Other Character Formats

Word also lets you specify small caps, word underline, dotted underline, double underline, strikethrough, all caps, outline, and shadow. You can experiment with these. As you can see from the mixture of styles in Figure 7-9, it is easy to overuse character styles. Most book and magazine publishers avoid using too many styles so that the text doesn't end up looking like an old-time circus poster.

The ImageWriter and LaserWriter printers for the Macintosh can handle superscripts and subscripts, although some letter-

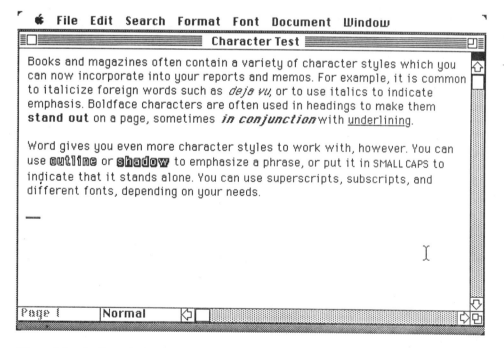

*Figure 7-9*   *Outline, shadow, and small caps added to text*

quality printers can't. It is always safe to specify these character formats in your documents even if your printer can't print them, since Word knows what your printer can and can't do and will compensate for it.

Superscripts and subscripts are chosen from the Position box of the Character command. These are often useful in scientific or technical papers. You can also use superscripts for footnotes (discussed in Chapter 9). Word lets you choose how high or low you want your superscript and subscripts.

To experiment with superscripts and subscripts, select the word "Superscripts" in the Character Test file, give the Character command, click the Superscript button, and then click the OK button. Figure 7-10 shows the effect on the word. Subscripts work the same way, with results like those in Figure 7-11.

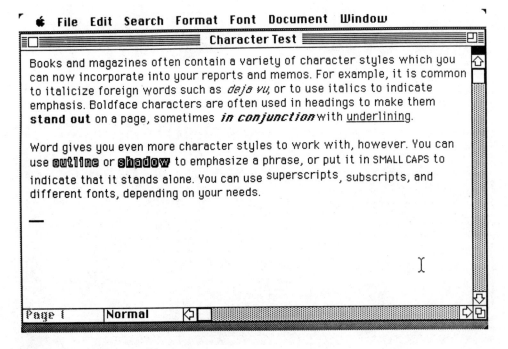

**Figure 7-10**   *Superscript in text*

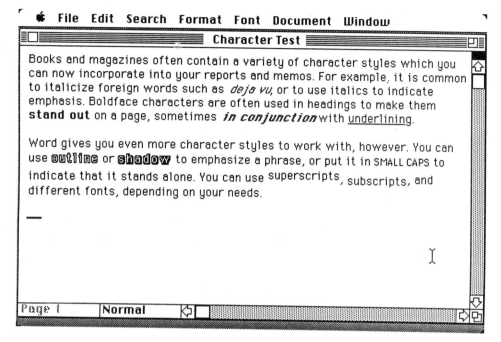

 ** File  Edit  Search  Format  Font  Document  Window

Character Test

Books and magazines often contain a variety of character styles which you can now incorporate into your reports and memos. For example, it is common to italicize foreign words such as *deja vu*, or to use italics to indicate emphasis. Boldface characters are often used in headings to make them **stand out** on a page, sometimes *in conjunction* with underlining.

Word gives you even more character styles to work with, however. You can use outline or shadow to emphasize a phrase, or put it in SMALL CAPS to indicate that it stands alone. You can use superscripts, subscripts, and different fonts, depending on your needs.

Page 1        Normal

**Figure 7-11**  *Subscript in text*

# LESSON 28  Using Other Fonts

As you probably have noticed, the Macintosh has many different fonts that you can use in your writing. These fonts are kept in the System file on the Word Program Disk. You may have as many or as few fonts available in Word as you desire, depending on whether you have used the Font/DA Mover (which is described in Appendix E).

If you have not experimented with fonts before, you will find that using different fonts creates different moods for your letters and reports. The following section covers the basics of type and fonts; if you are already familiar with fonts, feel free to skim through it.

## Introducing Type and Fonts

There are many ways to draw the standard alphabet. For instance, you may have very curly letters, very blocky ones, or letters with many intricate details. Each different alphabet set is called a *font*. Actually, a font contains more than just the letters of the alphabet: it contains all the numerals, punctuation marks, and special symbols as well.

Each font can have variations. The two major types of variation are *style* and *size*. You have already seen the different styles that Word can produce, such as underline, italics, and boldface. You may have noticed that when you applied a style with the Character command in the Format menu, the letters were still formed in much the way they were before.

The size of a font is defined as the amount of vertical space the letters take on a line. This size includes the amount that the letter goes above and below the *base line* (where the bottom of most letters line up) as well as the *leading,* which is the space between the very bottom of a letter and the very top of the letter on the next line. Figure 7-12 shows the elements that make up the size of a font.

Font size is measured in *points;* one point is 1/72 of an inch. For instance, the characters in a 12-point font are 1/6 of an inch high (including the leading). Fortunately, this is easy to translate to the Macintosh, since each dot (also called a *pixel*) on the screen is also 1/72 of an inch high.

Each font has many different characteristics that help define it. For instance, some fonts have *serifs,* which are little decorative lines used to finish off the stroke of a letter (fonts without serifs are called *sans serif*). Figure 7-13 illustrates the difference between serif and sans serif.

**Figure 7-12**    *Font sizes elements*

serif
sans serif

**Figure 7-13**    *Serif and sans serif*

Another common characteristic is whether the font uses *proportional spacing* or *monospacing*. In a proportional font, the letters have different widths; some of them may *kern,* or overlap another letter's space. In a monospace font, the letters and punctuation are all the same width. Figure 7-14 shows examples of each of these fonts.

Other characteristics include whether the type has wide or thin lines, what kinds of embellishments are used in the letters, and whether the letters can connect (as in a cursive font).

Each font on the Macintosh has a name (usually the name of a city). Figure 7-15 shows some of the fonts available with the Macintosh. Some of these may not be in the System file on your Word Program Disk; if you want to use them, you must install them with the Font/DA Mover.

## Changing Fonts

When you start entering text, you will notice that Word uses the Geneva font in 12-point characters (as you changed it in Chapter 1). You can easily change the font with the Character command. The dialog box (Figure 7-16) contains two lists:  one for the font

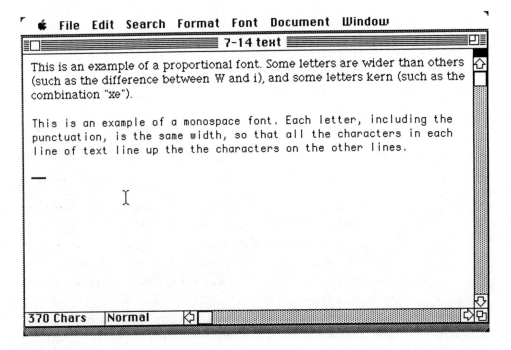

*Figure 7-14*    *Proportional and monospace fonts*

This is New York 12 **and New York 18.**

This is **bold,** underlined, outlined, shadow, *and italic.*

Some other fonts are **Chicago,** Geneva, Monaco, *Venice,*
London, Athens, *Los Angeles,* San Francisco,

and Toronto.

*Figure 7-15*   *Macintosh fonts*

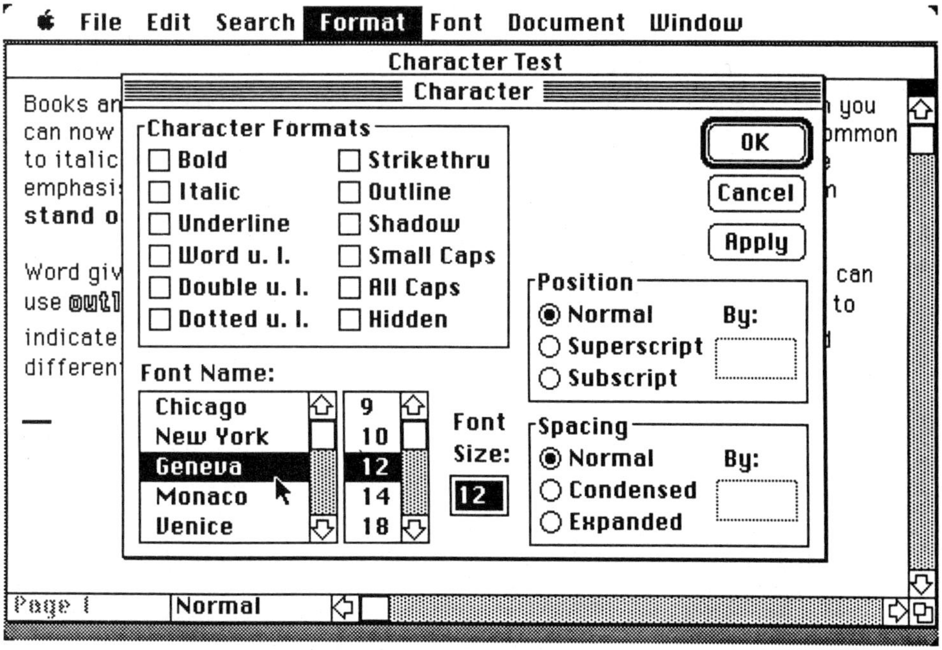

*Figure 7-16*   *Font and size choices*

names and the other for the font sizes. You can scroll through these to choose the size and style that you want to use. For each font, Word lists only the sizes that are available as installed fonts.

For practice, select the first paragraph of the text in the Character Test file and give the Character command. Click the Monaco font. Monaco comes in two sizes, 9 point and 12 point (as shown in Figure 7-17); click "9", then "OK". The selected paragraph will now appear as in Figure 7-18.

You can enter a font size that is not listed. To the right of the list of sizes is a box in which you can type a number. However, using font sizes that are not listed often causes the text to look jagged and poorly formed. Figure 7-19 shows how Monaco in 15-point type looks. Some fonts also look strange in boldface or outlined.

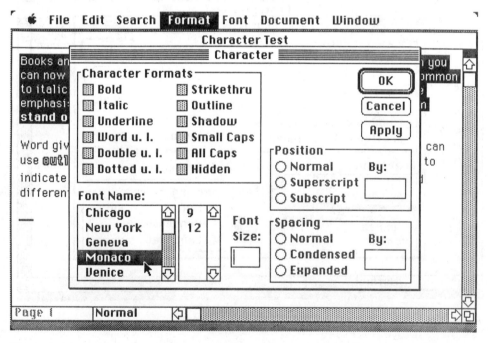

*Figure 7-17*    *Changing fonts*

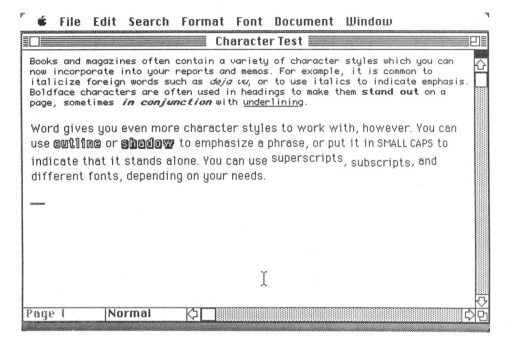

**Figure 7-18**    *Text after font change*

Many of the Macintosh fonts have international characters and symbols, as well as the standard alphabet. You can access these characters by holding down the OPTION key while pressing a character; you may need to hold down the SHIFT key as well. To see which characters correspond to the key combinations, use the Keycaps desktop accessory from the Apple menu.

Once you have experimented with all of the available character styles and some of the fonts, print out the file on your printer to see how it looks. Remember that Word does not mind if you request a style that your printer can't use; it will make its best guess about how the text should look based on your printer's capabilities. The ImageWriter can handle all of Word's capabilities, and your printed output will look just like the characters on the screen.

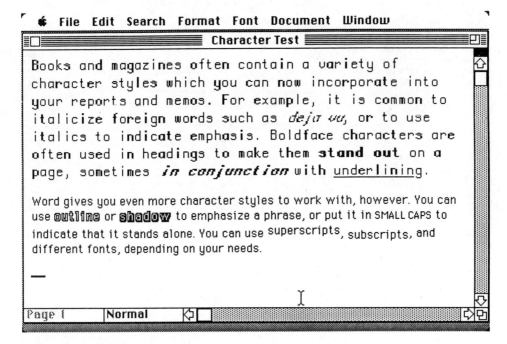

**Figure 7-19**   *Monaco in 15-point type*

# LESSON 29   Selecting Character Styles With the COMMAND Key

Using the Character command to change character styles can be tedious and slow since you need to give the command over and over. Word allows you to select character styles and fonts with key combinations.

Table 7-1 shows the key combinations used to select character styles and font sizes. As before, select the text you want to

**Table 7-1**   *Character Formatting with* COMMAND *Key Combinations*

| Format | Key Combination |
|---|---|
| Normal | COMMAND-SHIFT-SPACEBAR |
| Italic | COMMAND-SHIFT-I |
| Bold | COMMAND-SHIFT-B |
| Underline | COMMAND-SHIFT-U |
| Word underline | COMMAND-SHIFT-] |
| Double underline | COMMAND-SHIFT-[ |
| Dotted underline | COMMAND-SHIFT-\ |
| Small caps | COMMAND-SHIFT-H |
| All caps | COMMAND-SHIFT-K |
| Strikethrough | COMMAND-SHIFT-/ |
| Shadow | COMMAND-SHIFT-W |
| Outline | COMMAND-SHIFT-D |
| Subscript | COMMAND-SHIFT-MINUS |
| Superscript | COMMAND-SHIFT-PLUS |
| Increase font size | COMMAND-SHIFT-→ |
| Decrease font size | COMMAND-SHIFT-← |

change; then use the appropriate key combination. You also can change the font by pressing COMMAND-SHIFT-E followed by the font name.

Notice that using a key combination does not toggle the character style; it only adds it to the previous style. If words are in boldface, for instance, pressing COMMAND-SHIFT-I will show them in both boldface and italics. If you have combined many styles on some text, you need to use the Format menu commands to remove styles selectively. To do this, pull down the Character menu and drag to the style you want to remove. You can use COMMAND-SHIFT-SPACEBAR to remove all character styles.

For example, select the words "Books and magazines" in the previous file; then press COMMAND-SHIFT-I to put the words in italics. To add underlining, press COMMAND-SHIFT-U. The results will look like Figure 7-20. To make the words normal again, press COMMAND-SHIFT-SPACEBAR. You can use either upper- or lowercase letters with the above key combinations.

Word can show the Macintosh's graphics characters and it can also apply formatting to graphics that you paste in from other programs.

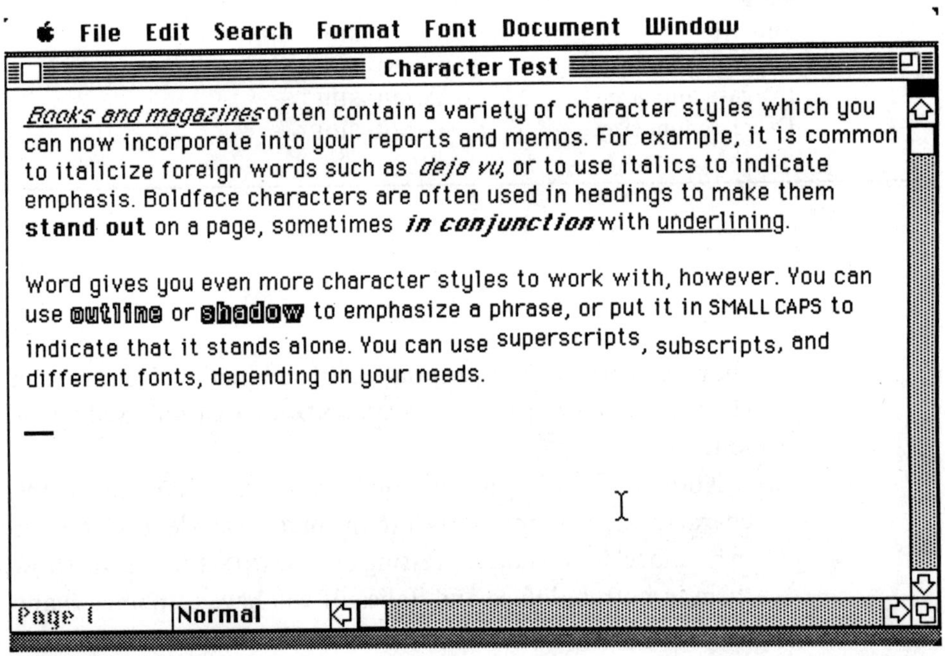

**🍎  File  Edit  Search  Format  Font  Document  Window**

**Character Test**

_Books and magazines_ often contain a variety of character styles which you can now incorporate into your reports and memos. For example, it is common to italicize foreign words such as _deja vu_, or to use italics to indicate emphasis. Boldface characters are often used in headings to make them **stand out** on a page, sometimes _**in conjunction**_ with <u>underlining</u>.

Word gives you even more character styles to work with, however. You can use outline or shadow to emphasize a phrase, or put it in SMALL CAPS to indicate that it stands alone. You can use superscripts, subscripts, and different fonts, depending on your needs.

Page 1   |   Normal

**Figure 7-20**   *Italics and underlined text from the keyboard*

# LESSON 30    Graphics and Graphics Characters

You may have noticed that the Macintosh screen can display a number of characters that are not on the keyboard. You can enter these characters into your text by pressing COMMAND-OPTION-Q and a number. If you use these characters in your Word document and use a printer that does not understand them, you can get unpredictable results (such as strange printing or large gaps in the printout). Letter-quality printers are usually not able to print special characters.

The characters available in Graphics font are shown in Table 7-2. Each font has a different set of characters available, including some numbers that are not shown in Table 7-2. Many of the characters are available by using the OPTION or SHIFT-OPTION keys. You can use the Key Caps desk accessory to find which key combinations produce specific characters.

Some characters are not available from the keyboard. To enter these characters, press COMMAND-OPTION-Q. The page box contains the word "Code," as shown in Figure 7-21.

Now type in the number of the character you want to insert and press RETURN. For example, if you type in 217, you will see the rabbit character (which is unavailable from the keyboard) shown in Figure 7-22.

For example, to change the "e" in "deja vu" to "é," delete it and use number 142. To change the "a" to "à," delete it and use number 136. The result is shown in Figure 7-23.

Most of the international characters with diacriticals also can be entered directly, although this procedure is confusing. It involves using the Macintosh *dead keys,* which are keys that do

***Table 7-2***   *Graphics Character Set*

| | | | | | | | | | |
|---|---|---|---|---|---|---|---|---|---|
| 33 | ! | 73 | I | 113 | q | 154 | ö | 194 | ¬ |
| 34 | " | 74 | J | 114 | r | 155 | õ | 195 | √ |
| 35 | # | 75 | K | 115 | s | 156 | ú | 196 | ƒ |
| 36 | $ | 76 | L | 116 | t | 157 | ù | 197 | ≈ |
| 37 | % | 77 | M | 117 | u | 158 | û | 198 | Δ |
| 38 | & | 78 | N | 118 | v | 159 | ü | 199 | « |
| 39 | ' | 79 | O | 119 | w | 160 | † | 200 | » |
| 40 | ( | 80 | P | 120 | x | 161 | ° | 201 | … |
| 41 | ) | 81 | Q | 121 | y | 162 | ¢ | 203 | À |
| 42 | * | 82 | R | 122 | z | 163 | £ | 204 | Ã |
| 43 | + | 83 | S | 123 | { | 164 | § | 205 | Õ |
| 44 | , | 84 | T | 124 | | | 165 | • | 206 | Œ |
| 45 | - | 85 | U | 125 | } | 166 | ¶ | 207 | œ |
| 46 | . | 86 | V | 126 | ~ | 167 | ß | 208 | – |
| 47 | / | 87 | W | 128 | Ä | 168 | ® | 209 | — |
| 48 | 0 | 88 | X | 129 | Å | 169 | © | 210 | " |
| 49 | 1 | 89 | Y | 130 | Ç | 170 | ™ | 211 | " |
| 50 | 2 | 90 | Z | 131 | É | 171 | ´ | 212 | ' |
| 51 | 3 | 91 | [ | 132 | Ñ | 172 | ¨ | 213 | ' |
| 52 | 4 | 92 | \ | 133 | Ö | 173 | ≠ | 214 | ÷ |
| 53 | 5 | 93 | ] | 134 | Ü | 174 | Æ | 215 | ◇ |
| 54 | 6 | 94 | ^ | 135 | á | 175 | Ø | 216 | ÿ |
| 55 | 7 | 95 | _ | 136 | à | 176 | ∞ | 217 | 🐇 |
| 56 | 8 | 96 | ` | 137 | â | 177 | ± | | |
| 57 | 9 | 97 | a | 138 | ä | 178 | ≤ | | |
| 58 | : | 98 | b | 139 | ã | 179 | ≥ | | |
| 59 | ; | 99 | c | 140 | å | 180 | ¥ | | |
| 60 | < | 100 | d | 141 | ç | 181 | µ | | |
| 61 | = | 101 | e | 142 | é | 182 | ∂ | | |
| 62 | > | 102 | f | 143 | è | 183 | Σ | | |
| 63 | ? | 103 | g | 144 | ê | 184 | Π | | |
| 64 | @ | 104 | h | 145 | ë | 185 | π | | |
| 65 | A | 105 | i | 146 | í | 186 | ∫ | | |
| 66 | B | 106 | j | 147 | ì | 187 | ª | | |
| 67 | C | 107 | k | 148 | î | 188 | º | | |
| 68 | D | 108 | l | 149 | ï | 189 | Ω | | |
| 69 | E | 109 | m | 150 | ñ | 190 | æ | | |
| 70 | F | 110 | n | 151 | ó | 191 | ø | | |
| 71 | G | 111 | o | 152 | ò | 192 | ¿ | | |
| 72 | H | 112 | p | 153 | ô | 193 | ¡ | | |

indicate that it stands alone. You can use superscripts, subscripts, and different fonts, depending on your needs.

Here is a new character: |
—

Code        Normal

**Figure 7-21**   *The page box*

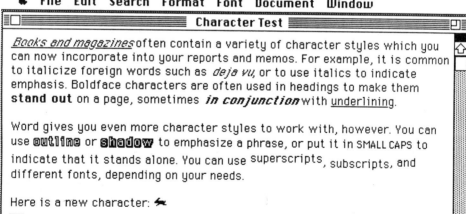

 **File   Edit   Search   Format   Font   Document   Window**

Character Test

*Books and magazines* often contain a variety of character styles which you can now incorporate into your reports and memos. For example, it is common to italicize foreign words such as *deja vu,* or to use italics to indicate emphasis. Boldface characters are often used in headings to make them **stand out** on a page, sometimes *in conjunction* with underlining.

Word gives you even more character styles to work with, however. You can use outline or shadow to emphasize a phrase, or put it in SMALL CAPS to indicate that it stands alone. You can use superscripts, subscripts, and different fonts, depending on your needs.

Here is a new character: 
—

**Figure 7-22**   *The rabbit character*

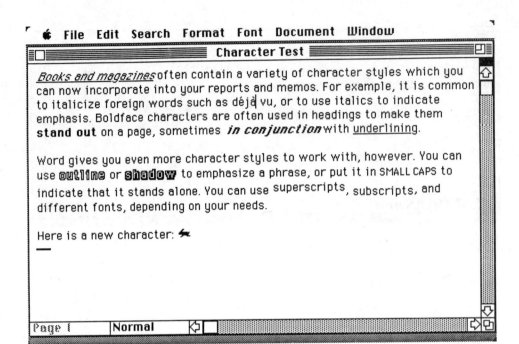

**Figure 7-23**    *International characters*

not print immediately, but cause the next key pressed to become a different character.

There are five dead keys that produce diacritical marks (listed in Table 7-3). To use them, press the dead key (such as OPTION-U), then press the letter you want the symbol over.

For example, another way to get "é" is to press OPTION-E (the dead key), then the letter "e." To get "à," press OPTION-` (the dead key), then the letter "a."

*Table 7-3*    *The Dead Keys*

| | Diacritical Mark | Dead Key |
|---|---|---|
| ~ | (tilde) | OPTION-N |
| ` | (grave accent) | OPTION-` |
| ´ | (acute accent) | OPTION-E |
| ¨ | (umlaut) | OPTION-U |
| ^ | (circumflex) | OPTION-I |

## Character Formatting and Graphics

Word treats graphics just like characters. Thus, you can use the character formatting you learned in this chapter with graphics that you put in your documents. There are two things you are most likely to do with graphics formatting: put a border around a graphic, and move it up and down on its line.

To format a graphic, select it as you learned in Chapter 5. Next, give the Character command in the Format menu and choose the character formatting you want. You can also format the box that you get with the Insert Graphics command in the Edit menu.

Word lets you put a border around a graphic using outline formatting. To see this, use the graphic that you created in Chapter 5 (see Figure 7-24). Select the graphic, give the Character command, and select Outline. The result is shown in Figure 7-25.

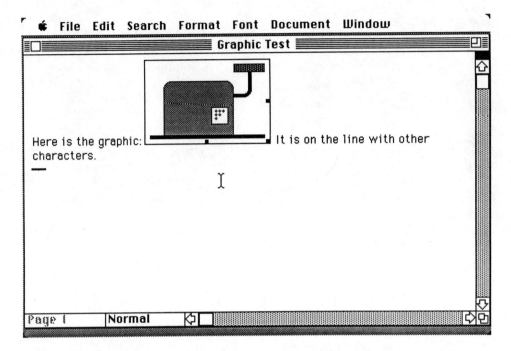

**Figure 7-24**   *The graphic selected*

Once you have an outline around your graphic, you can add other formatting. For instance, the outline and shadow features give a nice effect, as shown in Figure 7-26. Outline and bold give a darker box.

You can also use superscripts and subscripts to position the graphic within the line. Simply select the graphic and use the superscript and subscript formatting as you would for regular characters. This allows you to position graphics exactly where you want them.

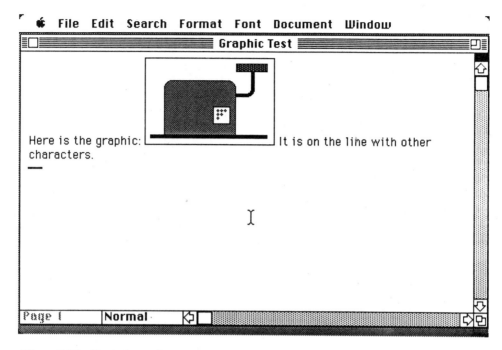

**Figure 7-25**  *Using the outline format*

# LESSON 31  Copying Character Formats

Now that you know how to apply a format to a character, you may be inclined to go back and add character formats to other files that you have created with Word. Giving the commands from the Character menu or entering COMMAND-key sequences

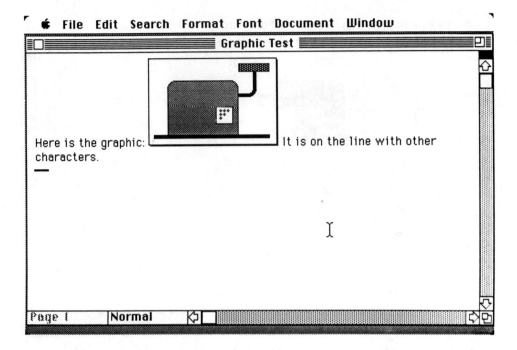

**Figure 7-26**   *Using the outline and shadow formats*

can get tedious, however, so Word allows you to copy the format of one set of characters to another without having to specify the actual format.

When you want to do this, you begin with one set of characters formatted the way you want (you will have to do this initially). The steps are

1. Select the formatted set of characters.

2. Press COMMAND-OPTION-V. The box in the lower left corner displays "Format to," as shown in Figure 7-27.

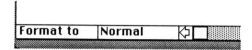

**Figure 7-27**  *Showing the "Format" message*

3. Select the characters to which you want to copy the format. Instead of highlighting them normally, Word uses a dotted underline.

4. Press RETURN. The characters you selected will be formatted and the selection moved to them.

These steps are best explained by example. Suppose that you want to change the first word in each sentence in the Character Test file to boldface (this is admittedly strange, but it's a good exercise). First, change the word "Books" to boldface with the Bold command; then press COMMAND-OPTION-V and select the word "For" in the second sentence, as in Figure 7-28. Press the RETURN key and the word "For" will be changed to bold, as in Figure 7-29.

Now press COMMAND-OPTION-V again and select the word "Boldface" in the third sentence. Press the RETURN key again. Figure 7-30 shows the results. You can continue to do this for any number of words or phrases.

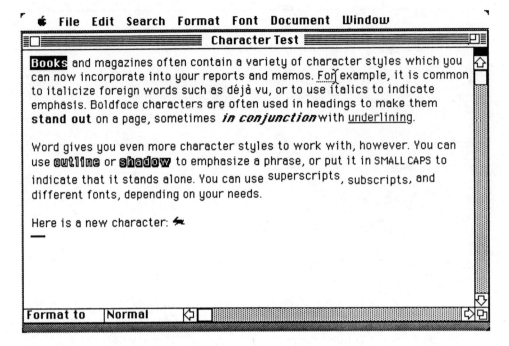

**Figure 7-28**    *"Books" in boldface, "For" selected*

# REVIEW

*1. Formatting characteristics*

Are the following formatting characteristics of characters, paragraphs, or sections?

   *a.* Headings at the top of each page

   *b.* Indentation of the first line of a paragraph

   *c.* Superscripted numbers

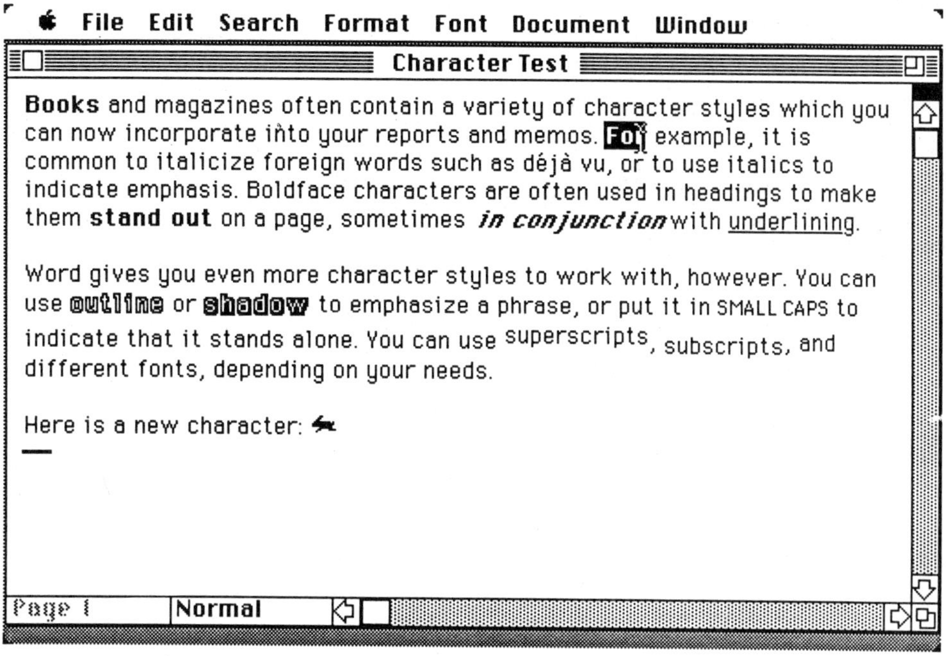

 **File   Edit   Search   Format   Font   Document   Window**

### Character Test

**Books** and magazines often contain a variety of character styles which you can now incorporate into your reports and memos. **For** example, it is common to italicize foreign words such as déjà vu, or to use italics to indicate emphasis. Boldface characters are often used in headings to make them **stand out** on a page, sometimes *in conjunction* with underlining.

Word gives you even more character styles to work with, however. You can use outline or shadow to emphasize a phrase, or put it in SMALL CAPS to indicate that it stands alone. You can use superscripts, subscripts, and different fonts, depending on your needs.

Here is a new character:

Page 1          Normal

*Figure 7-29   "For" in boldface*

2. *Changing text styles*

   Which character formats would be appropriate for the following?
   *a.* Book titles
   *b.* Emphatic sentences in an emergency procedures manual
   *c.* Footnote numbers

3. *Using the COMMAND key for Character commands*

   Give the procedure for first making a word boldface, then boldface and underlined, then plain text again.

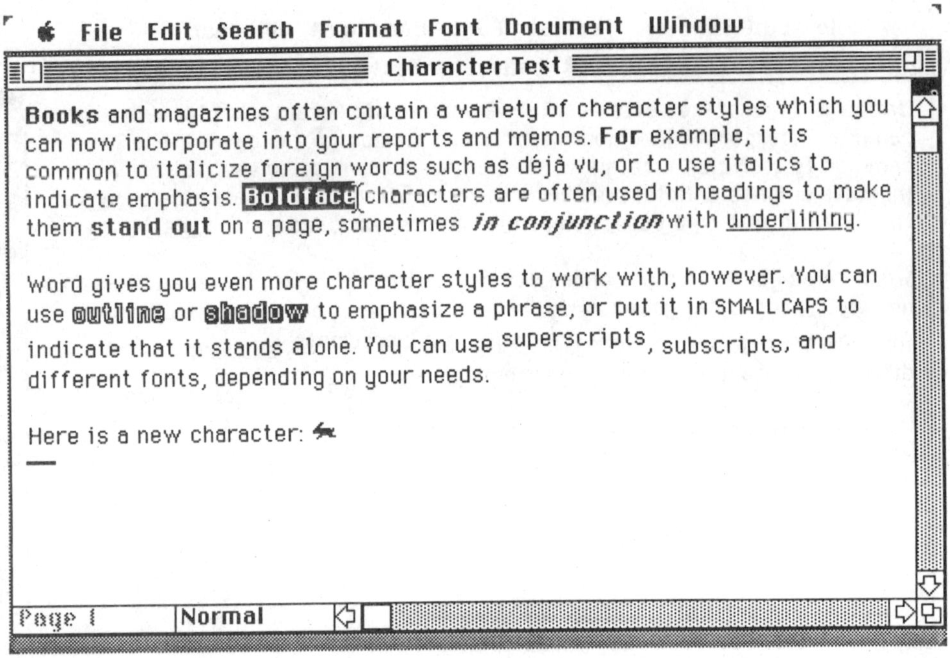

**Figure 7-30**  *"Boldface" in boldface*

4. *Copying character formats with the mouse*

   Copy the boldface and italics formats from the words "in conjunction" to the word "Sometimes" in the character test file. What is the procedure you used?

5. *International characters*

   How do you type "ü"?

# Chapter 8

## Formatting Paragraphs and Tables

One of the best ways to make letters and reports look professional is to use consistent formatting throughout the document. For example, if you indent your paragraphs, all paragraphs should be indented the same amount.

All headings should also be formatted consistently, so that the reader can quickly determine what you are saying. In a report, it is often important to see section headings and topics quickly. If your document is organized around an outline, your use of consistent formatting for each level of information will help the reader understand the meaning of the whole document.

Formatting paragraphs in Word is quite easy since Word associates a format with each paragraph. You can specify paragraph formatting when you enter the paragraph, and you can later change the formatting if you change your mind (just as you can with character formatting, described in Chapter 7). Word automatically uses the same format for each paragraph until you tell it otherwise. As a result, all of your text paragraphs will look the same until you give different formatting commands.

Tab stops are a format characteristic that you can set for a paragraph. Word's tab stops work just like those on a normal typewriter, but with one additional feature: if your writing includes figures and tables, you can easily use one set of tab stops for one table and a different set for another table.

There are many other interesting paragraph formatting features. For example, you can tell Word that you want a border (such as a solid line) around a paragraph; this makes headings stand out. You can also specify that you want two paragraphs to appear side-by-side.

## LESSON 32    Basic Formatting for Paragraphs

Word stores a paragraph's format in the mark at the end of the paragraph. You may have noticed that an extra blank character is inserted at the end of each paragraph after the period; this is the paragraph mark that is inserted when you press the RETURN key.

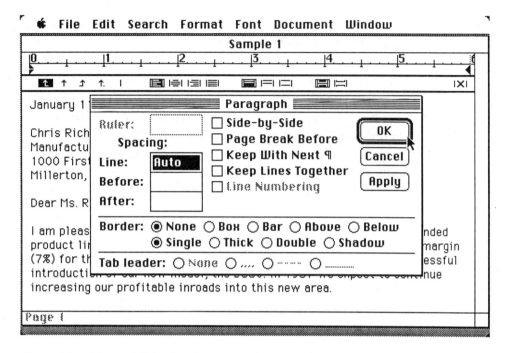

**Figure 8-1**   *Ruler and dialog box for Paragraph command*

You can choose from a variety of paragraph formatting options. To see a list of them, you can select any text in the paragraph and give the Paragraph command in the Format menu. For example, load the Sample 1 file into Word and put the insertion point in the first text paragraph. Now give the Paragraph command.

Notice that the top line of the file window changes to a ruler and that the dialog box is displayed in the middle of the screen, as in Figure 8-1. The ruler tells where your paragraph indentations are and where each tab stop is. The numbers on the ruler correspond to every inch; when you enter the settings for paragraph indentations, you normally give the position in inches, but you can change this with the Preferences command described in Chapter 13. You also use the ruler in this command to set tab stops, alignment, line spacing, and space around the paragraph. Figure 8-2 describes the parts of the ruler.

As in other Word menus, you simply choose the characteristics that you want the selected paragraph to have. The choices are described in the following lessons. Many of the paragraph formatting commands can be executed with COMMAND-key sequences (like those used in character formatting) instead of with the menu.

Remember that you can change the formatting of a paragraph at any time. Word has default settings for all of the paragraph formatting choices (sometimes called the "normal" choices), but it is likely that these will not be the best choices at all times. For example, you may enter some text in a memo with normal paragraph formatting and then decide later to indent the para-

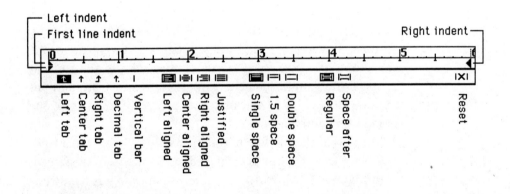

*Figure 8-2   Parts of the paragraph ruler*

graph from both margins to make it stand out on the page. You can change the margins, see how the paragraph looks, and decide to keep the new format. You can, of course, change it back at any time as well.

# **LESSON 33** Indenting Paragraphs

The most common changes that you will make to paragraph formats are to the indentation of the whole paragraph and of the first line. These can be changed with the left indent, first line, and right indent markers on the ruler. Throughout this section, remember that paragraph indentation is always relative to page indentation, which you will learn about in Chapter 10.

In common business letters and memos, the first line of each paragraph is indented from the margin by five spaces, or about half an inch. To do this in the Paragraph dialog box, simply move the first line indicator in the ruler to .5 inch, as shown in Figure 8-3. Click "OK", and notice that the paragraph is now indented, and the text is automatically wrapped around, as in Figure 8-4.

When you select the first line indicator in the ruler, the label in the top left of the Paragraph dialog box changes to "First" (see Figure 8-3). This is also true for the left indent, right indent, and tab stops. Instead of dragging the indicators, you can simply touch them and type in the value for the placement in the labeled box.

Sometimes you want to indent an entire paragraph from the left and right margins. This is common for direct quotations in reports. Indenting is also used a great deal in letters, especially for the date and closing (remember that these are considered paragraphs in Word). On a normal typewriter, you use the TAB

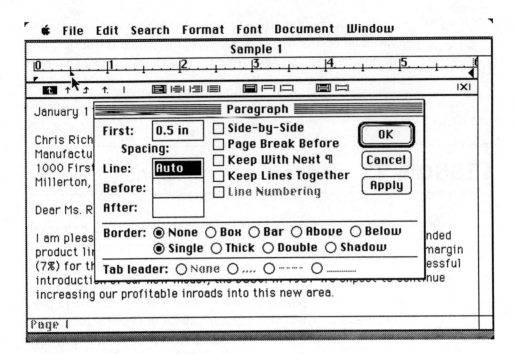

***Figure 8-3***   *Indenting the first line*

key or SPACEBAR to move to the place you want; in Word, you
simply indicate the indentation from the left margin. To see how
this is done, select the date at the beginning of the letter and use
the Paragraph command and drag the left indent indicator to 3
inches. To specify inches in the box, put the abbreviation "in"
after the number. Figure 8-5 shows the new position of the date.
If you move the date, you would probably indent the closing and
the name and address also.

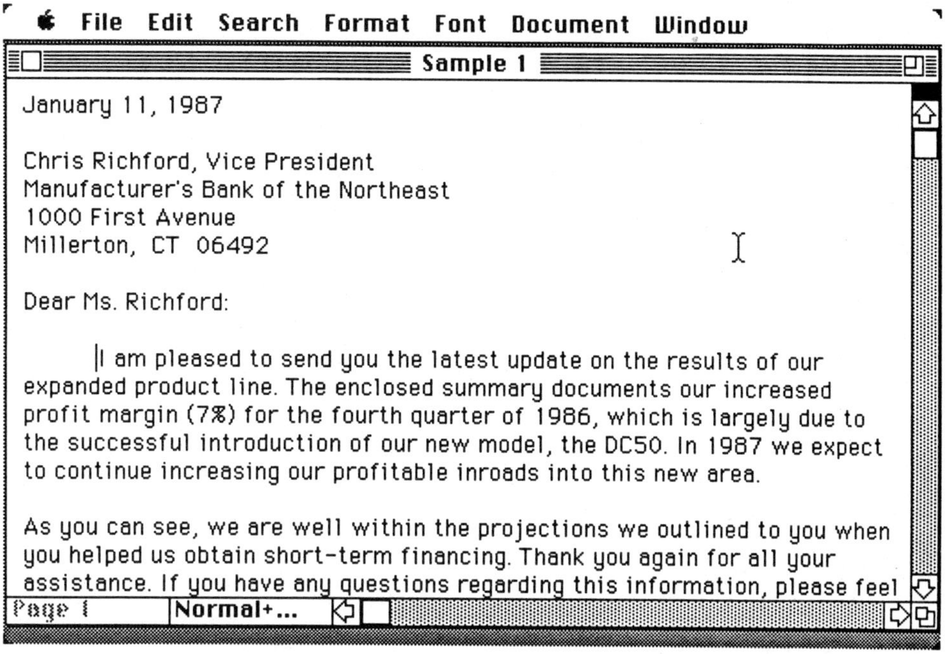

**&#x2665; File Edit Search Format Font Document Window**

≣ Sample 1 ≣

January 11, 1987

Chris Richford, Vice President
Manufacturer's Bank of the Northeast
1000 First Avenue
Millerton, CT  06492

Dear Ms. Richford:

 I am pleased to send you the latest update on the results of our
expanded product line. The enclosed summary documents our increased
profit margin (7%) for the fourth quarter of 1986, which is largely due to
the successful introduction of our new model, the DC50. In 1987 we expect
to continue increasing our profitable inroads into this new area.

As you can see, we are well within the projections we outlined to you when
you helped us obtain short-term financing. Thank you again for all your
assistance. If you have any questions regarding this information, please feel

Page 1        Normal+...

*Figure 8-4*    *First line indented*

The measurement indicated by the first line indicator is relative to that in the left indent indicator. That is, if you want to
indent the entire paragraph 1 inch and to indent the first line
half an inch beyond that, drag the left indent to 1 inch and the
first line to .5 inch. If you do not want to indent the first line but
want to move the entire paragraph 1 inch from the margin, you
would set the left indent to 1 inch and the first line to 0 inches. To
drag the left indent marker without moving the first line marker,
hold down the SHIFT key.

```
 ⌘  File  Edit  Search  Format  Font  Document  Window

▤□▤▤▤▤▤▤▤▤▤▤▤▤▤▤▤≡ Sample 1 ≡▤▤▤▤▤▤▤▤▤▤▤▤▤▤
                                  January 11, 1987                        ⇧

Chris Richford, Vice President
Manufacturer's Bank of the Northeast
1000 First Avenue
Millerton, CT  06492

Dear Ms. Richford:

        I am pleased to send you the latest update on the results of our
expanded product line. The enclosed summary documents our increased
profit margin (7%) for the fourth quarter of 1986, which is largely due to
the successful introduction of our new model, the DC50. In 1987 we expect
to continue increasing our profitable inroads into this new area.

As you can see, we are well within the projections we outlined to you when
you helped us obtain short-term financing. Thank you again for all your
assistance. If you have any questions regarding this information, please feel ⇩
Page 1       Normal+...    ⇦□                                           ⇦⇩
```

**Figure 8-5**   *The date indented*

This brings up an interesting situation:  what if you want the first line to start to the left of the rest of the paragraph? This format is called a *hanging indent* or an *outdent*. To see how this is formatted, select any part of the first full paragraph, give the Paragraph command, and set the left indent to 1 inch and the first line to −.5 (negative one-half) inch. The result is shown in Figure 8-6. Be sure not to set the left indent to a negative number.

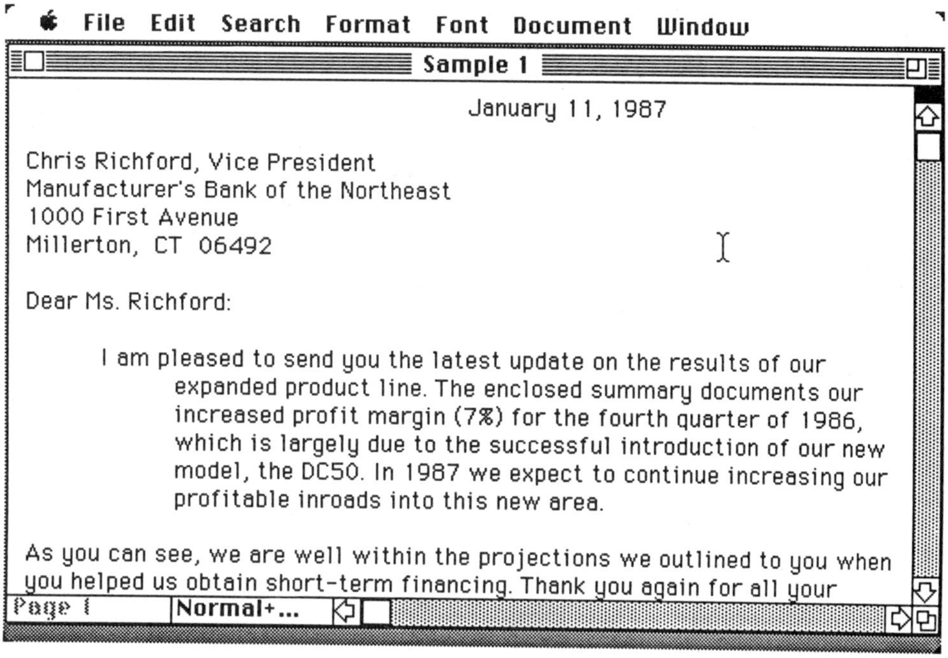

**&#xF8FF; File  Edit  Search  Format  Font  Document  Window**

Sample 1

January 11, 1987

Chris Richford, Vice President
Manufacturer's Bank of the Northeast
1000 First Avenue
Millerton, CT 06492

Dear Ms. Richford:

I am pleased to send you the latest update on the results of our
    expanded product line. The enclosed summary documents our
    increased profit margin (7%) for the fourth quarter of 1986,
    which is largely due to the successful introduction of our new
    model, the DC50. In 1987 we expect to continue increasing our
    profitable inroads into this new area.

As you can see, we are well within the projections we outlined to you when
you helped us obtain short-term financing. Thank you again for all your

Page 1     Normal+...

**Figure 8-6**  *First line outdented*

It is unlikely that you will change a paragraph's right margin unless you are also changing the left margin. Experiment by changing the right indent on the first full paragraph to 1 inch, as in Figure 8-7. As always, the Undo command will remove the effects of these changes.

Use the Show Ruler command (COMMAND-R) from the Edit menu to display the ruler. If you are displaying the ruler, you can set a paragraph's format by dragging the triangles and box

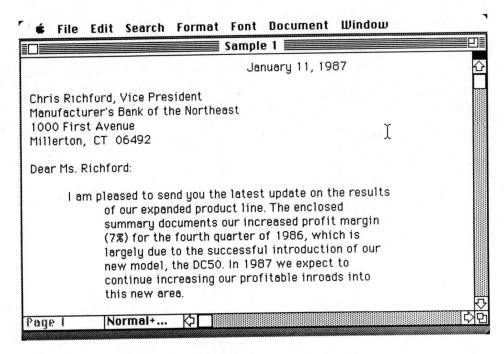

**Figure 8-7**   *Right margin indented*

around the ruler. For example, change your setting so that the first line will be indented by 1 inch by dragging the first-line triangle to the right by 16 jumps (each jump is 1/16 of an inch).

These indentation choices illustrate the reason that you want to treat related text as one paragraph by using NEWLINE instead of RETURN. Remember that you use NEWLINE (SHIFT-RETURN) to go to a new line without starting a new paragraph. When you change the margin with the Formats command, all the lines are formatted together since they are in one paragraph.

For example, assume that you want to move the lines with Thomas Mead's name, company, and address 3 inches from the left margin. If each line ends in a NEWLINE character, you can give just one command for the set of four lines, instead of having to format each line. To see how this works, change the paragraph's breaks to NEWLINE characters (if you did not use NEWLINE originally) by selecting the blank character at the end of each line, as shown in Figure 8-8. Replace the paragraph mark by typing in the NEWLINE character. Notice that the screen looks the same. Do this for all lines, and then select any part of this paragraph; give the Paragraph command and set the left indent to 3 inches. The lines now move together, with the result shown in Figure 8-9.

## LESSON 34   Line Spacing for Paragraphs

With Word you can modify the number of lines above, below, and inside a paragraph. In the examples that you have typed up to this point, you have inserted blank lines between paragraphs as if you were doing so on a typewriter—by pressing the RETURN key an extra time. Now you will see how to have Word do this automatically with the Formats command.

Although using this method is no easier than pressing the RETURN key, it allows you to enter text more consistently. Remember that one of the goals of using Word's formatting features is to make your documents look as consistent as possible. Instead of having to remember how many lines you want after each paragraph and pressing the RETURN key that many times, Word remembers to do this for you in the paragraph format.

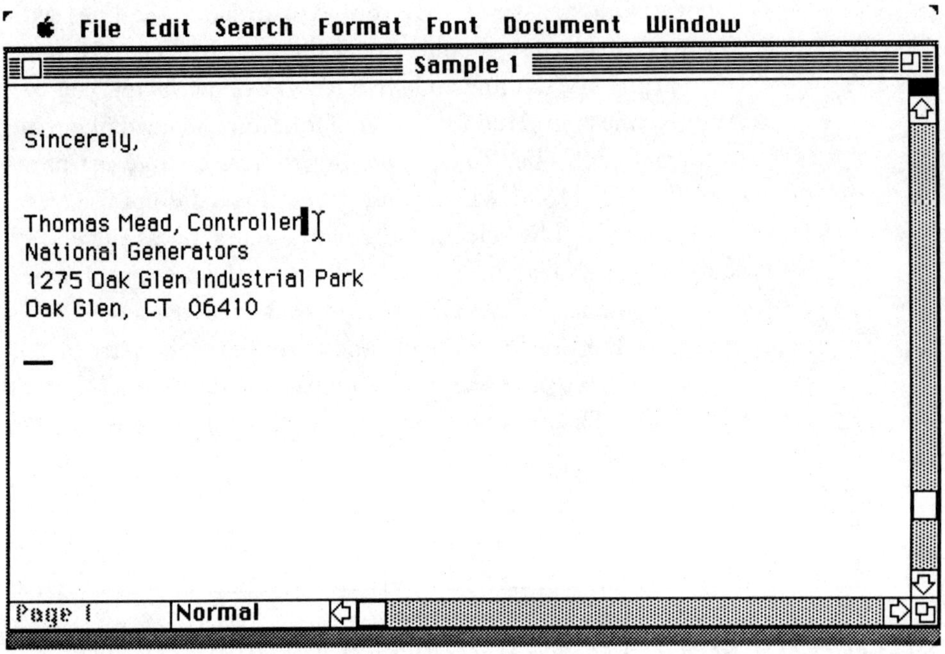

```
 ⚹  File  Edit  Search  Format  Font  Document  Window
```

```
▒▒▒▒▒▒▒▒▒▒▒▒▒▒▒▒▒▒▒▒ Sample 1 ▒▒▒▒▒▒▒▒▒▒▒▒▒▒▒▒▒▒▒▒

Sincerely,


Thomas Mead, Controller█]
National Generators
1275 Oak Glen Industrial Park
Oak Glen, CT  06410

▬

Page 1      Normal
```

*Figure 8-8*   *Paragraph mark selected*

If you want to insert blank lines between paragraphs, it is usually easier to specify them as space before the paragraph, not after. Thus, you should change "Before" to 12 points, or .166 inches, for the first text paragraph in Sample 1.

Unfortunately, you cannot simply type in **1 line** for the Before or After measurements; you must enter the number of points or inches. A point is approximately 1/72 of an inch, so 12 points is about 1/6 of an inch. After giving the command, the screen looks like Figure 8-10. You now need to eliminate the empty

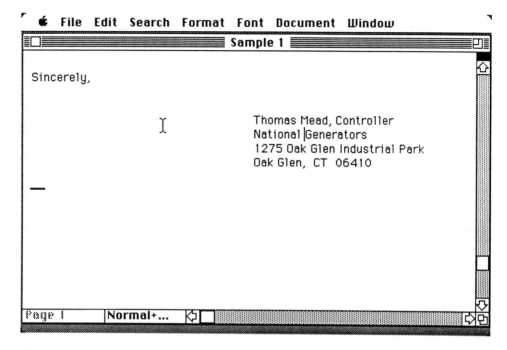

**Figure 8-9**   *Name and address indented*

paragraphs that you created when you used the RETURN key the second time. To do this, select the blank space at the end of a paragraph, as in Figure 8-11.

Press the BACKSPACE key; this makes the letter look as it did before by removing the second paragraph mark. Now reformat each paragraph in a similar fashion. The lines between the closing and Thomas Mead's name should be specified as two lines before the name.

Line spacing allows you to specify that a particular paragraph

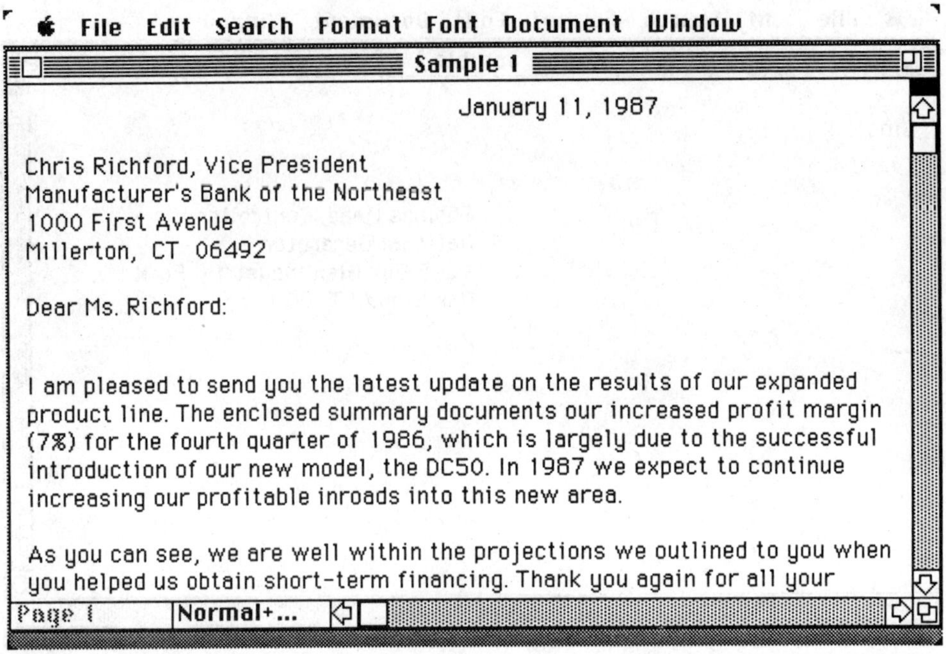

 ┌─────────────────────────────────────────────────────────────┐
 │  **⌘  File   Edit   Search   Format   Font   Document   Window**  │
 ├─────────────────────────────────────────────────────────────┤
 │ ▢▤▤▤▤▤▤▤▤▤▤▤▤▤▤▤▤▤▤▤▤  **Sample 1**  ▤▤▤▤▤▤▤▤▤▤▤▤▤▤▤  □ │
 │                        January 11, 1987                    ⬆ │
 │                                                              │
 │  Chris Richford, Vice President                              │
 │  Manufacturer's Bank of the Northeast                        │
 │  1000 First Avenue                                           │
 │  Millerton, CT  06492                                        │
 │                                                              │
 │  Dear Ms. Richford:                                          │
 │                                                              │
 │                                                              │
 │  I am pleased to send you the latest update on the results of our expanded │
 │  product line. The enclosed summary documents our increased profit margin │
 │  (7%) for the fourth quarter of 1986, which is largely due to the successful │
 │  introduction of our new model, the DC50. In 1987 we expect to continue │
 │  increasing our profitable inroads into this new area.       │
 │                                                              │
 │  As you can see, we are well within the projections we outlined to you when │
 │  you helped us obtain short-term financing. Thank you again for all your  ⬇ │
 ├─────────────────────────────────────────────────────────────┤
 │ Page 1      │ Normal+...   ◁ ▢                          ▷ │
 └─────────────────────────────────────────────────────────────┘

***Figure 8-10***    *First paragraph after formatting with 12 points before*

is double- or triple-spaced. Direct paragraph formatting does not allow you to specify line spacing for an entire document, so that if you entered a document with single spacing, you must then change each paragraph to double or triple spacing. However, you can enter a document with double or triple spacing by formatting the first paragraph and then typing in the others.

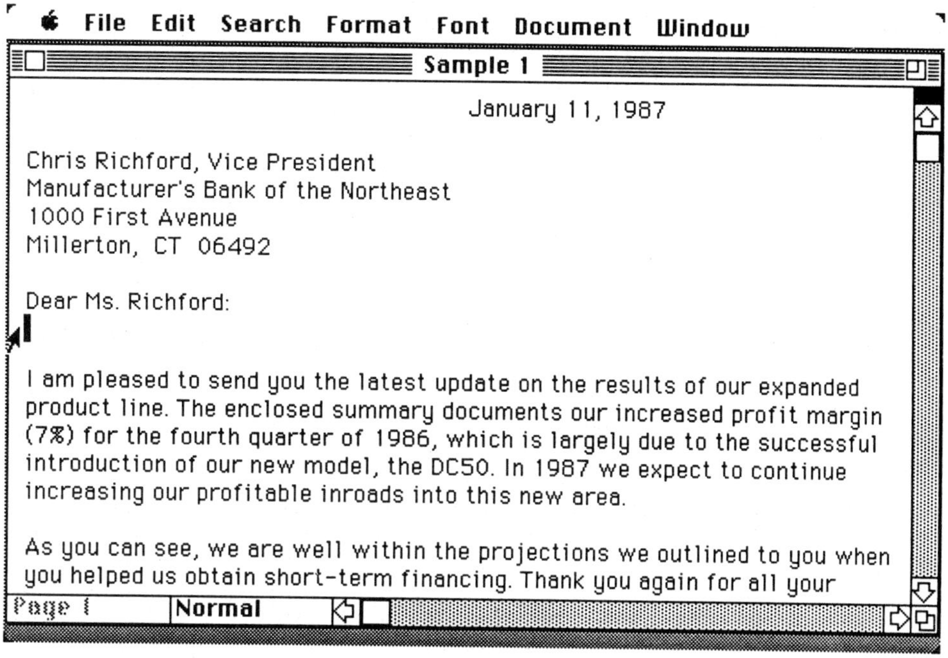

**Figure 8-11**    *Empty paragraph mark selected*

For instance, to double space the first paragraph in Sample 1, select it and type in **24 pt** for "Line". The result is shown in Figure 8-12. You can also click the double-space indicator on the ruler for the same result.

Word normally starts with the Spacing choice set to "Auto". This setting lets Word adjust the line height for you if you change font sizes and gives your text a generally open look.

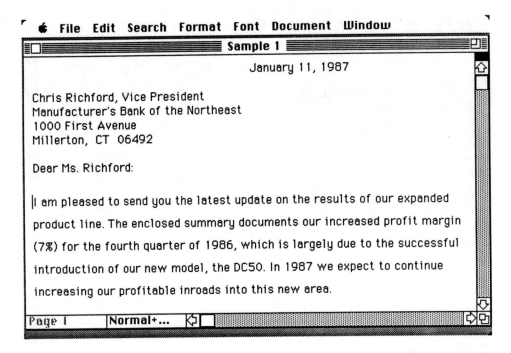

**Figure 8-12**   *Double-spaced paragraph*

---

# LESSON 35   Selecting Paragraph Styles With the COMMAND Key

---

You can choose many of the paragraph styles with COMMAND-key combinations, just as you did in Chapter 7 with character styles. Table 8-1 shows the styles available.

***Table 8-1***   *Paragraph Formatting With* COMMAND *Key Combinations*

| Format | Key Combination |
|---|---|
| Normal | COMMAND-SHIFT-P |
| Indent .5 in. | COMMAND-SHIFT-F |
| Decrease indent .5 in. | COMMAND-SHIFT-M |
| Increase indent .5 in. | COMMAND-SHIFT-N |
| 1 in. hanging indent | COMMAND-SHIFT-T |
| 1 line before | COMMAND-SHIFT-O |
| Left-aligned | COMMAND-SHIFT-L |
| Justified | COMMAND-SHIFT-J |
| Centered | COMMAND-SHIFT-C |
| Right-aligned | COMMAND-SHIFT-R |
| Side-by-side | COMMAND-SHIFT-G |
| Double-spaced | COMMAND-SHIFT-Y |

As you can see, some of these key combinations, such as COMMAND-SHIFT-M and COMMAND-SHIFT-N, do not set an absolute format. Instead, they change the current settings of the paragraph by a small amount. You can use these key combinations repeatedly to move the margins.

For instance, select any part of the first text paragraph of the letter; then press COMMAND-SHIFT-N. Notice that the paragraph moves one-half inch, as shown in Figure 8-13. If you press COMMAND-SHIFT-N again, the paragraph will move farther to the right as shown in Figure 8-14. To move it back, you can use COMMAND-SHIFT-M.

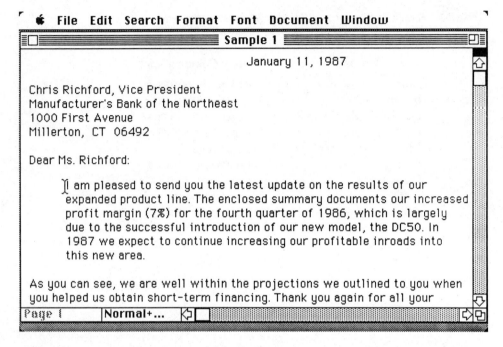

**Figure 8-13**   *First paragraph moved right one-half inch*

# LESSON 36   Aligning Paragraphs and Using Keeps

All of the paragraphs you have typed in so far have been *left-aligned*. This means that each line begins at the left margin and is formatted with wordwrap, but the right margin is ragged. Books and magazines often use *justified* margins, which means that, in addition to beginning at the left margin, the lines are filled with spaces so that each one ends on the right margin (for instance, this book uses justified margins). Many people find justified text easier to read, and it gives a professional look to reports.

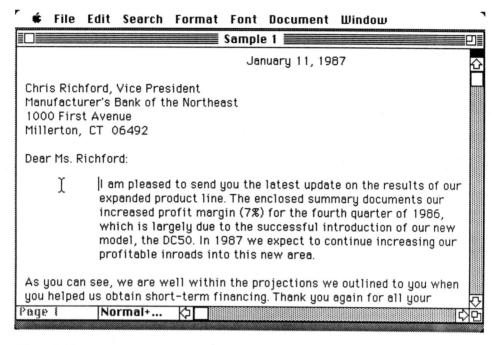

**Figure 8-14**   *First paragraph moved right one-half inch more*

Almost all of your writing will be either left-aligned or justified; however, Word also lets you center each line of text in a paragraph, which is often useful for headings or for text that needs to stand out on a page, such as warnings. For a trendy look, you can even format right-aligned text, which makes the left margin ragged and aligns the right margin. The four styles of paragraphs (left-aligned, justified, centered, and right-aligned) are illustrated in Figure 8-15.

Clear the Sample 1 file from your screen and enter the text for each paragraph in Figure 8-15. Then use the Paragraph command to set the alignment from the ruler. Experiment by adding text to the centered and right-aligned paragraphs to see how Word shuffles the characters as you type them.

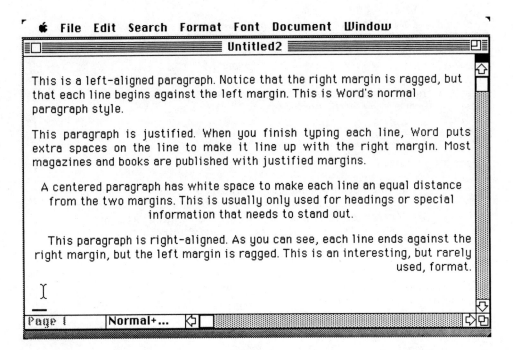

**Figure 8-15**   *Four paragraph styles*

Remember that you can use the NEWLINE character to start a new line without starting a new paragraph. You can use NEWLINE together with the centered format to make text stand out on a page. For example, enter the text in Figure 8-16 as a single paragraph with NEWLINE characters. Now use the Formats command to center the paragraph. The result should be as in Figure 8-17.

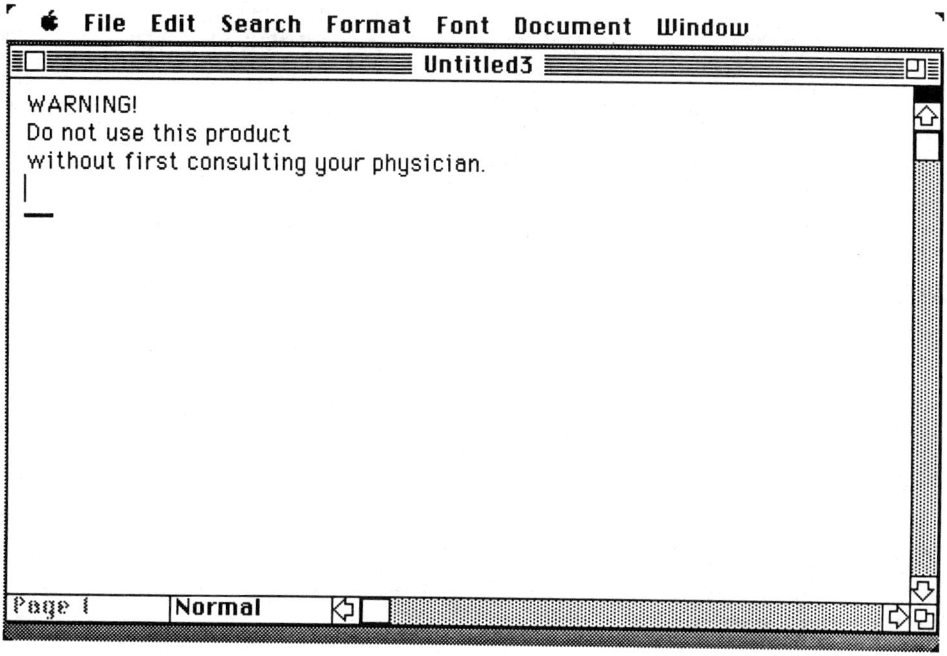

```
 ⌐        🍎  File  Edit  Search  Format  Font  Document  Window              ¬
 ┌──────────────────────────────────── Untitled3 ────────────────────────────┐
 │ WARNING!                                                                ⇧  │
 │ Do not use this product                                                    │
 │ without first consulting your physician.                                   │
 │ |                                                                          │
 │ ▬                                                                          │
 │                                                                            │
 │                                                                            │
 │                                                                            │
 │                                                                            │
 │                                                                            │
 │                                                                         ⇩  │
 │ Page 1      Normal      ◁ □                                          ▷    │
 └────────────────────────────────────────────────────────────────────────┘
```

**Figure 8-16**   *Paragraph with* NEWLINE

When you write memos and reports that are longer than one page, you may find that Word breaks the last paragraph on the page in an inappropriate place. Word automatically prevents *widows* (only the last line of a paragraph on the top of a page) and *orphans* (only the first line of a paragraph on the bottom of a page) by moving lines to or from a page as necessary. Word will never leave one line of a paragraph stranded on a page unless you turn this feature off in the Page Setup command.

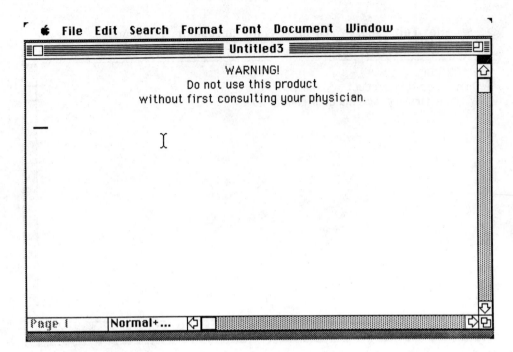

***Figure 8-17***   *Paragraph with* NEWLINE *centered*

There are times when you will want to keep the whole paragraph together. For instance, in tables or figures where blank space at the bottom of a page is preferable to splitting up the information. To keep a paragraph together, click the Keep Lines Together button in the Paragraph dialog box.

If you want to keep the selected paragraph with the paragraph that follows it, click "Keep With Next ¶ ". This tells Word that the two paragraphs must stay on the same page, which can be useful for keeping a heading with the text that follows it, or a caption under a quotation.

# LESSON 37    Creating Side-by-Side
Paragraphs

So far, you have learned how to create paragraphs that sit on a line by themselves. There are many times when you would want two paragraphs to be next to each other, however. For example, imagine that you were preparing a list of events and participants. You could create the list of participants before each event as shown in Figure 8-18. But it might be more useful to list the participants to the side as in Figure 8-19. You cannot do this easily with the table-making techniques you have learned so far, because here you need Word to wrap both the left and right columns.

Instead, use the Side-by-Side option of the Paragraph command. Before you do, however, you must determine the width of

Keller, Stanley, Anderson, Thatcher

Customer service seminar for all C.S. staff. Receptionists are invited to seminar.

Nolan, Timmer, Fellston

Group dynamics seminar for engineering staff and quality control technicians.

*Figure 8-18*    *Participants listed above events*

---

Keller, Stanley,          Customer service seminar for all C.S. staff.
Anderson, Thatcher        Receptionists are invited to this seminar.

Nolan, Timmer, Fellston   Group dynamics seminar for engineering staff
                          and quality control technicians.

---

**Figure 8-19**    *Participants listed next to events*

both paragraphs and their placement between the page margins. Word does not make this particularly easy, because you must know what the line length for your document is when you make these decisions. You will learn more about determining the page margins in Chapter 11; for this discussion, assume a line length of 6 inches.

In the previous example, you want the left paragraph to be 2 inches wide, the white space between the paragraphs to be .25 inch, and the right paragraph to be 3.75 inches. Since the text width is 6 inches, to make the left column 2 inches wide, set the right indent to 4 inches.

Follow these steps when you want to create side-by-side paragraphs:

1. Type in the text for both paragraphs.

2. Determine the layout of the page, as in the previous example.

3. Select the left paragraph and give the Paragraph command. Set the left indent to 0, the right indent to the width of the text on the page minus the width of the paragraph, and select the Side-by-Side option. In the previous example, the right indent would be 4 inches.

4. Select the right paragraph and give the Paragraph command. Set the left indent to the beginning of the paragraph, the right indent to 0, and select the Side-by-Side option. In the previous illustration, the left indent would be 2.25 inches.

Notice that the two paragraphs are not aligned on the screen. When you print your document, or view it in Page Preview mode, discussed in Chapter 9, Word aligns the columns properly. You can use the Side-by-Side option to put up to six paragraphs on the same line. The method is similar to the one used here, but you must set both the left and right indents for all the middle paragraphs.

Using the Side-by-Side option does not prevent you from using Word's paragraph formatting. In the previous example, both paragraphs are left-aligned. You can specify other formats just as easily.

## LESSON 38   Using Tabs

Setting up tables in your text is often one of the hardest chores in word processing. Even if the tabs are set just right, your data often does not fit on the page. Adding a column of text can be nearly impossible. However, if you set the tabs correctly with Word, you will find that making tables is very easy.

You set and move tabs with the Paragraph command. This command displays the ruler with the currently active tabs, as shown in Figure 8-20. Remember that the left and right triangles are the indentation settings. In your text, you skip to the tab stop the same way you do on a typewriter: by pressing the TAB key.

Word comes with a set of tabs defined as the default. These

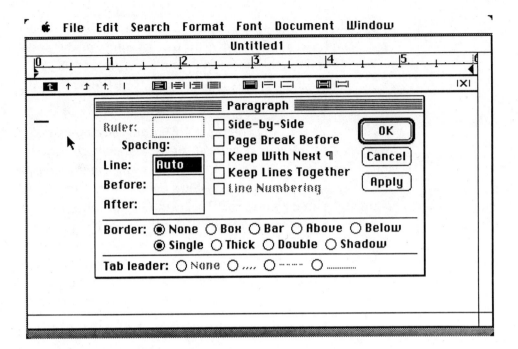

***Figure 8-20***   *Tabs displayed on ruler*

are set to every half inch. This is useful when you are typing letters and memos that don't require any special tab stops. You can change the setting for the default tab distance in the Page Setup command. When you enter a new tab stop, Word automatically erases all the default tabs to the left of that new tab.

Word has four different types of tabs: *left, center, right,* and *decimal.* The type of tab indicates where the text will line up against it. A left tab is like a tab stop on a typewriter: the text begins at the tab stop and continues to the right. A right tab is the opposite of a left tab: the text starts to the left of the tab stop and ends at the tab stop.

The example in Figure 8-21 should clear up any confusion

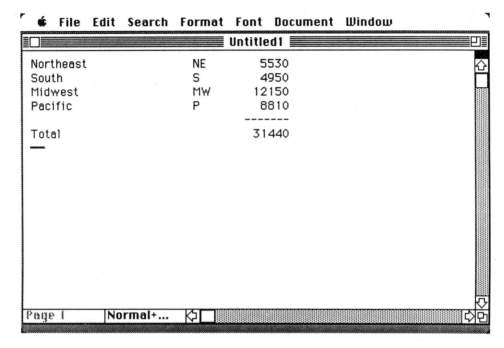

**Figure 8-21**   *Left and right tabs*

between these two types of tabs. The first tab (at 2.2 inches) is a left (normal) tab stop, and the second (at 3.5 inches) is a right tab stop. Notice that the numbers in the third column all end at the tab. In general, left tabs are used for text and right tabs are used for numbers. Right tabs are especially useful if you include a sum for the group of numbers, since numbers of different lengths then line up correctly.

A center tab causes the text to be centered around the tab stop, much like a centered paragraph; this tab is useful for headings of columns. A decimal tab causes numbers with decimal points to line up with the decimal point on the tab. In the next example in Figure 8-22, the tab stop at 1.5 inches is a

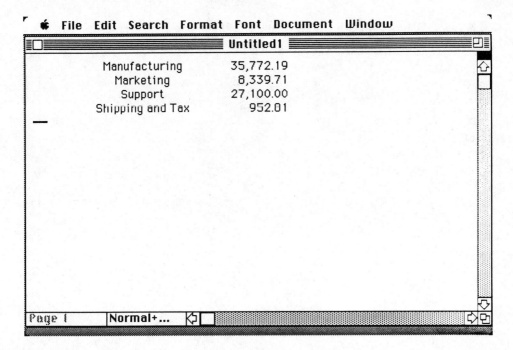

**Figure 8-22**   *Center and decimal tabs*

center tab and the tab stop at 3.5 inches is a decimal tab. These two types of tabs are used much less frequently than left and right tabs. Figure 8-23 shows how text and decimal numbers line up with the different types of tabs.

Word has another type of tab you should know about. The *vertical bar* is not really a tab because it does not affect the way you use tab characters, but you place it on the tab line in the ruler. Setting the vertical bar causes Word to draw a vertical line through the paragraph at that position. This is useful for drawing forms, as you will see in Chapter 19.

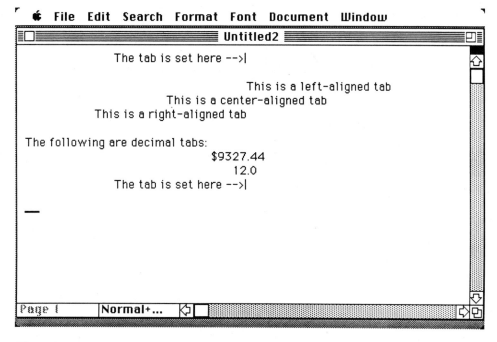

**Figure 8-23**   *Lining up text and numbers with tabs*

# LESSON 39   Setting Tabs

Setting tabs with the Paragraph command is fairly easy. You select the type of tab you want from the lower left position of the ruler (see Figure 8-24). Then you point to the upper part of the ruler and click where you want the tab to be set. You can repeat this for as many tabs as you want. To delete a tab stop, drag it down off the ruler. When you are done, click "OK". For

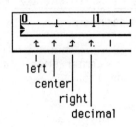

**Figure 8-24**   *Types of tabs in the ruler*

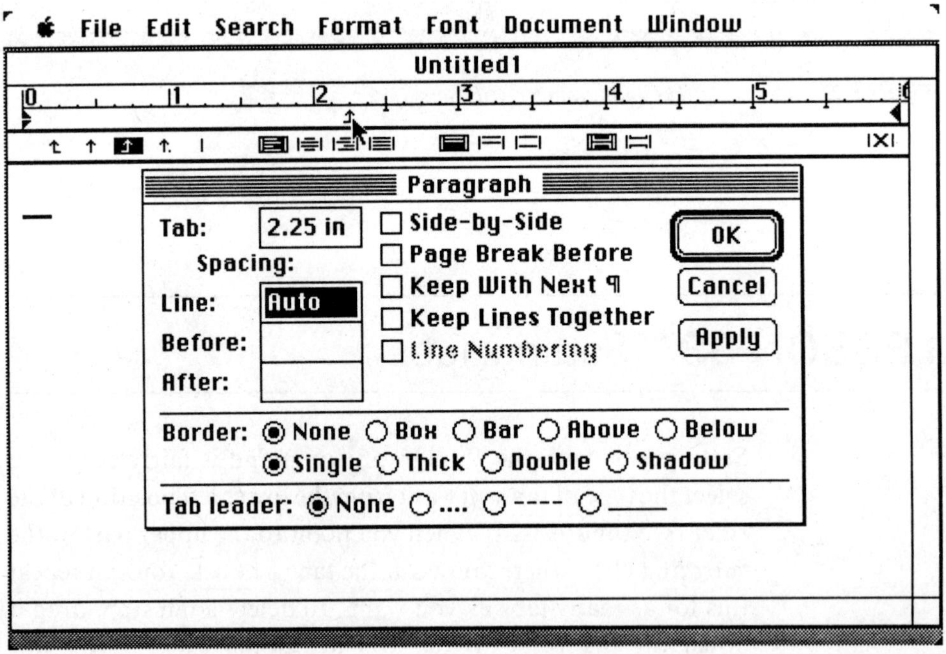

**Figure 8-25**   *Setting up a right tab*

instance, to set a right tab at 2.25 inches, click the icon for the
right tab stop in the ruler and then point at the space between 2
and 2.5 inches in the ruler, as shown in Figure 8-25. You can
move a tab setting on the ruler line by dragging it around. For
instance, drag the tab you just set to 2.5 inches. You can also
specify a tab by typing its position in the Tab box (see Figure
8-26).

Set up the table shown in Figure 8-27 for practice. The second
column is right-aligned, the third column is left-aligned, and the
fourth column is decimal-aligned. (If you need help, the three
tab stops are a right-aligned tab at 2.1 inches, a left-aligned tab
at 3.1 inches, and a decimal tab at 4.5 inches.)

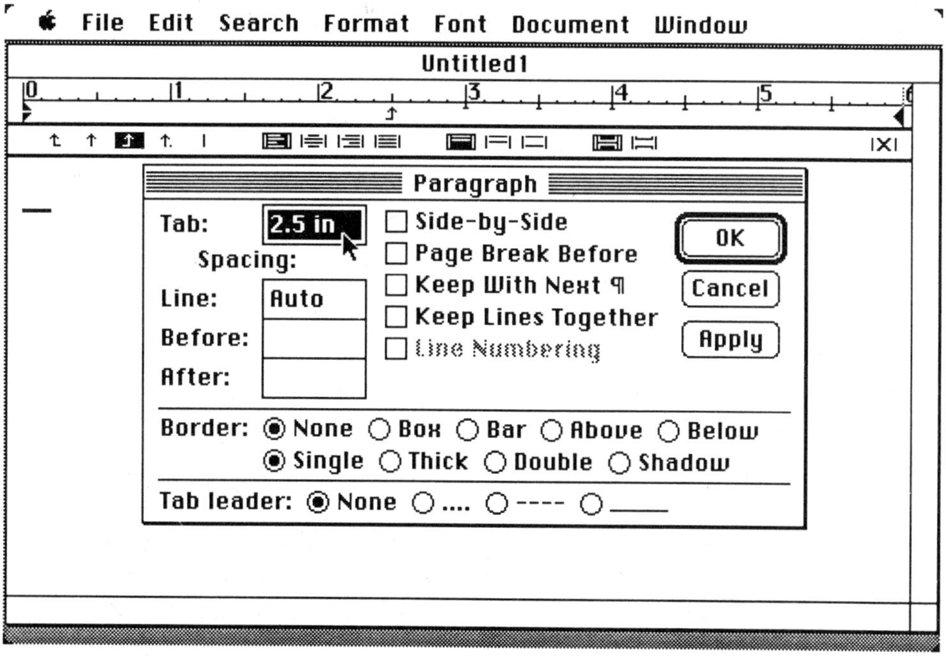

**Figure 8-26**  *Moving a tab setting*

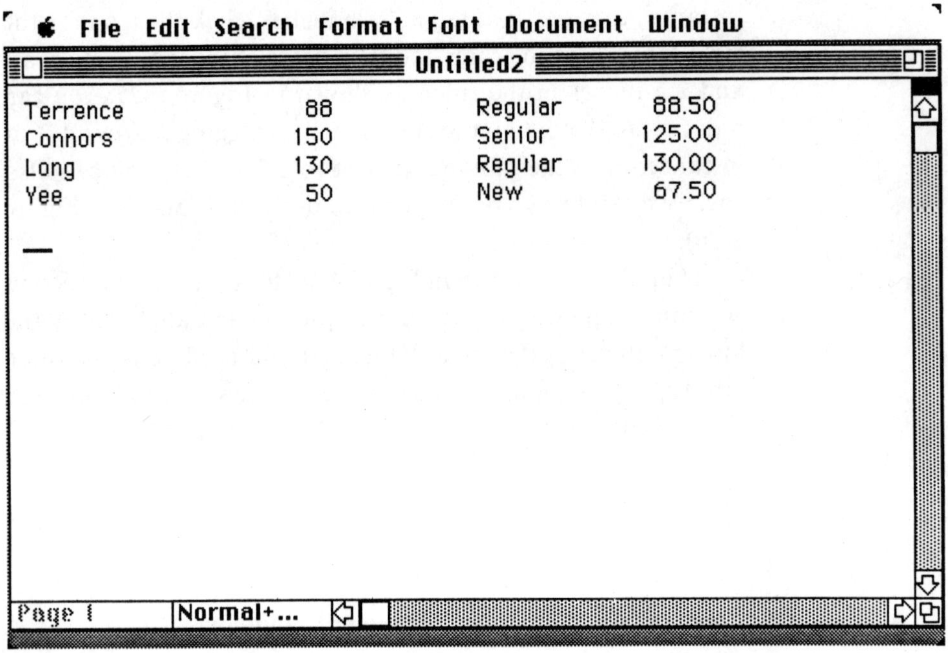

```
 ⌘  File  Edit  Search  Format  Font  Document  Window
═════════════════════════ Untitled2 ═════════════════════════
Terrence            88        Regular       88.50
Connors            150        Senior       125.00
Long               130        Regular      130.00
Yee                 50        New           67.50
—




Page 1      Normal+...
```

**Figure 8-27**  *Practice table*

# LESSON 40  Using Leader Characters and Making Tables

You may have noticed the Tab leader choice in the Paragraph dialog box. Many tables, such as financial summaries, often use characters to connect the columns of information across the page. These characters, usually dots, are called *leader characters* because they lead to the text at the next tab stop. Unless you specify otherwise, Word will assume that you want a blank leader character.

For practice, change the first tab stop in the previous example to include a dot leader character. Click on the tab stop on the ruler, then click the "...." button, as in Figure 8-28. The table will then look like Figure 8-29. This is, of course, a great deal easier than typing all the periods yourself. It is also easy to change to another type of leader character in a table since you don't have to erase the old characters and type in the new characters for each entry. For instance, change the leader character to a dash, as shown in Figure 8-30. The table now looks like Figure 8-31. You can also use underscores as leader characters.

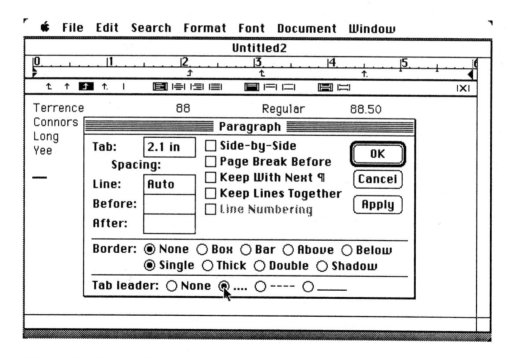

**Figure 8-28**   *Selecting dot leader characters*

```
 🍎  File  Edit  Search  Format  Font  Document  Window
═══════════════════════════ Untitled2 ═══════════════════════════
Terrence..............................88        Regular        88.50
Connors............................ 150         Senior        125.00
Long.................................. 130       Regular       130.00
Yee....................................50         New           67.50

━


Page 1      Normal+...
```

*Figure 8-29*   *Dot leader characters in table*

When making a complex table, it is a good idea to use graph paper and pencil before setting your tabs. Figure out where on the line you want each item to appear and mark that place; then use the Paragraph command.

The table in Figure 8-32 uses a number of different types of tabs; see if you can figure out which ones were used. Note that the table makes use of underlining and boldfacing to make the

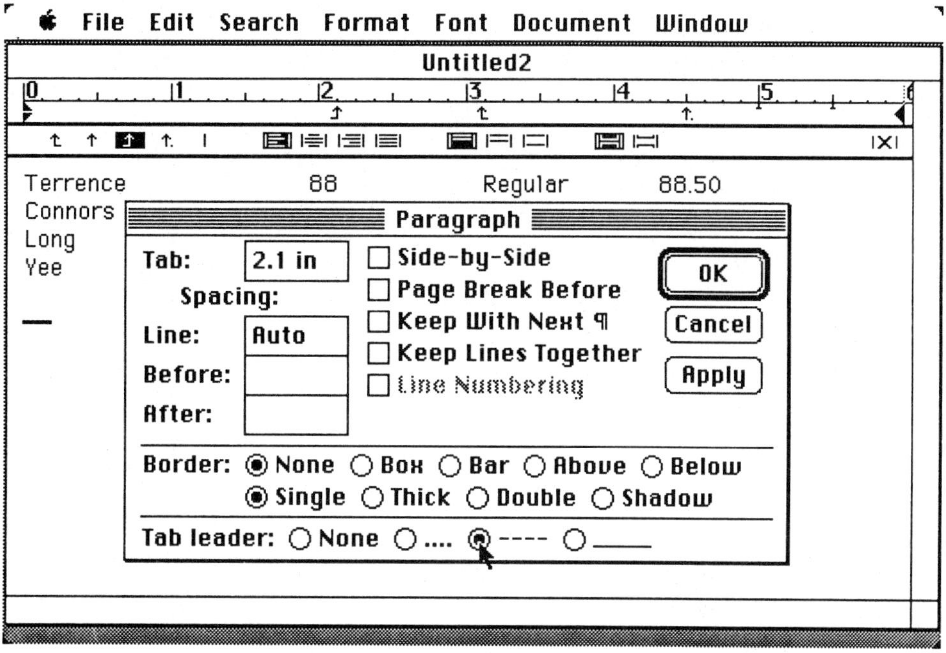

**Figure 8-30**   *Selecting dash leader characters*

report clearer. The dots before the first tab stop were produced as leader characters.

Feel free to experiment with the different types of tabs, and determine which will be most useful in your report writing. Try moving tabs around in a table to determine the best amount of room between columns. You will find that editing tables is fairly easy and that the more you experiment with tab settings, the better your tables will look.

```
 ┌ ⌘  File  Edit  Search  Format  Font  Document  Window  Utils        ┐
 ├─□──────────────────────── Untitled2 ──────────────────────────┤
 │ Terrence------------- 88        Regular      88.50             │⇧│
 │ Connors------------- 150        Senior      125.00             │ │
 │ Long---------------- 130        Regular     130.00             │ │
 │ Yee----------------- 50         New          67.50             │ │
 │                                                                │ │
 │ ▬                                                              │ │
 │                                                                │ │
 │                                                                │ │
 │                                                                │ │
 │                                                                │⇩│
 │ Page 1      Normal+...   ◁ □                              ◁  ▷ │▫│
 └────────────────────────────────────────────────────────────────┘
```

***Figure 8-31***   *Dash leader characters in table*

# LESSON 41   Working With Columns

If you are editing a table, you may want to move or delete a
column of data. For example, in the previous table you may
want to have the current year in the right-most column and the
previous year to its left. To make such a move you need a way of
selecting a single column.

There are other times when you would want to manipulate
columns of text. If you have created a table and you want to add

```
 ⌘  File  Edit  Search  Format  Font  Document  Window
═════════════════════ Ice Nine Annual Report ═════════════════════
                          Ice Nine Music Corp.
                         Annual Report for 1987
                      Consolidated Statements of Income

(Dollars in thousands)                    1987         1986
Net sales...................................982,769      583,061
Costs and expenses
      Cost of sales.........................505,765      288,001
      Research and development...............60,040       37,979
      Marketing and distribution............229,961      119,945
      General and administrative.............57,364       34,927
                                           853,130      480,852
Operating income...........................129,639      102,209
Interest, net...............................16,483       14,563
Income before taxes on income..............146,122      116,772
Provision for taxes on income...............69,408       55,466
Net income.................................. 76,716       61,306

Page 1        Normal+...
```

**Figure 8-32**   *Table with different types of tabs*

a column in the middle, you need to add a new column of tab characters. To format all the numbers in a column you could select the whole column and only give the Character command once.

To select a column of text:

1. Put the insertion point at one corner of the column, as in Figure 8-33. Usually, you should select a character in the upper-left corner.

2. Press the OPTION key to activate the column selection feature.

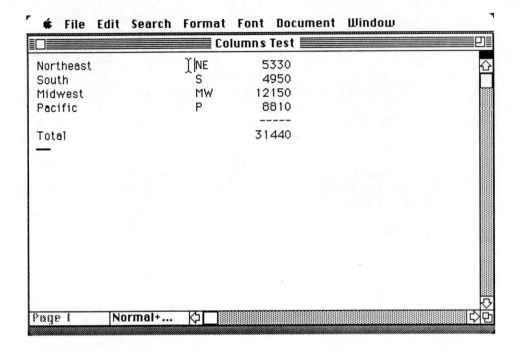

**Figure 8-33**   *Selecting the corner*

3. Extend your selection by dragging to the end of the column. If you are editing a table, be sure to include the tab characters in your selection (see Figure 8-34).

You can select more than one column at a time with this method. Word will simply treat everything that you select as a single column.

Once you have selected a column of text, you can treat it like any other text. You can cut it, copy it to the Clipboard, and so on. Thus, to switch the position of two columns, you would select the right column, cut it, point to the first character of the remaining column, and give the Paste command.

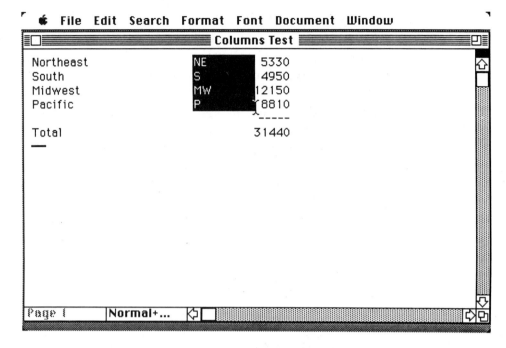

**Figure 8-34**    *Extending the selection*

# LESSON 42    Copying Paragraph Formats

In Chapter 7 you learned how to copy character formats from one set of characters to other sets; here you will learn the similar process for copying paragraph formats. Copying paragraph formats is an excellent way to format tables, since you can make the table without worrying about the format, choose the format for one section, and then copy it throughout the table.

You may recall that character formats are copied by selecting the text with the format that you want to apply, pressing COMMAND-OPTION-V, and pressing RETURN. Paragraph formats are copied in much the same way, except that you select the paragraph you want to copy the format from instead of selecting just the characters.

In Figure 8-35, the first paragraph is left-aligned, while the second is right-aligned. To right align both paragraphs, select the second paragraph and press COMMAND-OPTION-V, as shown in Figure 8-36. Now click in the first paragraph and press the RETURN key to copy the formatting to the first paragraph. Figure 8-37 shows the results: two right-aligned paragraphs.

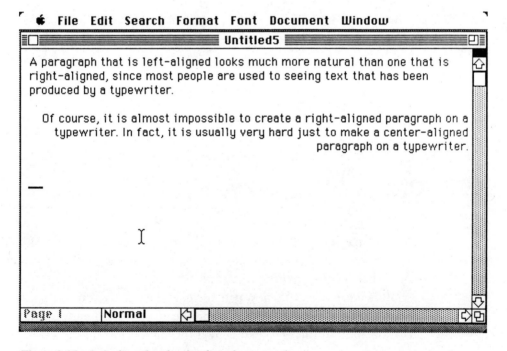

**Figure 8-35**   *Left-aligned and right-aligned paragraphs*

**File   Edit   Search   Format   Font   Document   Window**

Untitled5

A paragraph that is left-aligned looks much more natural than one that is right-aligned, since most people are used to seeing text that has been produced by a typewriter.

Of course, it is almost impossible to create a right-aligned paragraph on a typewriter. In fact, it is usually very hard just to make a center-aligned paragraph on a typewriter.

Format to    Normal+...

*Figure 8-36   Copying a paragraph format*

# LESSON 43   Adding Text to a Graphic

As you saw in Chapter 5, Word treats graphics just like characters. If you make a graphic a paragraph by itself, you have a one-character paragraph. This arrangement allows you to add text to graphics.

To add text directly to a graphic, the text must consist of the

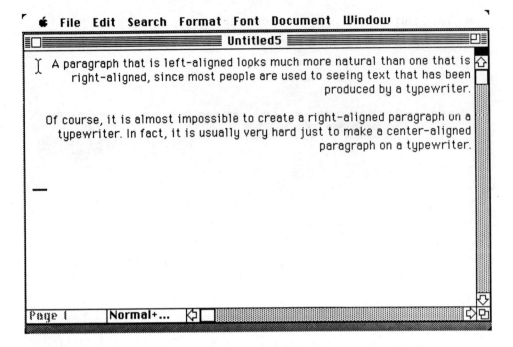

**Figure 8-37**   *Two right-aligned paragraphs*

paragraph immediately following the graphic, as shown in Figure 8-38. The steps are

1. Make sure that the graphic is the only element in the paragraph.

2. Select the text paragraph and give the Paragraph command in the Format menu.

3. Set the indentation for the text paragraph. If you want the text to appear to the right, this indentation will be greater than that of the graphic. Figure 8-39 shows the setting for the indentation of the text to be .25 inches. Click the OK button.

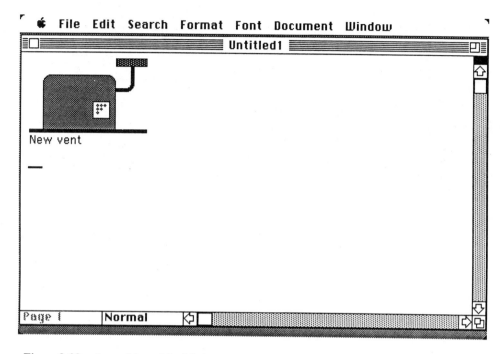

**Figure 8-38**   *A graphic and its labeling text*

4. Now select both paragraphs and give the Paragraph command again. Set the Side-by-Side option and click OK.

5. You can check the results by giving the Page Preview command in the File menu and looking at the appropriate page, as shown in Figure 8-40. The text may or may not appear on the screen. You can use the magnifying glass to check the exact placement. If it is not correct, you can change the indentation on both paragraphs to fix the alignment.

Remember that you can control the vertical placement of the text by altering the Space Before option of the text paragraph.

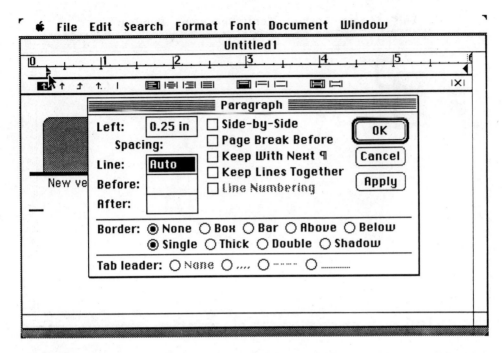

**Figure 8-39**   *Indenting labeling text*

# LESSON 44   Highlighting Paragraphs with Borders and Bars

Word lets you emphasize a paragraph by surrounding it with a border or by placing a bar above it, below it, or to the left of it. You have a wide selection of borders and bars.

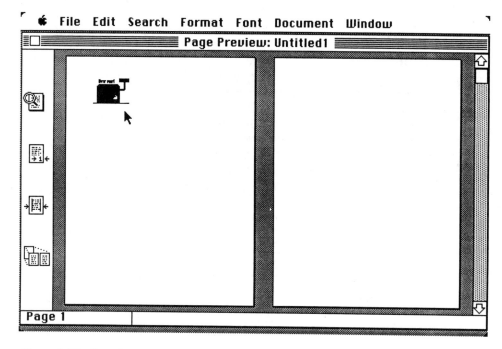

**Figure 8-37**    *Page Preview of the graphic and its labeling text*

To add a border to a paragraph, select any part of the paragraph and give the Paragraph command. Select the type from the Border option section, as shown in Figure 8-41. For example, to make a heading stand out, you might want to put a thin box around it. Select "Box" and "Single". Another interesting method is to use a shadow bar below the paragraph. These options are shown in Figure 8-42.

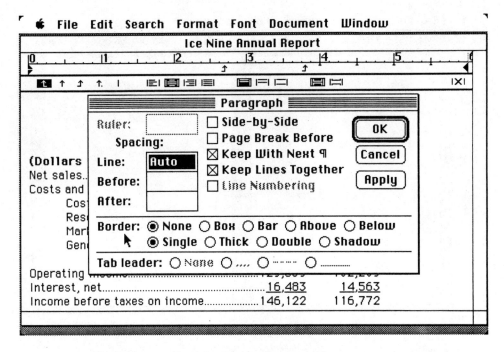

**Figure 8-41** *The Border section of the Paragraph command*

## REVIEW

*1. Formatting paragraphs*

Which of the following characteristics are changed with the
Paragraph command?

    *a.* Fonts

    *b.* Single and double spacing

    *c.* Page margins

    *d.* Indentation

    *e.* Justification

**File    Edit    Search    Format    Font    Document    Window**

### Ice Nine Annual Report

| Ice Nine Music Corp. |
| :---: |
| Annual Report for 1987 |
| Consolidated Statements of Income |

| (Dollars in thousands) | 1987 | 1986 |
| :--- | ---: | ---: |
| Net sales............................................. | 982,769 | 583,061 |
| Costs and expenses | | |
|     Cost of sales................................ | 505,765 | 288,001 |
|     Research and development.............. | 60,040 | 37,979 |
|     Marketing and distribution............. | 229,961 | 119,945 |
|     General and administrative.............. | 57,364 | 34,927 |
| | 853,130 | 480,852 |
| Operating income............................... | 129,639 | 102,209 |
| Interest, net...................................... | 16,483 | 14,563 |
| Income before taxes on income............. | 146,122 | 116,772 |
| Provision for taxes on income.............. | 69,408 | 55,466 |
| **Net income**........................................ | **76,716** | **61,306** |

Page 1    Normal+...

*Figure 8-42*    *Two highlighted paragraphs*

### 2. *Indenting paragraphs*

Describe how paragraphs with the following formatting would look:

*a.* Left indent 1.2 in., first line 0 in., justified

*b.* Left indent 3 in., right indent 3 in., centered

*c.* Left indent 1 in., first line −1 in., left-aligned

### 3. *Centering text*

Enter the text in Figure 8-43.

What steps would you use to make the paragraph look like Figure 8-44?

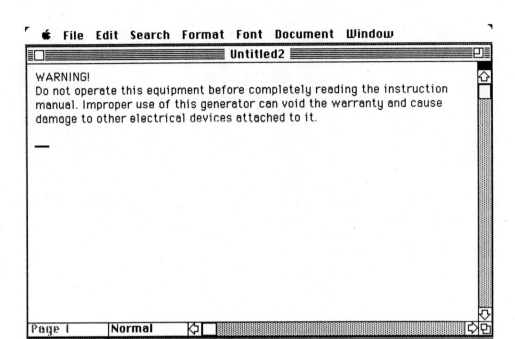

**Figure 8-43**   *Text of review paragraph*

4. *Changing the line spacing of paragraphs*

   When would you use triple-spaced paragraphs?

5. *Aligning paragraphs with the margins*

   If a paragraph is 12 lines long when it is formatted with left alignment only, how long will it be if you change to a justified margin?

6. *Keeping a paragraph together on a page*

   Should you use the Keep With Next ¶ button of the Formats command to be sure that Word does not split a paragraph after the first line?

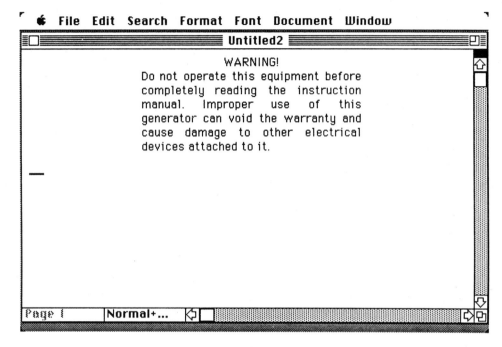

**Figure 8-44**   *Formatted review paragraph*

7. *Using tabs*

What type of tab stop would be appropriate for the following?
   *a.* Dollar amounts
   *b.* Column headings
   *c.* Lists of numbers

8. *Columns*

How do you select a column of a table?

# Chapter 9

## Formatting Pages and Footnotes

So far you have learned how to format characters and paragraphs to improve their appearance. The third unit that requires formatting is the section, which allows you to specify the page formatting of your text when it is printed out. Page layout generally consists of the page margins and the position of running heads (the text at the top and bottom of each page, such as the page number and the chapter name).

Most often you will use the same page layout throughout a document. Sometimes, however, you may use a few different page layouts in one document; for instance, the preface of a report may have a different style than the main text. Word lets you change the page layout for each section (which generally can be considered a chapter).

Use the Section command in the Format menu and Document menu to change the format for each section. The formatting characteristics of each section are kept in the section marker at the end of the section, just as paragraph characteristics are stored in the markers at the end of paragraphs. To create a new division, press COMMAND-ENTER and Word will display a series of colons, as in Figure 9-1.

It is important to remember that these formatting characteristics show up when you print out your text; except for the section marker, none of them appear on the screen. (In fact, you will not see any screen changes when you give the Section command.) For instance, if you specify the placement of the page number at the top of each page, you won't see the number on the screen, only on the printed page.

Even though the section changes are not visible when you make them, you do not need to print out your document to see these changes. Word's Page Preview command in the File menu lets you preview what your work will look like. The Page Preview command is covered in detail in the next section.

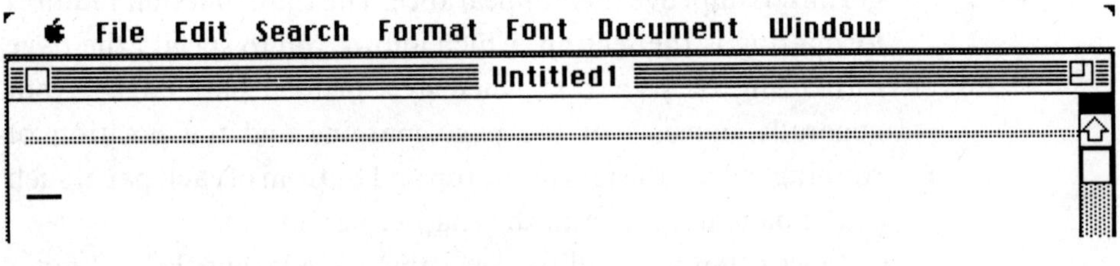

**    File  Edit  Search  Format  Font  Document  Window**

Untitled1

**Figure 9-1**   *The section marker*

A concept basic to many of the choices in the section commands is that of odd and even pages. If you examine books and magazines, you will find that they always begin on the right page (for example, look at the beginning of this book). This means that all right-hand pages have odd numbers (1, 3, 5, . . .) and all left-hand pages have even numbers (2, 4, 6,. . .). Knowing whether a page is odd or even often helps in formatting your pages, as you will see in this chapter.

In order to tell Word that you are differentiating between odd and even pages, you must set the Facing Pages option in the Page Setup command of the File menu. This procedure is shown in Figure 9-2.

When you give the Section command, you see the dialog box shown in Figure 9-3. The Section Start option, which specifies

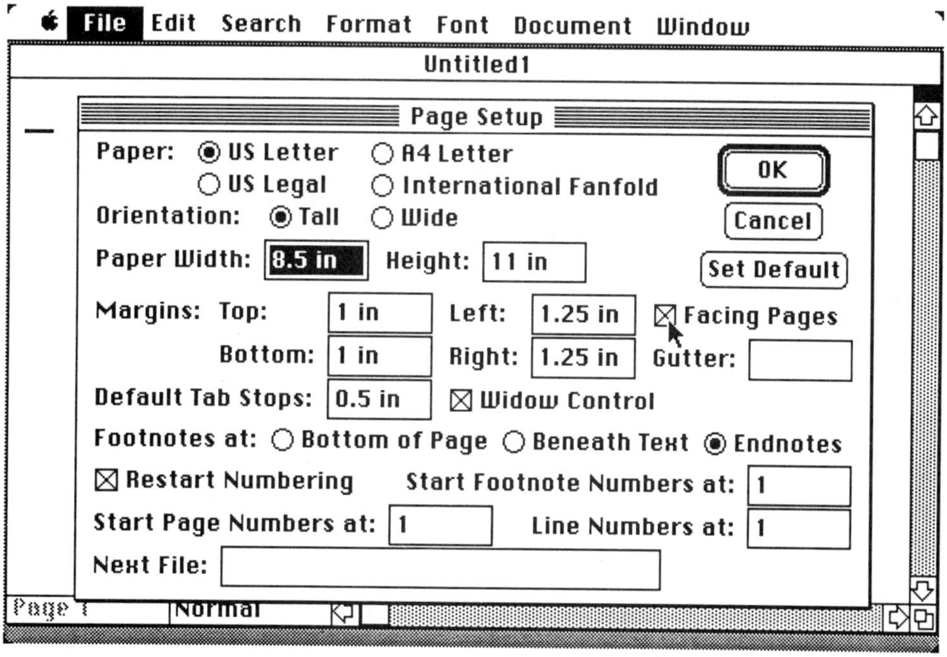

*Figure 9-2*  *Setting the Facing Pages option in the Page Setup command*

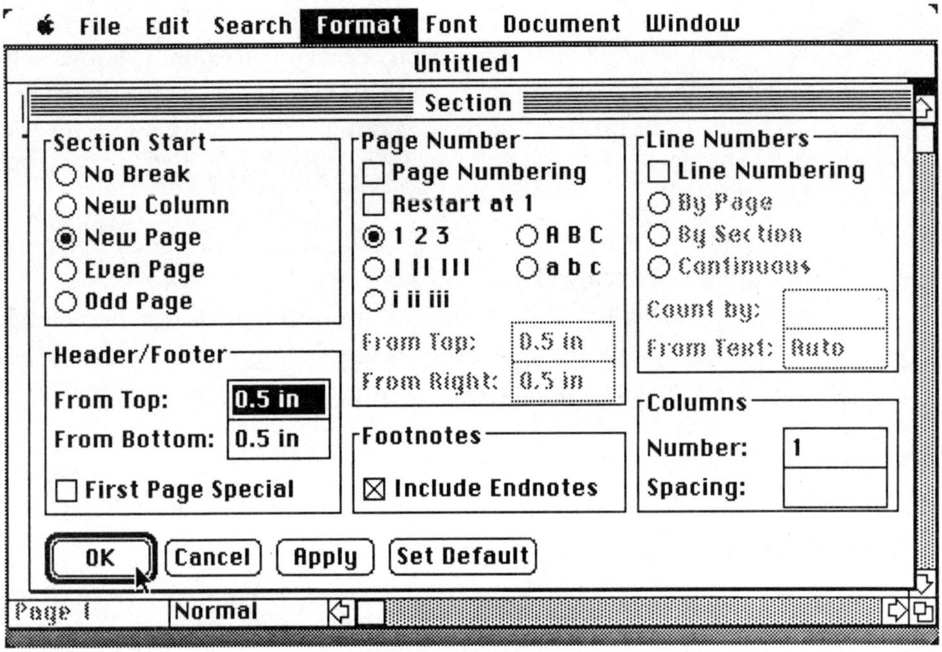

**&#xF8FF;  File   Edit   Search   Format   Font   Document   Window**

Untitled1

Section

**Section Start**
- ○ No Break
- ○ New Column
- ● New Page
- ○ Even Page
- ○ Odd Page

**Page Number**
- ☐ Page Numbering
- ☐ Restart at 1
- ● 1 2 3          ○ A B C
- ○ I II III       ○ a b c
- ○ i ii iii

From Top:    0.5 in
From Right:  0.5 in

**Line Numbers**
- ☐ Line Numbering
- ○ By Page
- ○ By Section
- ○ Continuous

Count by:
From Text:  Auto

**Header/Footer**

From Top:      **0.5 in**
From Bottom:   0.5 in
☐ First Page Special

**Footnotes**
☒ Include Endnotes

**Columns**

Number:   1
Spacing:

[ **OK** ]   ( Cancel )   ( Apply )   ( Set Default )

Page 1      Normal

*Figure 9-3*   *Section choices*

where to start the beginning of the section, lets you choose whether you want the section to continue on the same page as the previous section or to start on a different page. These choices are defined in Table 9-1.

Figure 9-4 is a summary of a funding proposal. It will be used to illustrate formatting throughout this chapter and the next one. You do not need to type the report into Word; however, you may want to type in sections when trying out the examples.

***Table 9-1***    *Choices for Beginning a New Section*

| Choice | Result |
| --- | --- |
| No Break | Continue from previous division without break |
| New Column | Start division in the next column (for multi-column text) |
| New Page | Start division on the next page |
| Even Page | Start division on the next even page |
| Odd Page | Start division on the next odd page |

# LESSON 45    Using Page Preview

Word's Page Preview command lets you see exactly how your document will look when it is printed. Even though what you see on the screen is generally what your document looks like when printed, it is not exact. For instance, you cannot see what the margins look like, or how side-by-side paragraphs will appear.

Using the Page Preview command is faster than printing out your documents (and it doesn't waste paper). You can use the command at any time. When you give the Page Preview command, Word opens a window in your document and shows the contents of two pages, as shown in Figure 9-5.

---

**Excerpts from a Proposal for Bank Funding**

## I.  Introduction

National Generators has the opportunity over the next five years to take a commanding lead in our established markets and to penetrate a new market, the construction industry, where our products will be particularly attractive. This report is intended to provide an overview of the company's business development strategies along with a description of those areas for which we require funding.

National Generators can become the premier producer of electrical generation equipment for the entertainment and exposition industries. Our portable yet sturdy generators have acquired a solid reputation in these fields. As the number of outdoor concerts, large conventions, and other events that use portable generators continues to increase each year, we will be better able than our competitors to satisfy the demand for reliable equipment.

While accelerating efforts aimed at our existing base of industrial users, we propose to enter the construction industry. We have already begun developing a small, quiet generator for this market. Research is also under way to design a larger, more efficient generator for heavy construction projects that can replace several smaller ones.

## II.  Market Analysis

National Generators currently has a 42% share of the markets we now serve. Our nearest competitor, Regional Outdoor Electricity, has 34%, with the rest divided among other manufacturers. We believe that our superior products will ensure that we will increase our share of sales to the entertainment and exposition industries. Some of our competitors will be unable to match our new technology, and we will pick up their business.

Over the next five years, we anticipate gaining 15% of the market for generators in the construction industry.[1] Two important trends favor our planned new products over any now available or known to be coming on the market. Anti-noise pollution legislation restricts the level of noise at urban construction sites, while OSHA legislation protects workers from damage to their hearing caused by equipment.

---

[1] Based on trends and growth in the construction industry, detailed in U.S. Department of Labor projections for 1985–1990.

---

*Figure 9-4   Business report*

### III.   Expansion Costs

In order to carry out the entrance into the construction industry and to keep ahead of growth in the entertainment and exposition industries, we will require $4MM to be allocated in three areas:

1.   Research and development of new products
2.   Marketing for new business opportunities
3.   Additional staffing for R and D and for marketing.

We will need to add one senior mechanical engineer and two technicians in R and D. We will also need a technical services manager, two product managers, and a merchandising manager in marketing. The advertising budget will include campaigns in trade magazines and attendance at national trade shows.

### IV.   Current and Projected Earnings

National Generators has shown a profit each year since its founding in 1974. Pretax profits in 1986 were $3.25MM on sales of $17.5MM (20%). This year, sales are expected to reach $19MM and a pretax profit of $4.2MM (22%). Five year projections call for $50MM in sales and pretax profit of $12MM (25%) by 1991.[2]

### V.   Company Directors

National Generators is a privately held company. The founders have a controlling interest (70%), and the remainder of the stock is held by the Joffee Group and Japanese-American Enterprises. The members of the board of directors are:

Samuel Ross, President (founder)
Albert Normandy, V.P., research and development (founder)
Irene Yashimoto, V.P., operations
Philip Bushnell, V.P., marketing
Hon. Louise B. Dart, The Joffee Group
Yuji Ko, Japanese-American Enterprises

---

[2]Based on constant 1987 dollars, using U.S. Department of Commerce inflation and growth estimates.

---

**Figure 9-4**   *Business report* (continued)

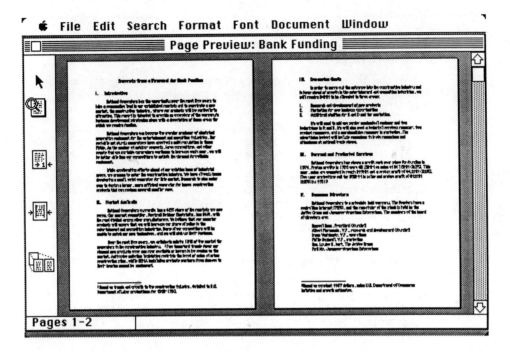

**Figure 9-5**   *Page Preview window*

The four icons on the left of the window (from the top) are

- Magnifying icon

- Page number icon

- Margins icon

- Single-to-double page view icon

You can see different pages in the page preview mode by using the scroll bar on the right of the window.

To close the Page Preview window, click on its Close button. You can also give the Print command while viewing the Page Preview window. This is useful for comparing a printed version to what you see on the screen.

Of course, you may want to see the actual text in your document, not just a picture of how things appear. To do this, click on the magnifying icon. Notice that the pointer is now a little magnifying glass. Move the pointer to the part of the page that you want to view in detail, as shown in Figure 9-6. Click the page, and Word displays that area in the full window, as Figure 9-7 shows.

You can switch back to the general view by clicking the magnifier again. You can also move around in the magnified view using the scroll bars.

If the paper you are using is larger than 8.5 by 11 inches, or you are using a large-screen Macintosh, you may want to use the single-page display mode instead of the double-page display. To switch, click the single-to-double page view icon.

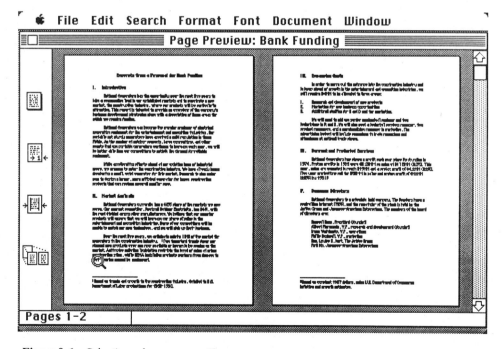

**Figure 9-6**  *Selecting where to magnify*

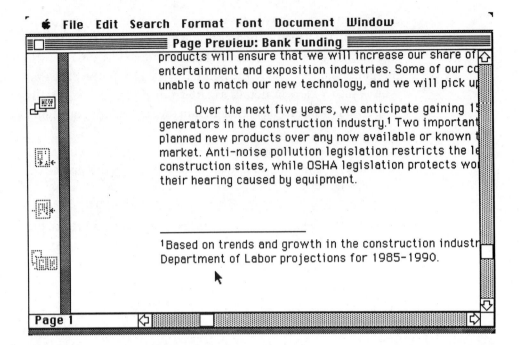

**Figure 9-7**    *The magnified view*

The page number and margins icons are used to change the location of the page numbers and the margins. These topics are discussed later in this chapter. You can change the margins by clicking on the margins icon and dragging the lines around. To see the effect of your changes, double-click on the page after dragging the margin line.

# LESSON 46   Creating Multi-Column Text

Word can be used to print out newsletters and other material formatted with two or more columns on a page. When you use more than one column, Word adjusts whatever formatting commands you have given so that they work within the columns. For this reason, you can keep the Section Start choice set at "New Page" for the division formatting.

The choices you set to produce multi-column text are "Number" and "Spacing" (the amount of white space between two columns in the columns box). For example, to make a three-column document with .25 inch between each column, set the characteristics as shown in Figure 9-8. Remember that you won't see the multiple columns on the screen, only on the printout or in Page Preview; however, the screen displays the single column as it will appear on the page.

Splitting a page into columns greatly reduces the number of words per line, so you should probably format the paragraphs as left aligned, rather than as justified. You will also want to use as many nonrequired hyphens as you can to make the lines more even. Justifying narrow columns usually results in a great deal of white space between words. For example, compare the paragraphs in Figure 9-9 and in Figure 9-10.

Even though multi-column text is not often used in business documents, you may find that it enhances the appearance of some reports. Figure 9-11 shows part of the report printed in two columns with .5 inch between them. Multi-column text is often used in newsletters, which are covered in Chapter 19.

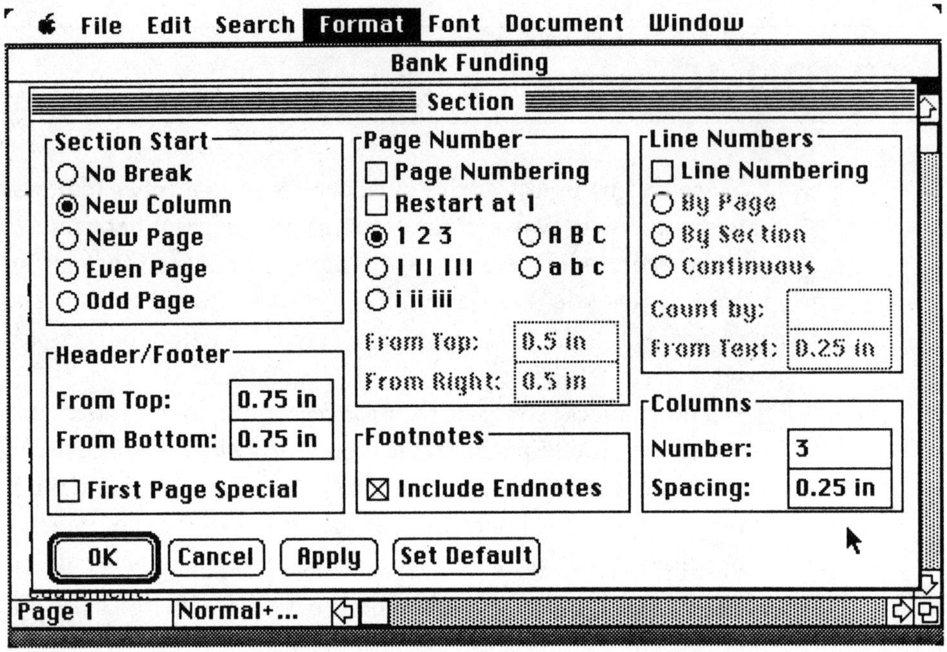

**Figure 9-8**   *Formatting a multi-column page*

# LESSON 47   Using Headers, Footers, and Page Numbering

Word allows you to put *headers* and *footers* at both the top and bottom of the page, and to change their text as often as you want. Your headers and footers can be more than one paragraph, or they can be just a page number on the page.

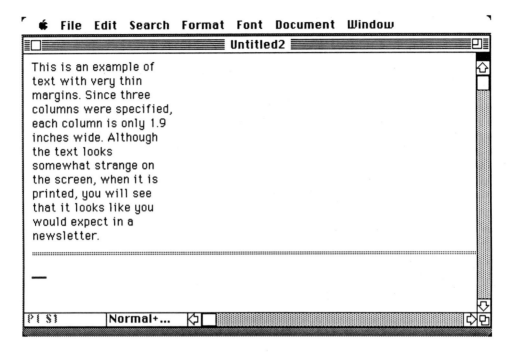

**Figure 9-9** *Column with left-aligned paragraph*

## Positioning the Page Number

In the Page Number section of the Section command, Word allows you to choose whether or not to display the page number, where on the page to display it ("From Top" and "From Left"), what number to start at, and the format of the number. However, you will most often want to have page numbers and some text (headers and footers) on the page; in this case, you should use the Open Header and Open Footer commands, not the page number choices in the Section command, as you will see.

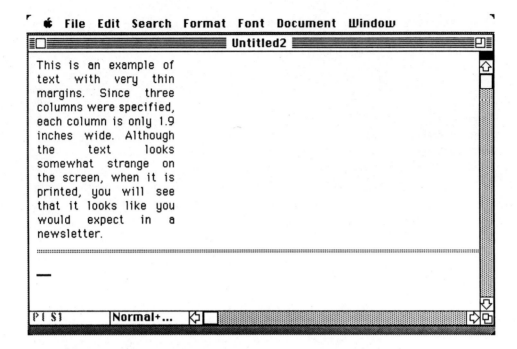

***Figure 9-10***   *Column with justified paragraph*

If you do not want page numbers in your document, or if you want headers and footers that include page numbers, do not click the Page Numbering button. If you do want just numbers, you have to decide where you want them. If you want just the page number in the report, you can, for instance, place it in the lower left-hand corner of each page, about .5 inch up and .25 inch to the right. To do this, set the characteristics as shown in Figure 9-12.

Page numbering can start at 1 in each section, at the number after the last page of the previous section, or at a number you specify. If you do not select the "Restart at 1" blank, Word will continue numbering from the previous section in the file; if this is the first section, it will start at 1.

**Excerpts from a Proposal for Bank Funding**

**I.  Introduction**

National Generators has the opportunity over the next five years to take a commanding lead in our established markets and to penetrate a new market, the construction industry, where our products will be particularly attractive. This report is intended to provide an overview of the company's business development strategies along with a description of those areas for which we require funding.

National Generators can become the premier producer of electrical generation equipment for the entertainment and exposition industries. Our portable yet sturdy generators have acquired a solid reputation in these fields. As the number of outdoor concerts, large conventions, and other events that use portable generators continues to increase each year, we will be better able than our competitors to satisfy the demand for reliable equipment.

While accelerating efforts aimed at our existing base of industrial users, we propose to enter the construction industry. We have already begun developing a small, quiet generator for this market. Research is also under way to design a larger, more efficient generator for heavy construction projects that can replace several smaller ones.

**II.  Market Analysis**

National Generators currently has a 42% share of the markets we now serve. Our nearest competitor, Regional Outdoor Electricity, has 34%, with the rest divided among other manufacturers. We believe that our superior products will ensure that we will increase our share of sales to the entertainment and exposition industries. Some of our competitors will be unable to match our new technology, and we will pick up their business.

Over the next five years, we anticipate gaining 15% of the market for generators in the construction industry.[1] Two important trends favor our planned new products over any now available or known to be coming on the market. Anti-noise pollution legislation restricts the level of noise at urban construction sites, while OSHA legislation protects workers from damage to their hearing caused by equipment.

**III.  Expansion Costs**

In order to carry out the entrance into the construction industry and to keep ahead of growth in the entertainment and exposition industries, we will require $4MM to be allocated in three areas:

---

[1] Based on trends and growth in the construction industry, detailed in U.S. Department of Labor projections for 1985–1990.

**Figure 9-11**  *Business report in two columns*

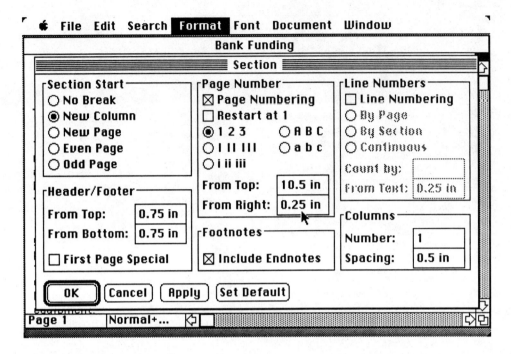

**Figure 9-12**   *Auto page numbering*

You can also choose a format for page numbers. This is extremely useful when you submit articles and reports for publication, since many publishers have guidelines about the format of page numbers. Table 9-2 shows the formats for the page numbers that are available on Word.

If you wish, you can position the page number in Page Preview mode. To do this, give the Page Preview command, then click the page number icon. You can now click it any place on the page and Word will automatically update the placement in the Section command. This method lets you experiment easily with different placements.

***Table 9-2*** *Page Number Formats*

| Format | Choice |
| --- | --- |
| Numeric | 1 2 3 |
| Roman (upper) | I II III |
| Roman (lower) | i ii iii |
| Alphabetic (upper) | A B C |
| Alphabetic (lower) | a b c |

## Headers and Footers

If you are going to use headers or footers in your document, do not click the Page Numbering button. Having a header or footer prevents the page number options from working. However, you can include a header or footer that contains only a page number at the top or bottom of a page. The Open Header and Open Footer commands allow you to do this. Also, since you can't specify odd or even pages with the page number options, using running heads gives you more flexibility if you print your document on both sides of the paper.

A header or footer can appear on odd or even pages, and on the first page of a division. Depending on your requirements, you can have up to six different running heads in a document. Often, however, you will have similar or identical text at the top or bottom of even or odd pages, or no text at all.

Word allows you to include the current page number, date, or time as part of the text on a page (for instance, if you want to print the number 5 on page 5). The page number is printed in the format you choose in the Section menu.

You should generally use a header or footer for the page

number instead of the page number positioning method discussed in the last section. In this way you can quickly change the positioning by changing the format of just the header or footer instead of having to change the entire section format. This also makes it possible to include text around the page number, as in "Page 5" or "-5-".

Creating and positioning headers and footers is fairly easy. First, decide what information you want to present; then decide which part of that information should be at the top or bottom of the page. Make these settings in the Header/Footer part of the Section command.

You can change the settings in the Page Preview mode by dragging the header and footer area around. To do this, give the Page Preview command, click the margins icon, select the header or footer box, and drag it to the new position you want.

For instance, if you want to show just the page number and chapter name, you may want the chapter name centered at the top and the page number centered at the bottom. Figure 9-13 shows this format for the second page of the report.

Next, decide if there should be a distinction between even and odd pages. If your text will be printed back-to-back (on both sides of the paper), you should put the headers and footers on the right side of odd-numbered pages and the left side of even-numbered pages, so that the information appears on the outside edge of the printed document (unless you want it centered).

Finally, decide whether you want running heads on the first page of the section. You usually will not, since this distracts the reader from the chapter title. Once you have decided on a layout, you can incorporate it.

You use a few commands to format headers and footers in Word. First, use the Section command to position the running heads relative to the top and bottom edges of the page. Then use the Header and Footer commands in the Document menu, and then format the paragraphs as you want them to appear (such as its alignment or use of character styles).

Funding Proposal

## III.  Expansion Costs

In order to carry out the entrance into the construction industry and to keep ahead of growth in the entertainment and exposition industries, we will require $4MM to be allocated in three areas:

1.  Research and development of new products
2.  Marketing for new business opportunities
3.  Additional staffing for R and D and for marketing.

We will need to add one senior mechanical engineer and two technicians in R and D. We will also need a technical services manager, two product managers, and a merchandising manager in marketing. The advertising budget will include campaigns in trade magazines and attendance at national trade shows.

## IV.  Current and Projected Earnings

National Generators has shown a profit each year since its founding in 1974. Pretax profits in 1986 were $3.25MM on sales of $17.5MM (20%). This year, sales are expected to reach $19MM and a pretax profit of $4.2MM (22%). Five year projections call for $50MM in sales and pretax profit of $12MM (25%) by 1991.[2]

## V.  Company Directors

National Generators is a privately held company. The founders have a controlling interest (70%), and the remainder of the stock is held by the Joffee Group and Japanese-American Enterprises. The members of the board of directors are:

Samuel Ross, President (founder)
Albert Normandy, V.P., research and development (founder)
Irene Yashimoto, V.P., operations
Philip Bushnell, V.P., marketing
Hon. Louise B. Dart, The Joffee Group
Yuji Ko, Japanese-American Enterprises

---

[2]Based on constant 1987 dollars, using U.S. Department of Commerce inflation and growth estimates.

*Figure 9-13*   *Chapter name at top, page number at bottom of page*

To specify the position of the running head on the page, use the Header/Footer option of the Section command. For instance, Figure 9-14 shows the running heads set .5 inch from the edge of the paper.

Now you can actually create the header. To create a header that says "Funding Proposal, page (page)" on the right side of the page (for odd pages):

1. Be sure the Facing Pages option of the Page Setup command is selected. If it is, you will see four commands at the beginning of the Document menu, as shown in Figure 9-15. Give the Open Odd Header command; its window is shown in Figure 9-16.

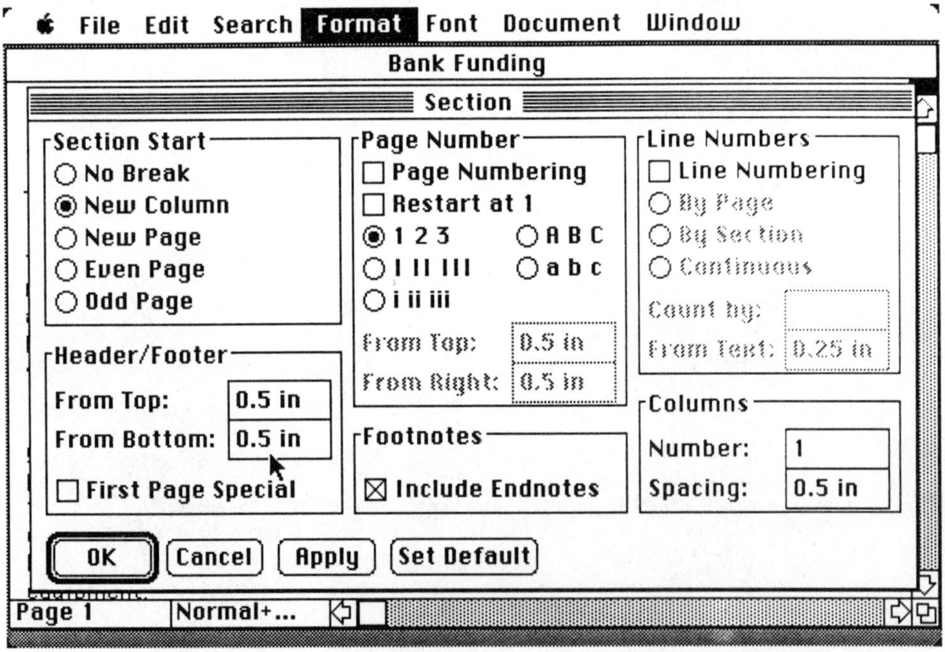

*Figure 9-14*   *Header/Footer settings*

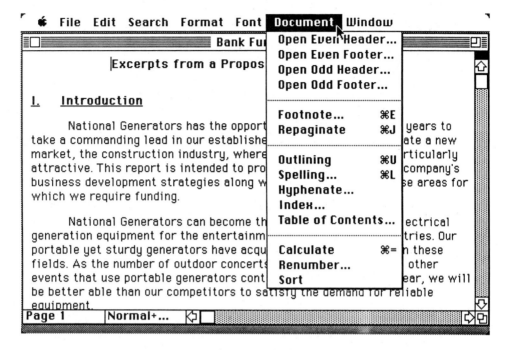

**Figure 9-15**   *The Document menu with four Open options*

2. Add the text **Funding Proposal, page** followed by a space.

3. Click the page number icon (the one on the left near the top), as shown in Figure 9-17.

4. Word inserts the page number in the heading. Don't worry that it shows an actual page number; it will print the real page number during Page Preview or printing.

5. Click the close box of the header. Word asks you whether you want to save this header; click "Yes."

Enter other headers and footers in the same way.

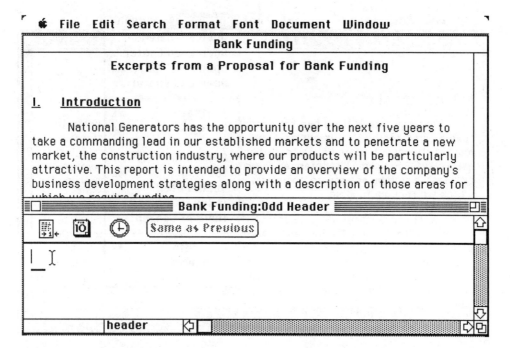

**Figure 9-16**   *The Header window*

You can also include the date and time in a header or footer by clicking the the other two icons in the header window. When you print, the date and time reflect the time of printing.

If you want to have a different header or footer on the first page of a section, you must select First Page Special in the Section command. When you do this, Word puts two additional commands in the Document menu (Open First Header and Open First Footer). You can mix any combination of headers and footers.

You can make the header appear in the text section (that is, inside the page margins) by using a negative number for the margin measurement. Even though this number is negative, Word understands that you really want the positive measure-

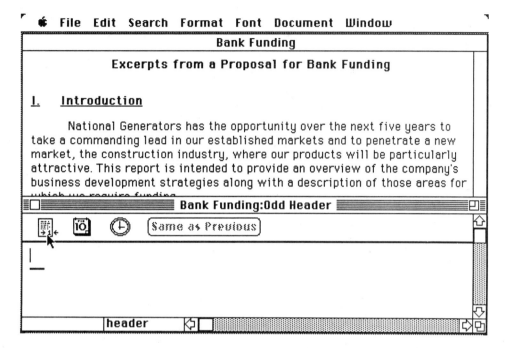

**Figure 9-17**   *Clicking the page number icon*

ment. However, this negative number prevents Word from changing the margin for the header, as it normally would. You will see applications for this in Chapter 19.

# LESSON 48   Using Page Breaks

The Section command does not allow you to go to a new page without creating a new section. However, pressing SHIFT-ENTER inserts a page break wherever you enter it (this is similar to using

NEWLINE to go to a new line without making a new paragraph). Word prints a line of dots across the screen to indicate the forced page break, as shown in Figure 9-18.

If you want to move from page to page, you can use the Go To command in the Search menu. When you give the command, Word prompts you for the page number you want to go to. Enter a page number, and Word moves the selection indicator to the beginning of that page. If your document has more than one section, you can also use the Go To command to go to a particular page in a particular section. For example, to go to page 7 of section 3, enter **P7S3** in the Go To command.

As you will see in Chapter 11, Word shows you page marks after it prints your text. Once you have printed a file, the Go To command will use these page marks, as well as those you specify with SHIFT-ENTER, to determine which page to move to. If you edit a file and want to see the new page breaks, use the Repaginate command in the Document menu (COMMAND-J).

If you want to be sure that a particular paragraph appears at the top of a page, you can format the paragraph to cause a page break instead of inserting a page break. To do this, give the Paragraph command and select "Page Break Before."

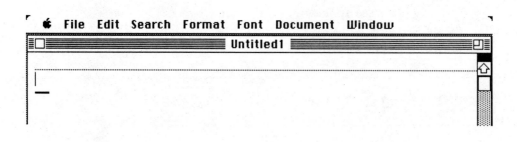

*Figure 9-18*   *Page break marker*

# LESSON 49   Using Footnotes

Many writers find footnotes hard to incorporate in text correctly; however, Word lets you include footnotes easily. In general, footnotes are used for two purposes: to give the reference for a quotation or an idea, or to give a supplementary note. They are most commonly used in academic and scholarly papers, but they are becoming more common in financial reports.

Footnotes consist of the reference mark (usually an asterisk or a number) and the footnote text. To enter these parts, use the Footnote command in the Document menu. Most people prefer to use sequentially numbered footnotes: Word will keep track of the current footnote number and will even renumber your footnotes if you take one out. When you later print your document, you can choose if you want the footnotes to be printed on the page where they are referenced or at the end of the text (using the Page Setup command).

To insert a footnote, you position the insertion point at the place where you want the reference mark. When you give the Footnote command, Word shows the dialog box that appears in Figure 9-19. If you enter a character (or up to 10 characters) for the reference mark, Word will use that as the reference mark; if you click the Auto-numbered Reference button, Word will automatically number the footnote in sequence.

When you execute the Footnote command, Word splits the main text window and creates a footnote area. You can then enter and edit the footnote text in this area and go back to your normal text. To return to where you were before you entered the footnote, drag the split bar to the bottom of the window or press COMMAND-OPTION-Z to leave the window open. If you want to open the footnote window without creating a footnote, press the SHIFT key when you drag down the split bar. If you leave the Footnote window open as you scroll through your document,

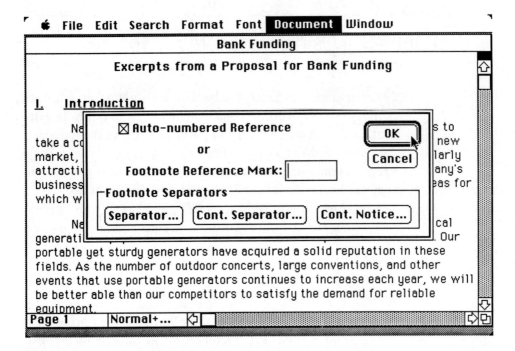

**Figure 9-19**   *Dialog box for the Footnote command*

Word will scroll the Footnote window to the first footnote of the page you are on.

To see how footnoting works, assume that you want to add another footnote to the report. Move the insertion point to just after the period following the words "trade shows" at the end of the third section, as in Figure 9-20. Give the Footnote command and click "OK", since the automatic numbering choice is already selected. Now enter the text for the additional footnote, as in Figure 9-21.

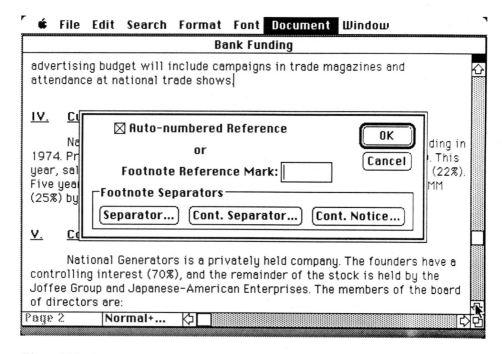

**Figure 9-20**   *Inserting a footnote reference*

Notice that Word automatically renumbered the footnote that follows your new footnote. If you use automatic numbering, Word will keep track of footnotes that you insert or delete and correctly number them. To delete a footnote, simply delete its reference mark.

Word lets you change the appearance of the footnotes, the footnote markers, and the separators between the text and the footnotes. This gives you greater flexibility in determining how your documents appear.

```
 ⌐   ⚫ File  Edit  Search  Format  Font  Document  Window      ⌐
╔════════════════════════════ Bank Funding ═══════════════════════╗
║ ▢ □                                                          ▢▢║
║ attendance at national trade shows.2                          ⬆ ║
║                                                                 ║
║ IV.   Current and Projected Earnings                            ║
║                                                                 ║
║     National Generators has shown a profit each year since its founding in ║
║ 1974. Pretax profits in 1986 were $3.25MM on sales of $17.5MM (20%). This   ║
║ year, sales are expected to reach $19MM and a pretax profit of $4.2MM (22%).║
║ Five year projections call for $50MM in sales and pretax profit of $12MM  ⬇ ║
╠═════════════════════════════════════════════════════════════════╣
║ 2An itemized breakdown of costs is attached.                  ⬆ ║
║ 3Based on constant 1987 dollars, using U.S. Department of Commerce inflation and growth ║
║ estimates.                                                      ║
║                                                                 ║
║ ▬                                                               ║
║                                                                 ║
║                                                               ⬇ ║
║ Footnote    Normal      ◁□▭▭▭▭▭▭▭▭▭▭▭▭▭▭▭▭▭▭▭▭▭▭▭▭▭▭▭▭▭▭▭▷▢ ║
╚═════════════════════════════════════════════════════════════════╝
```

***Figure 9-21***   *Adding text for a footnote*

You can change the formatting of the footnote text and foot-note markers with the direct formatting commands. In addition, you can change their appearance with the style commands that you will learn about in Chapter 10.

The three buttons you saw in the Footnote command allow you to change the characters Word uses as separators. Clicking on the Separator button opens a window with the bottom-of-page separation text, which is normally a short line. The Cont. Separator button lets you edit the line for footnotes that carry over from one page to the next, and the Cont. Notice button lets you edit the continuation notice.

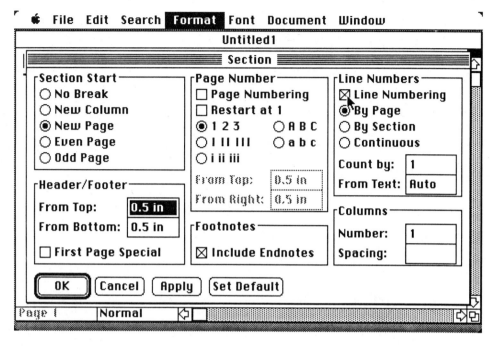

*Figure 9-22*   *Line Numbering options of the Section command*

# LESSON 50   Numbering Lines in Your Document

The legal profession often requires that line numbers be printed on documents such as pleadings and depositions. One method is to use forms with line numbers already printed on them, but this limits the kind of text you can include. For example, footnotes (which are common in pleadings) do not line up with the numbers on preprinted forms.

Word's Line Numbering option enables lawyers (and anyone else who requires numbered lines) to edit and print documents easily. To turn on Line Numbering, simply use the Line Numbers portion of the Section command, shown in Figure 9-22. Line numbers only appear on the printed document and in Page Preview mode.

Once you select Line Numbering, you can also tell Word how you want the lines numbered. Generally, you will want the numbering to begin with 1 on each page, so you should select "By Page." If, instead, you want the lines of your document numbered from beginning to end, choose "By Section" (for numbering in each section) or "Continuous" (for the whole document).

You also can specify whether to show every line number or only a few. For example, if you enter 5 for "Count By," Word will only print every fifth line number. You can also specify how close the line numbers appear to the text by using the From Text option.

Usually, you will want to number the lines in all the paragraphs in your document. If you want to exclude some paragraphs from line numbering, select them and give the Paragraph command. Unselect the Line Numbering option.

# REVIEW

*1. Setting up page characteristics*

Which of the following can be set with the Section command?
   a. Number of columns
   b. Underlining of running heads
   c. Justification
   d. Type of numbers used in page numbers

2. *Formatting multi-column text*

Reformat the report into two columns with a half-inch space between them. What steps did you use? What things should you do to your text if you are using multi-column printing?

3. *Using running heads and page numbering*

How would you specify a centered running head like "(page 33)"?

4. *Page breaks*

What does Word do when it sees a SHIFT-ENTER character if it is printing a document?

5. *Footnotes*

How do you choose between showing footnotes on the bottom of each page or at the end of a document?

6. *Formatting front matter*

Make a title page for the report that includes the report title, company name, and date. Each line should be centered. Give two methods for separating such a title page from the text.

# Chapter 10

## Formatting With Styles

Up to this point you have had to specify the formatting characteristics for each paragraph in your text. Microsoft Word also allows you to define a set of styles for your documents that is automatically used when you format. When you use styles instead of formatting each paragraph, you specify the style for each type of paragraph (such as "normal paragraph" or "section heading"), and Word formats the paragraph by finding the corresponding style in the document's style sheet.

The term *style sheet* (or *style list*) is Microsoft's jargon for this feature. Word is one of the few word processors offering formatting styles, so even if you are familiar with many other word processing packages, this concept is probably unfamiliar to you. (If you use IBM mainframe computers, you may have used the Generalized Markup Language [GML], which is similar to styles.)

A style sheet can be thought of as a formatting guide that contains a list of types of paragraphs and the formats associated with them. For example, to format a "normal paragraph" in your text, your instructions might be "justified text, indent the first line .5 inch, and skip a line before the paragraph." Instead of having to format each paragraph this way when you enter or edit the text, you simply tell Word that you are entering a "normal paragraph". When you print the text, Word looks up the formatting for your "normal paragraph" in the style sheet.

Using styles in Word consists of two steps. First, you must create the style list by defining the types of styles you want. To do this, you use the Define Styles command in the Format menu. After you design the styles, you format your document by labeling its elements with styles. As you will see, you use the Styles command in the Format menu to specify the styles used in your documents. You can also apply a style from the keyboard. Word lets you easily copy style sheets from document to document.

One of the excellent features of formatting with styles is that you can have many different style sheets in different documents that use the same style elements but format them differently. Thus, a "normal paragraph" in one style sheet might be double-spaced and ragged right, but single-spaced and justified in another. You might use the first style sheet to print rough drafts so you can correct mistakes easily, and then use the second style sheet to print your final document.

Word lets you specify the types of styles you want and allows you to modify and add styles easily; you do not need to stick to predefined styles. You might have styles for "normal paragraph", "long quotation", "normal running head", "section heading", and so on.

Using styles does not prevent you from using direct formatting; however, you will probably find that using styles almost exclusively will make writing and printing easier. If you have used only styles and want to change the format of one type of paragraph in all of your different documents, you do not need to change any of them: simply change your style lists. When you print the document, your new formatting will automatically be used. Of course, you cannot do this with direct formatting. While you can use style lists for most of your text, you can also use some direct formatting when it is faster or when you are sure you will not want to change the format.

Another big advantage of styles is that you can easily change a format without having to change anything in your documents. For example, you may have a style called "normal heading" that corresponds to boldface and centered text. If you later want all the normal headings to be underlined and left-aligned, you only need to change the style, not search through all of your files to change the headings.

If you want to begin using styles but do not want to create your own at first, you can use the default styles supplied by Microsoft. Of course, you can modify these default styles if you wish.

The next lesson shows you how to create two styles from scratch and how to specify your own style elements. The lesson after that shows how to save your style list in your document. You will then learn how to specify styles in your documents.

# LESSON 51   Creating a Style Sheet

Now that you understand the concept behind style sheets, the next step is to build a small style sheet that you can experiment with.

The rest of this chapter will use the report shown in Chapter 9 for its examples. You may want to enter the first section heading and the first few paragraphs of the report so you can try out examples as they are presented. When you enter the text, be sure not to use any direct formatting commands.

To start making styles, give the Define Styles command in the Format menu. You see the menu shown in Figure 10-1.

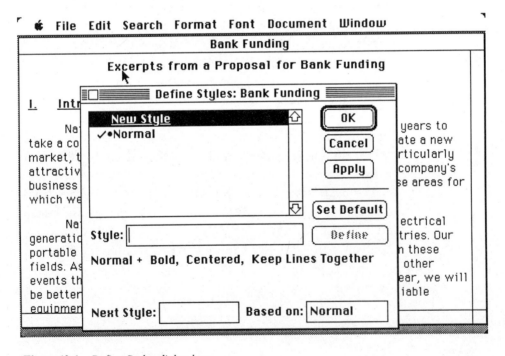

*Figure 10-1*   *Define Styles dialog box*

You will create two styles for this sample sheet: a paragraph style for section headings, and another paragraph style for normal paragraphs.

There are two ways to define a style. You can format a paragraph with the style you want, then give the Define Styles command, or you can start with a normal paragraph and give the formatting commands that define the style. The second method generally is easier.

To begin, select the first heading paragraph. This is currently "Normal" text like everything else in the document. You can see what style is used on any paragraph by looking in the style box next to the page number at the bottom of the window, as shown in Figure 10-2.

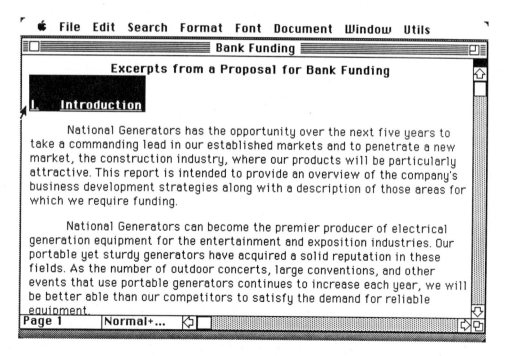

*Figure 10-2*  *The style box*

Now give the Define Styles command. Make sure that "New Style" is selected in the list of styles, and enter the new style's name in the box labeled "Style:". For this example, type **Heading**.

Next, define the formatting characteristics for that style. In the case of "Heading", you should make it bold, underlined, left-aligned, with two lines above, lines kept together, and a tab stop at 0.4 inches.

To do this, you can use the Character and Paragraph commands in the Format menu, just as if you were using direct formatting. However, if you already have formats in your paragraph, Word uses the paragraph formats as a starting base for the style.

As you give the Character and Paragraph command, notice that the style that began "Normal +" contains all the style attributes. When you are finished giving the formats, click the Define button. Next, click the OK button, which defines the style and applies it to the paragraph you selected. Notice that the style box (shown in Figure 10-3) shows the new style.

Next, change the style for normal paragraphs. Give the Define Styles command again and select "Normal" from the style sheet. Notice that "Normal" has a bullet next to it; this indicates that it is one of Word's default styles.

You can change the formatting of the default styles, and this change will continue to be used every time you run Word. You can, of course, change it back. Remember that we changed this default style in the Getting Started section to have normal text appear in Geneva font instead of New York font.

Add the new formatting as you would for a new style. In this case, change "Normal" to have the first line indented 0.5 inches and justified. Next, click on the Default button. Word asks if you are sure you want to change the default; click "Yes," then "OK." Notice how all the other paragraphs now change to this new format. If you want to change the definition of "Normal" for just this document, don't click "Default"; instead, click "Define."

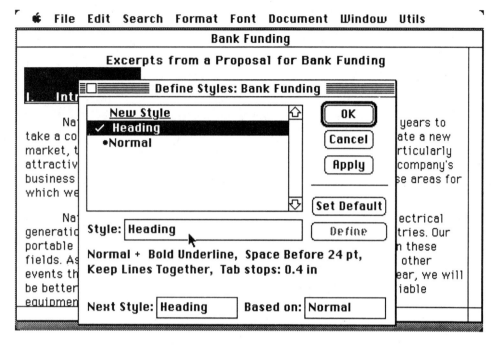

**Figure 10-3**   *The new style*

# LESSON 52   Using Styles in Your Documents

Now that you have a style sheet, you can start applying styles to your documents. When you use Word, you can either set up a style sheet and then enter the styles as you type in new text, or you can convert a directly formatted document to styles.

If you convert a directly formatted document to styles, you should first unformat the entire document. Word requires that you do this since you can use both style sheets and direct formatting at the same time. To unformat a document, select the

File   Edit   Search   Format   Font   Document   Window

**Bank Funding**

Excerpts from a Proposal for Bank Funding
I.      Introduction
National Generators has the opportunity over the next five years to
take a commanding lead in our established markets and to penetrate a new
market, the construction industry, where our products will be particularly
attractive. This report is intended to provide an overview of the company's
business development strategies along with a description of those areas for
which we require funding.
National Generators can become the premier producer of electrical
generation equipment for the entertainment and exposition industries. Our
portable yet sturdy generators have acquired a solid reputation in these
fields. As the number of outdoor concerts, large conventions, and other
events that use portable generators continues to increase each year, we will
be better able than our competitors to satisfy the demand for reliable
equipment.
While accelerating efforts aimed at our existing base of industrial
users, we propose to enter the construction industry. We have already begun
developing a small, quiet generator for this market. Research is also under

Page 1          Normal

**Figure 10-4**   *Plain document*

entire document before attaching a style sheet, press
COMMAND-SHIFT-P to make all paragraphs normal, and then
press COMMAND-SHIFT-SPACEBAR to remove all character
formatting. You now have a very plain document that is ready to
have styles applied, as shown in Figure 10-4.

You are now ready to start applying styles. You can give text a
style by selecting the text, pressing COMMAND-SHIFT-S, and
typing the name of the style you want to apply. The page number
in the lower left of the window becomes the word "Style," as

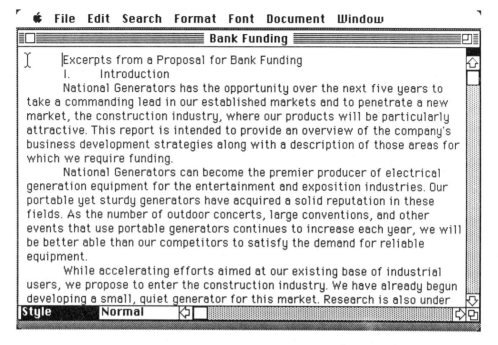

**Figure 10-5**    *The style name box*

shown in Figure 10-5. As you type, your style name appears there. If you change your mind, press COMMAND-PERIOD to cancel the command.

For example, select the first section heading, "I. Introduction," as shown in Figure 10-6. Now press COMMAND-SHIFT-S and type **Heading** to indicate that this is a section heading. The result is shown in Figure 10-7. Notice that the paragraph is now formatted properly and that "Heading" now appears in the style box.

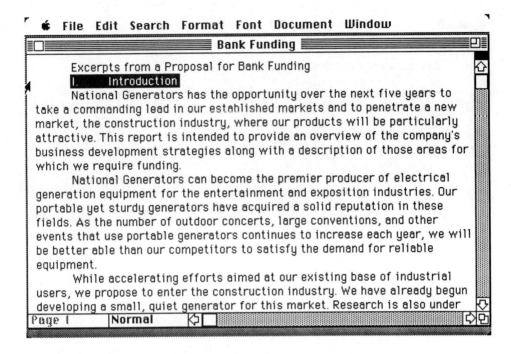

**Figure 10-6**   *Section heading selected*

To see the power of style lists, suppose that you decide not to justify the normal paragraphs and want to change them to left-aligned. Simply give the Define Styles command and change the formatting of "Normal" to left-aligned. Save this new default. As soon as you return to editing, your document has changed to the new style, as shown in Figure 10-8.

# LESSON 53   Saving Style Sheets in Files

Although style sheets are saved with each document, you may want to create your own "master" style sheet. For example, this may hold all the definitions that you normally use. Create a document with all these styles and save it with the name "Master."

The next time you want all the style definitions included in a document, give the Define Styles command; then, while the

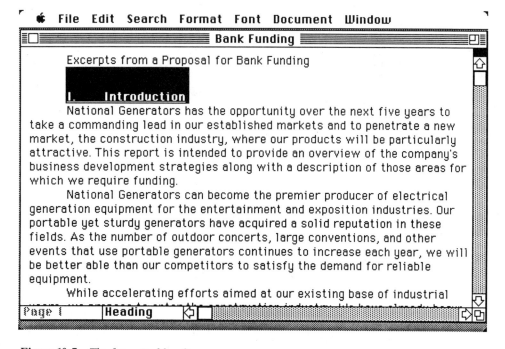

*Figure 10-7*   *The formatted heading*

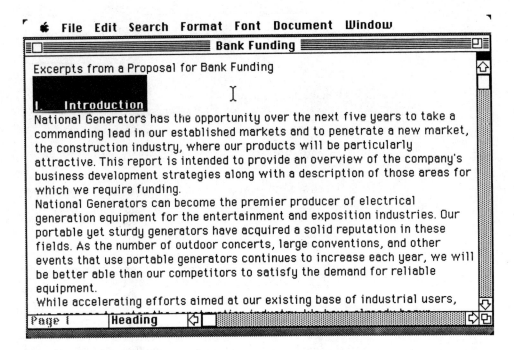

**Figure 10-8**   *Left-aligned normal paragraphs*

Define Styles dialog box is open, give the Open command in the File menu. Select "Master," and the style sheet from "Master" will be included in your current document.

This method for keeping style sheets opens up new areas for using Word's styles. For example, it is usually most convenient to edit text on the screen when it is single-spaced (so that more lines fit on the screen) but more convenient to edit it on paper when it is double-spaced (so that you can write additions or corrections between the lines). You can keep a document that has its "Normal" paragraph formatted for double-space. When you open this file's style sheet in a document, it causes all the "Normal" paragraphs to be double-spaced, but causes everything else to be left the same. You can then print the document,

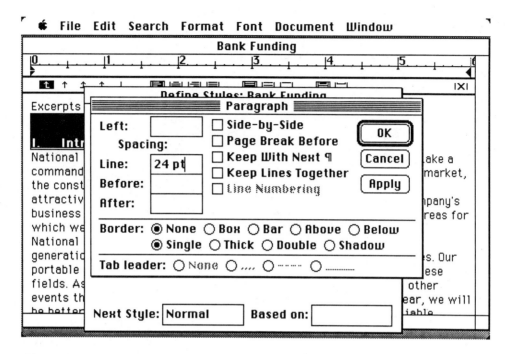

**Figure 10-9**   *Double-spaced in normal paragraphs*

and close it without saving the changes (in this case, the double-spacing).

To print your style sheet, give the Define Styles command and, while the dialog box is open, give the Print command. Word will show you each style and its elements.

You can now easily make a style sheet for double-spaced (24 point) drafts of reports. Open a new document and change the line spacing of normal paragraphs to two lines, as shown in Figure 10-9. Save this style sheet as "Double space." Now whenever you want to print a draft of a report, it takes almost no effort to double space it, since all you have to do is open this style sheet.

# LESSON 54 Getting the Most Out of Style Sheets

Style sheets can make formatting all your documents, from letters to entire books, a much easier task. Even for large reports it is unlikely that your style sheet will contain more than 15 styles, and only five or so will probably be used with any frequency. If you want, you can remove styles in a style sheet by using the Cut command.

You will find that style sheets have many advantages over direct formatting, and in the few places where styles are not appropriate, you can still format directly. Once you start thinking in terms of style elements ("this is a heading", "this is a normal paragraph", and so on), you will find that your printed documents will be much clearer, since they will be presented in a more organized manner.

Copying styles from one piece of text to another is identical to copying direct formats. It is thus easy to convert files that use direct formatting to style-sheet formatting simply by applying a style to one paragraph and then copying that style to all other paragraphs to which it applies.

Word even gives you a way to search just for styles in your documents. This is useful, for example, if you have a style for headings and want to find the next heading quickly. Simply select the paragraph with the style you want to find and press COMMAND-OPTION-R. Word moves the selection to the next paragraph that has that formatting.

# REVIEW

1.  *Using style sheets*

    Briefly describe the advantages of style sheets over direct formatting.

2.  *Creating new styles*

    Create a new style for the title of the sample report.

# Chapter 11

## Printing Your Text

Word has many advanced features that make printing easier. When you edit and format text, for example, you do not need to know what type of printer your text will be printed on. Instead, when you are ready to print, you simply tell Word what type of printer you are using, and it will determine what it needs to do in order to use as many of the formats you specify as it can.

This is important, since there is no standard method for instructing different printers how to perform certain tasks, such as printing superscripts. Most of the instructions are complex and involve strange character codes. Word does not require you to remember these arcane codes, however; it stores the text formatting with your file, and when you print, it reads a special Macintosh file called a *printer driver* to determine how to use your printer's special features so they correspond to the format. The Macintosh printer drivers are the files on your Master Disk in the Printer Drivers folder.

Figure 11-1 shows typical output from two printers. Different printers, of course, produce output of different quality; they also print at different speeds, have different special features, and range in cost from around $250 to over $10,000.

Although you learned a bit about printing in Chapter 1, this chapter gives you the rest of the information you need to tell Word what type of printer you have and to use the options of the Print command.

## LESSON 55   Selecting a Printer Driver

Microsoft has Macintosh printer drivers for many brands of printers. If you are printing with one or more of the printers in the Printer Drivers folder, be sure the driver is on your Program Disk. You can delete the other drivers from your Program Disk (do not erase them from your Master Disk).

Many printers that are not included in the Printer Drivers folder respond to the same codes from your computer as those on the list; for instance, many letter-quality printers take the same codes as the Diablo 630. If there is a printer equivalent to yours on the list, you can use the indicated printer driver. You can find out if your printer acts like some other printer by asking your dealer.

If you have a printer from a manufacturer of one of the supplied drivers with a model number that is slightly different from the one in the file name, try the listed driver before following the suggestions below. Note that many printer manufacturers supply drivers for their printers.

January 11, 1987

Chris Richford, Vice President
Manufacturer's Bank of the Northeast
1000 First Avenue
Millerton, CT 06492

Dear Ms. Richford:

I am pleased to send you the latest update on the results of our expanded
product line. The enclosed summary documents our increased profit margin
(7%) for the fourth quarter of 1986, which is largely due to the successful
introduction of our new model, the DC50. In 1987 we expect to continue
increasing our profitable inroads into this new area.

As you can see, we are well within the projections we outlined to you when
you helped us obtain short-term financing. Thank you again for all your
assistance. If you have any questions regarding this information, please feel
free to call me.

Sincerely,


Thomas Mead, Controller
National Generators
1275 Oak Glen Industrial Park
Oak Glen, CT 06410


January 11, 1987

Chris Richford, Vice President
Manufacturer's Bank of the Northeast
1000 First Avenue
Millerton, CT  06492

Dear Ms. Richford:

I am pleased to send you the latest update on the results of our expanded
product line. The enclosed summary documents our increased profit margin
(7%) for the fourth quarter of 1986, which is largely due to the successful
introduction of our new model, the DC50. In 1987 we expect to continue
increasing our profitable inroads into this new area.

As you can see, we are well within the projections we outlined to you when
you helped us obtain short-term financing. Thank you again for all your
assistance. If you have any questions regarding this information, please feel
free to call me.

Sincerely,


Thomas Mead, Controller
National Generators
1275 Oak Glen Industrial Park
Oak Glen, CT  06410

*Figure 11-1*   *Letter printed on the ImageWriter (top) and a letter-quality printer (bottom)*

Don't worry if your printer is not included in the Printer Driver folder and you do not know whether it emulates one of the included printers. You can use Word's all-purpose printer driver, the Typewriter driver discussed earlier in Chapter 1, for whatever type of printer you have. The only difference is that some formatting features (such as italics or subscripts) will not appear on your output. Also, if you use character formats a great deal, it may take slightly longer to print with all-purpose drivers.

Regardless of the type of printer you have, be sure that it is turned on and that it has paper before giving the Print command. Also be sure the cable between the printer and the computer is attached properly.

# LESSON 56   Setting the Printer Options

Before you give the Print command, you should tell Word about your printer with the Chooser command in the Apple menu. The dialog box for this command looks like Figure 11-2. Select the icon of the printer you are going to use.

If you are not sure about the pitch or baud rate, check your printer manual. Of course, it is easy to determine which port connects your printer to your Macintosh by looking at the back of the Mac. When you are finished with the Chooser dialog box, click the close button.

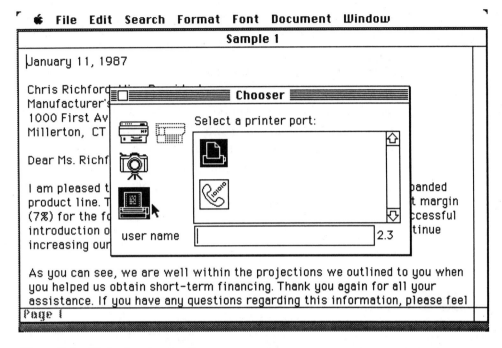

**Figure 11-2**   *Dialog box for the Chooser command*

---

# LESSON 57   Using the Page Setup Command

You should give the Page Setup command in the File menu to tell Word the type of paper you are using, as well as to set the page margins and other settings. The dialog box is shown in

Figure 11-3. The default settings are usually correct for most users, and you will not need to give the Page Setup command often.

The Paper choice tells Word what type of paper you are using. "US Letter" corresponds to standard 8.5-by-11-inch paper, while "US Legal" corresponds to 8.5-by-14-inch paper. "A4 Letter" and "International Fanfold" are for paper that conforms to international standards. The Orientation choice specifies how you have loaded the paper into the printer: "Tall" (the normal fashion), "Tall Adjusted" (same as tall, but prints pictures in proportion to the page), and "Wide" (loading the paper sideways in the printer).

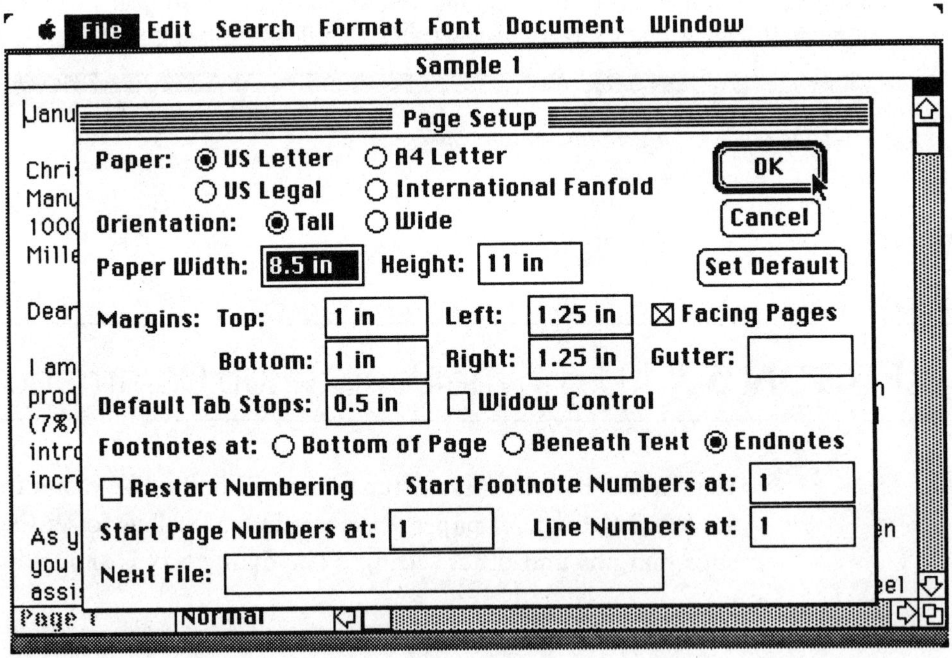

***Figure 11-3***   *Dialog box for the Page Setup command*

Other settings are used to specify the page margins and the gutter width. It is important to remember that there is a difference between the left and right page margins and the left and right paragraph margins. The page margins are measured from the edge of the paper (determined by the paper length and width); the paragraph margins are measured from the left and right page margins.

The top and bottom margins are set by default to 1 inch, and the left and right margins are set to 1.25 inches. These four values are the ones you are most likely to reset. Word gives you wide margins so that your running heads do not appear too near the edge of the page.

You can now see how Word decides on the line length of a page:

*line length = page width − (left margin + right margin) − gutter*

In all of the examples so far, the page width has been 8.5 inches, the left and right margins 1.25 inches, and there has been no gutter so the line length is 6 inches.

You may, however, need different settings. For example, many publishers insist on a 1.5-inch border around text submitted for publication. To create this margin, you would set the characteristics as shown in Figure 11-4.

If you are going to bind the document, you may want to set a gutter width after selecting Facing Pages. The *gutter* is the space on a page that is not used in printing; in this case, it is the amount of space that is used in binding the document. Since binding a document takes up a certain amount of space from the left side of odd-numbered pages and the right side of even-numbered pages, Word allows you to stretch the margins, alternating between left and right pages. Set the gutter width to the amount that would be lost in binding; when your pages are printed and bound, the text will not run into the gutter and will thus be easier to read.

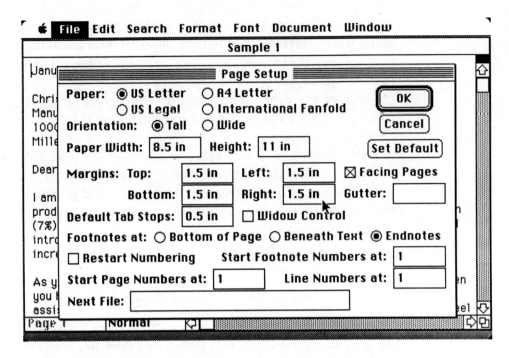

**Figure 11-4**   *Changing the page margins*

The other choices in the Page Setup command let you specify

- The default tab stops for the paragraphs for which you don't set tab stops

- Whether to use widow and orphan control (you will almost always want to leave this set)

- Where to place the footnotes in the document

- Whether to start the footnote, page, and line numbers at 1

- The name of the next file for keeping the numbering consistent

If you click the Default button, Word will make the current choices the default for the Page Setup command. For instance, if you always use the Facing Pages option, you can make that the default.

# LESSON 58    Giving the Print Command

The last set of print options that Word offers is in the Print command in the File menu. You use the Print command when you are ready to print your text (you can use COMMAND-P for the command). Word presents the dialog box in Figure 11-5.

The Quality choices let you decide how your text is printed; this affects both the appearance of the printed output and the speed at which your printer runs. Click the Faster button if you want normal printing or the Best button if you want Word to use the slower, but better-looking, high-quality printing. Click the Draft button if you want to speed up the printing process; doing this, however, means that you will not see character formats.

You can choose to print only certain pages from your document by using the Pages option. You can instruct Word to print the entire document ("All" is the normal setting), to print the text on particular pages or to print just the selection. If you click the From button, you can then enter the page numbers. If your document has more than one section, you can specify the section number and the page number in the range. For example, "5S3" indicates page 5 from section 3.

If you want to print more than one copy of a file, use the Copies option. This is a convenient way to print many copies of a letter or memo without having to give the Print command over and over.

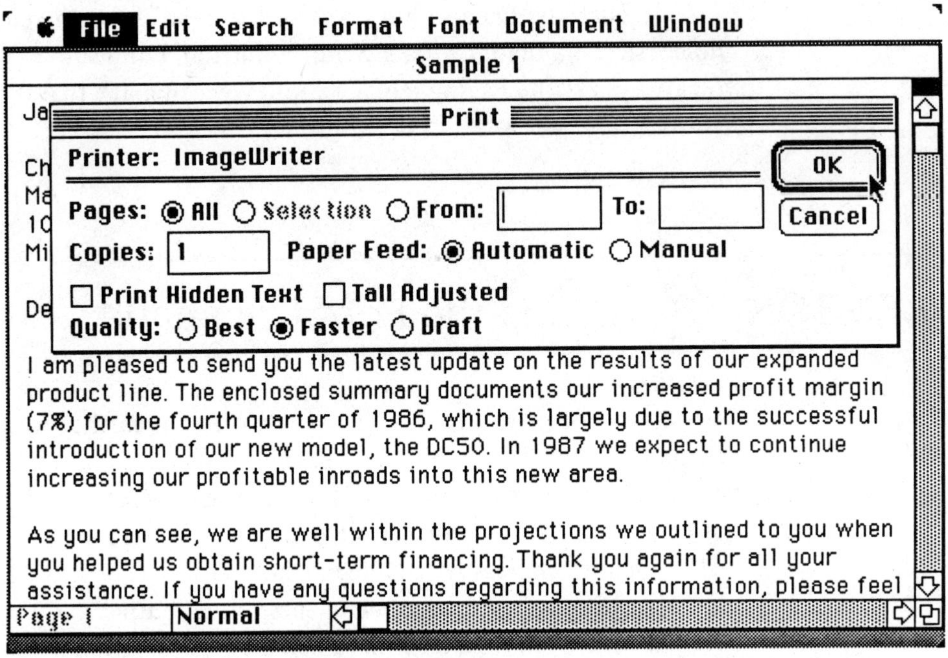

**Figure 11-5**   *Dialog box for the Print command*

The Paper Feed option tells Word how your printer handles the paper you are printing on. Click the Automatic button to indicate continuous form paper or the Manual button to indicate single sheets of paper. You can also tell Word to print hidden text. When you have made all of your choices, click the OK button, and Word begins printing your text. While you are printing, Word displays the message in Figure 11-6.

The Print command can also print out a style sheet or a glossary. To do so, give either the Styles command or the Glossary command; while either dialog box is open, give the Print command.

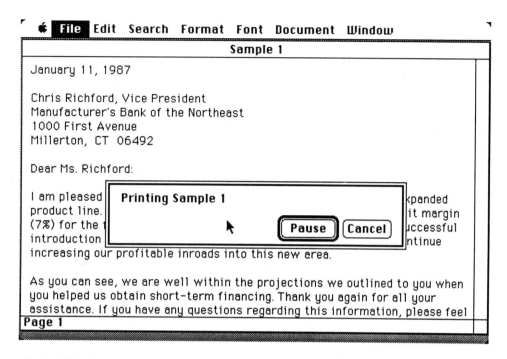

*Figure 11-6*   *Screen display while printing*

# REVIEW

1. *Selecting a printer driver*

   What printer driver do you use if Word does not provide a driver designed for your printer?

2. *Choosing other print options*

   What three commands affect the printed output? How do you tell Word that you are not using continuous-form paper?

# Part 3

## Adapting Word
## To Your Special Uses

# Chapter 12

## Using Merge for Form Letters

About seven years ago, only a few word processing programs included features that let you create form letters from a file of names and addresses. This feature is sometimes referred to as *mail merge*. Today, many programs give you this capability in a limited fashion. The merge feature in Word is more sophisticated than in other word processing programs and produces letters that look much more personalized.

The basic concept behind Word's merge feature is fairly simple. Your *main document* contains the letter you want to send to many people, with special place holders (*fields*) for the parts that change from letter to letter (like the recipient's name and address). Your *datafile* contains the information that Word puts into the fields in the main document; all the fields for each letter are on one line (called a *record*) of the datafile.

Your main document tells Word which file is to be the datafile. You create the main document with Word and create the datafile either with Word, a data base management system, or with a programming language like BASIC. The format of the datafile is very easy to understand, so it is easy to set up datafiles to go with your main documents.

When you print your file with the Print Merge command in the File menu, Word reads the first record from the datafile, substitutes the fields into your main document, formats your letter, prints it, reads the next record from the datafile, and so on. You can have as many as 256 fields in a letter, as long as each field matches the information in the datafile.

You can include fields in the middle of a paragraph, and Word will format the paragraph with the new information in it (few other programs will format the paragraph after putting in the new information). Thus, if you have a field called "amount", and that field in one record of your datafile is equal to 1533, Word would properly reformat a paragraph that contained the sentence "You still owe us $1533, which we would like you to send immediately."

# LESSON 59   Using Merge Fields

Each field can have a name consisting of as many as 65 letters or hyphens, such as "amount" or "last-payment". The field name is used in both the main document and the datafile, and the names must match. However, the order in which the names are used in the main document does not need to match the order in which the fields appear in the datafile. In fact, you can use the data in a field many times in your main document.

The body of your main document is entered just as you normally enter text with Word. When you want to enter a field name, you surround it with << and >> symbols, which you enter by typing OPTION-\ and OPTION-SHIFT-\, respectively. You also enclose all merge instructions and keywords with the << and >> symbols. Note that you must enter these symbols with OPTION-\ and OPTION-SHIFT-\, not by using the less-than and greater-than keys, < and >.

Type in the example in Figure 12-1,which is a main document that could be used to inform customers of balances due. The fields are "company", "name", "address", "city", "state", "zip", "amount", and "last-payment".

```
 File  Edit  Search  Format  Font  Document  Window

                      Payment 1 Letter

«DATA Payment 1 Data»
                              August 15, 1987


«company»
«name»
«address»
«city», «state»  «zip»


Dear «name»:

Our records show that your outstanding balance is $«amount», and that we
have not received any payment from you since «last-payment». If there is a
disagreement about this, please feel free to call us about it.


                       Sincerely,


                       Sharon Myers
                       National Manufacturing

Page 1      Normal
```

*Figure 12-1*   *Example of a main document*

Each main document must begin with a DATA instruction, which names the datafile. For example, if the name of your datafile is Payment 1 Data, your data statement is "≪DATA Payment 1 Data≫". In general, the datafile should have a name that indicates that the file is data.

# LESSON 60   Using the Datafile Format

The first record in a datafile, the *header,* is a list of fields in the order in which they appear in all the other records, with the field names separated by commas. The other records contain the data, with each field separated by a comma. Enter the datafile for the main document shown in the last lesson, as in Figure 12-2. When you create your datafile, it is often useful to see the main document at the same time; this is a perfect use for Word's windows (discussed in Chapter 4).

Since commas in the datafile indicate the boundaries of fields, commas in your data could cause Word to be confused. However, Word allows you to enclose any field with quotation marks, so that a comma within a quoted field will not be considered a field boundary. The second record in the datafile shows this use. (You should also use quotes in any field that contains a TAB character.)

Since any text field might have a comma in it, it cannot hurt to enclose all text fields in quotation marks. If you are preparing your datafile with Word, however, this is not necessary as long as you are careful to enclose all fields containing a comma with quotes.

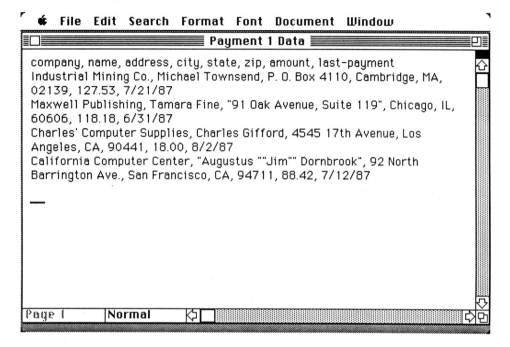

**Figure 12-2** *Datafile for the main document*

The WRITE# statement in most BASIC programming languages, including Microsoft BASIC, will enclose all strings in quotes for you. If your quoted fields have quotation marks in them, you need to put two quotation marks instead of one inside the field. This is shown in the fourth record of Payment 1 Data.

Some applications programs that can write out datafiles may not be able to write out the header record. In this case, Word lets you have two datafiles: one with just the header record, the other with the data. If you use this scheme, you need to alter your DATA instruction to indicate both files: you would give the name of the header file first and then the name of the datafile. For instance, if Payment 1 Head has the header record and Payment 1 Data has the data records, your DATA instruction would read "<<DATA Payment 1 Head, Payment 1 Data>>".

---

# LESSON 61   Printing Your Document

---

Printing with merge is very similar to regular printing. Give the Print Merge command from the File menu after setting up your printer with the Page Setup and Chooser commands.

Figure 12-3 shows the letters Word prints out when you merge the Payment 1 letter. As you can see, Word filled in the fields in the body of the paragraph and correctly wrapped the text.

---

# LESSON 62   Using Merge Instructions

---

The previous example showed a simple merge file with a DATA instruction and many fields. A unique feature of Word that makes letter writing even easier is *conditional insertion*. You can check the value of a field and insert different text depending on the value of the field. For instance, if the "amount" field is over 1000, you can insert a sentence describing the dire consequences of not paying promptly. Or your datafile can have a field called "regular-customer" that contains a "Y" or "N", and you can use

***Table 12-1***   *Word Merge Instructions*

| Instruction | Use |
|---|---|
| ASK | Has Word prompt you to fill in a field when each letter is printed |
| DATA | Identifies the datafile |
| IF ... ENDIF<br>or<br>IF ... ELSE<br>... ENDIF | Conditionally inserts text if a field in the datafile has a particular value. You can use the $=, >,$ or $<$ operators for numeric fields or the $=$ operator for string fields. |
| INCLUDE | Inserts another Word file in the main document |
| NEXT | Has Word read the next record in the datafile |
| SET | Sets the contents of a field or has Word prompt you for the value once at the beginning of printing |

this to decide what type of salutation to use. The merge feature has a number of options that you can use; these are listed in Table 12-1.

The main document in Figure 12-4 is similar to the last one except that it has an IF instruction used with a text field. The IF instruction checks the value of the "sales-rep" field and prints one of two possible sentences, depending on whether "sales-rep" is "none" or some other value. The datafile, shown in Figure 12-5, is also similar to the previous one. Figure 12-6 shows the new output.

Notice the results of the IF instruction. You can also use the IF instruction with integer fields to test whether a number is greater than, less than, or equal to a field value. For instance, if your datafile has a field "cust-years" that is, the number of years a customer has been with your firm, you might include the following sentence in a letter: "$\ll$ IF cust-years$>$5$\gg$We value your long-standing relationship with us.$\ll$ENDIF$\gg$".

August 15, 1987

Industrial Mining Co.
Michael Townsend
P. O. Box 4110
Cambridge, MA  02139

Dear Michael Townsend:

Our records show that your outstanding balance is $127.53, and that we have
not received any payment from you since 7/21/87. If there is a
disagreement about this, please feel free to call us about it.

Sincerely,

Sharon Myers
National Manufacturing

August 15, 1987

Maxwell Publishing
Tamara Fine
91 Oak Avenue, Suite 119
Chicago, IL  60606

Dear Tamara Fine:

Our records show that your outstanding balance is $118.18, and that we have
not received any payment from you since 6/31/87. If there is a
disagreement about this, please feel free to call us about it.

Sincerely,

Sharon Myers
National Manufacturing

*Figure 12-3   Payment 1 letters printed*

August 15, 1987

Charles' Computer Supplies
Charles Gifford
4545 17th Avenue
Los Angeles, CA  90441

Dear Charles Gifford:

Our records show that your outstanding balance is $18.00, and that we have
not received any payment from you since 8/2/87. If there is a disagreement
about this, please feel free to call us about it.

Sincerely,

Sharon Myers
National Manufacturing




August 15, 1987

California Computer Center
Augustus "Jim" Dornbrook
92 North Barrington Ave.
San Francisco, CA  94711

Dear Augustus "Jim" Dornbrook:

Our records show that your outstanding balance is $88.42, and that we have
not received any payment from you since 7/12/87. If there is a
disagreement about this, please feel free to call us about it.

Sincerely,

Sharon Myers
National Manufacturing

**Figure 12-3**   *Payment 1 letters printed* (continued)

```
 ⌘  File  Edit  Search  Format  Font  Document  Window
```

```
═══════════════════ Payment 2 Letter ═══════════════════

«DATA Payment 2 Data»
                            August 15, 1987


«company»
«name»
«address»
«city», «state»  «zip»

Dear «name»:

Our records show that your outstanding balance is $«amount», and that we
have not received any payment from you since «last-payment». «IF sales-
rep="none"»Our accounts receivable manager, Holly Watson, will call you
about this.«ELSE»Your sales representative, «sales-rep», will call you about
this.«ENDIF»

                            Sincerely,

Page 1        Normal
```

**Figure 12-4**   *Payment 2 main document*

The IF instruction can be used to check whether there is anything in the field or not. For example, the following command determines if there is any value in the "owner" field: "Dear <<IF owner>><<owner>><<ELSE>>Store Owner<< ENDIF>>". This prints the contents of the "owner" field if it exists, or the phrase "Store Owner" if it does not.

The SET and ASK instructions allow you to enter information when you print. The SET instruction sets a field once for all

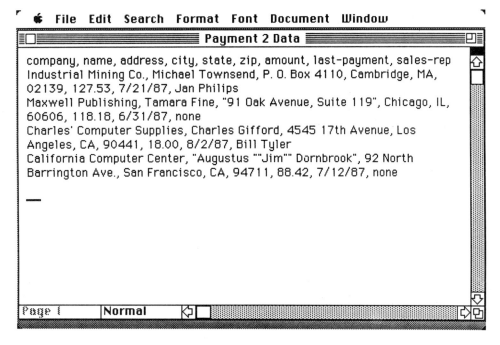

*Figure 12-5*  *Datafile for Payment 2*

letters, whereas the ASK instruction prompts you for a new value for each letter. You can include a string that Word will prompt you with.

For instance, instead of typing the date into a main document, you should include a SET instruction, as in Figure 12-7. This would set the "date" field. You use the "date" field at the place you want the date in your document, just as if it were a field in your datafile.

August 15, 1987

Industrial Mining Co.
Michael Townsend
P. O. Box 4110
Cambridge, MA  02139

Dear Michael Townsend:

Our records show that your outstanding balance is $127.53, and that we have not received any payment from you since 7/21/87. Your sales representative, Jan Philips, will call you about this.

Sincerely,

Sharon Myers
National Manufacturing

August 15, 1987

Maxwell Publishing
Tamara Fine
91 Oak Avenue, Suite 119
Chicago, IL  60606

Dear Tamara Fine:

Our records show that your outstanding balance is $118.18, and that we have not received any payment from you since 6/31/87. Our accounts receivable manager, Holly Watson, will call you about this.

Sincerely,

Sharon Myers
National Manufacturing

*Figure 12-6*   *Payment 2 letters printed*

August 15, 1987

Charles' Computer Supplies
Charles Gifford
4545 17th Avenue
Los Angeles, CA  90441

Dear Charles Gifford:

Our records show that your outstanding balance is $18.00, and that we have
not received any payment from you since 8/2/87. Your sales representative,
Bill Tyler, will call you about this.

Sincerely,

Sharon Myers
National Manufacturing

August 15, 1987

California Computer Center
Augustus "Jim" Dornbrook
92 North Barrington Ave.
San Francisco, CA  94711

Dear Augustus "Jim" Dornbrook:

Our records show that your outstanding balance is $88.42, and that we have
not received any payment from you since 7/12/87. Our accounts receivable
manager, Holly Watson, will call you about this.

Sincerely,

Sharon Myers
National Manufacturing

**Figure 12-6**   *Payment 2 letters printed* (continued)

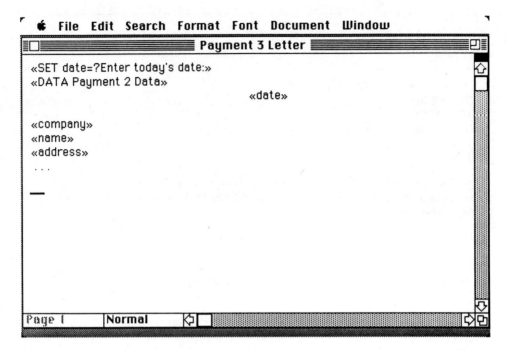

**Figure 12-7**   *SET instruction for date*

The INCLUDE instruction allows you to bring the contents of other files into your Word document. This is useful if you want to include some standard information in a letter but do not want to copy the information until the file is printed. For instance, if you have a table that is updated often, instead of inserting it in the file, use the INCLUDE command so that the printout will have the latest version of the table.

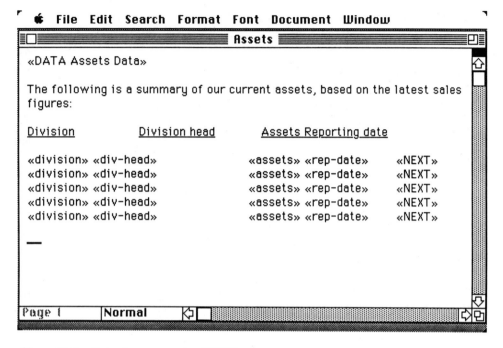

**Figure 12-8**   *Main document using NEXT*

You can use the NEXT instruction to read in more than one record for each main document, for example, if you are using Word to read a list of data to make a report. Figure 12-8 is a main document that reads five records from a file and prints a report of the data in one document. Figure 12-9 is the datafile, Assets Data, that goes with the report. Figure 12-10 shows the output of the report. Notice that all the records appear on the same output.

```
 ⚫ File  Edit  Search  Format  Font  Document  Window
┌───────────────────────── Assets Data ─────────────────────────┐
│ □                                                              │
│ division, div-head, assets, rep-date                        ⬆  │
│ Pacific, Anita Yee, 1315000, 8/15/87                        ▯  │
│ Mid-West, Sam Horn, 875000, 8/14/87                            │
│ South, Margaret Miller, 1105000, 8/14/87                       │
│ North-East, Kim Taylor, 2660000, 8/15/87                       │
│ Foreign, Noriko Takayama, 397000, 8/12/87                      │
│                                                                │
│ ▬                                                              │
│                                                                │
│                                                             ⬇  │
│ Page 1    Normal      ◁ □                                   ▷  │
└────────────────────────────────────────────────────────────────┘
```

**Figure 12-9**   *Assets Data datafile*

---

The following is a summary of our current assets, based on the latest sales figures:

| Division | Division head | Assets | Reporting date |
|----------|---------------|--------|----------------|
| Pacific | Anita Yee | 1315000 | 8/15/87 |
| Mid-West | Sam Horn | 875000 | 8/14/87 |
| South | Margaret Miller | 1105000 | 8/14/87 |
| North-East | Kim Taylor | 2660000 | 8/15/87 |
| Foreign | Noriko Takayama | 397000 | 8/12/87 |

---

**Figure 12-10**   *Assets report printed*

# REVIEW

1. *Printing documents with merge features*

   Briefly describe what you need in order to use the merge feature.

2. *Typing in merge instructions and field names*

   Which keys do you use to enter the $\ll$ and $\gg$ characters?

3. *Using fields*

   Create a merge letter for an insurance firm to remind clients to renew their auto insurance policy. In addition to standard form-letter fields (name, address, and so on), add fields for expiration date and policy type. How would you
   
       *a.* tell readers about a home insurance policy if they don't already have one?
   
       *b.* explain new features of their policies?

4. *Setting up a datafile with fields*

   What precautions must you take if your data contains commas?

5. *Using merge instructions*

   Which merge instruction do you use
   
       *a.* to insert text from another file?
   
       *b.* to set a field before printing each letter?
   
       *c.* to test a field's value?

# Chapter 13

## Using Word's Options

Word has commands that allow you to set various options. For example, you can adjust the way Word's screen looks and the amount of information that Word gives you.

## LESSON 63  Setting the Options

The Preferences command in the Edit menu lets you set the way Word takes measurements and displays text. These choices are only cosmetic and do not affect the way your printed output will look. The dialog box in Figure 13-1 shows the measurements and display choices.

275

**File**  **Edit**  **Search**  **Format**  **Font**  **Document**  **Window**

### Sample 1

January 11, 1987

Chris Richfc
Manufacture
1000 First
Millerton, C

Dear Ms. Ric

I am pleased
product line

**Preferences**

┌**Measure**┐
  ⊙ **Inch**
  ○ **Cm**
  ○ **Points**

☒ **Display As Printed**
☒ **Show Hidden Text**

**Keep in Memory:** ☐ **File**  ☐ **Program**

[ **OK** ]

[ **Cancel** ]

panded
t margin

(7%) for the fourth quarter of 1986, which is largely due to the successful
introduction of our new model, the DC50. In 1987 we expect to continue
increasing our profitable inroads into this new area.

As you can see, we are well within the projections we outlined to you when
you helped us obtain short-term financing. Thank you again for all your
assistance. If you have any questions regarding this information, please feel

Page 1      Normal

**Figure 13-1**   *Preferences dialog box*

The Measure option lets you set the units that Word uses
when it prompts you for linear measurement, as in the Paragraph and Section menus. You select the choice you want to use
when you give measurements. Table 13-1 shows the meaning of
each choice.

The Display as Printed option is only changed if you are
going to print your text on a printer with proportional spacing.
With Display as Printed selected, Word spaces each line exactly
as it will come out on the type of printer you chose with the
Chooser command. You also can specify whether or not you
want to see hidden text on the screen with the Preferences
command.

The Show ¶ command in the Edit Menu (COMMAND-Y) allows you to see the paragraph and NEWLINE markers on the screen. This is especially useful if you are reformatting tables, since you can quickly tell which lines are connected in a paragraph. For instance, the Sample 1 file would look like Figure 13-2. Nonrequired hyphens (when they are used) are also shown. Table 13-2 shows the characters displayed.

Unfortunately, the Show ¶ command continuously causes Word to run more slowly, since it has to display much more on the screen. You should weigh the speed costs of using this command against its usefulness in showing the characters.

*Table 13-1*   *Measurement Choices in the Preferences Command*

| Choice | Meaning |
|--------|---------|
| Inch | Inches (1 in. = 2.5 cm.) |
| Cm | Centimeters (1 cm. = 0.4 in.) |
| Points | 1 point = 1/72 in. Points are used for measurement by typesetters and are described in Chapter 7. |

*Table 13-2*   *Characters Displayed by the Show  ¶  Command*

| Character | Meaning |
|-----------|---------|
| ¶ | Paragraph end |
| ⌐ | NEWLINE |
| . | Normal space (nonbreaking spaces are indicated by a blank) |
| → | TAB |
| — | Nonrequired hyphens |

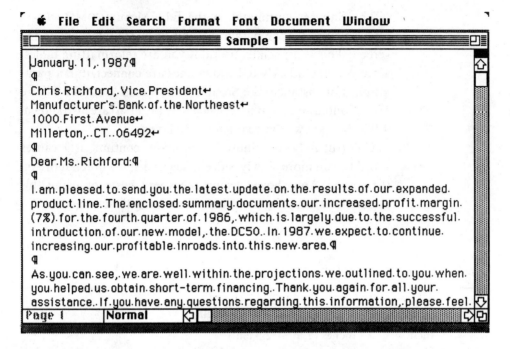

*Figure 13-2*   *Paragraph and NEWLINE markers shown on screen*

# LESSON 64   Customizing Word's Menus

Most Macintosh programs only let you work with the menus that come with the program. Word, on the other hand, lets you add items to some of the menus, and also lets you add a special menu, called the Work menu, to make using Word easier.

The Work menu holds the names of documents, the names of glossary entries, and the names of styles. The Format menu holds the names of character, paragraph, and section formats, and the Font menu holds the names of additional fonts.

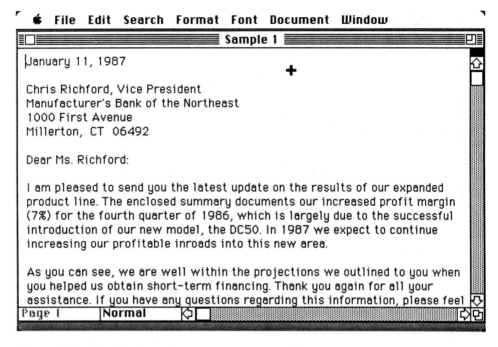

**Figure 13-3**    *The plus-shaped pointer*

To add one of these items to a menu, press COMMAND-OPTION-+. The pointer turns into a bold plus sign, as shown in Figure 13-3. You then select the item you want added, and Word adds it to the menu.

For example, assume that you want to add the Sample 1 file to the Work menu. Press COMMAND-OPTION-+, then give the Open command. Select Sample 1 from the list box (as shown in Figure 13-4), and click the Open button. Although "Sample 1" is not opened, it is added to the Work menu, as shown in Figure 13-5.

Glossary entries and style names are added to the Work menu in a similar way. Press COMMAND-OPTION-+, then give the Glossary or Styles command.

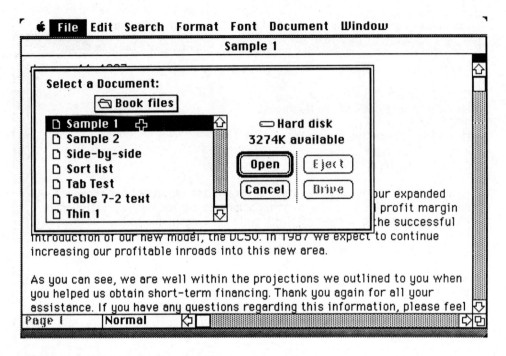

**Figure 13-4**   *Selecting the Sample 1 file*

To add entries to the Format or Font menus, press COMMAND-OPTION-+, then give the Character, Paragraph, or Section command. Select the items you want to add (such as a font name or a paragraph format), and click the OK button. You even can add alignment or spacing options from the paragraph ruler to the Format menu.

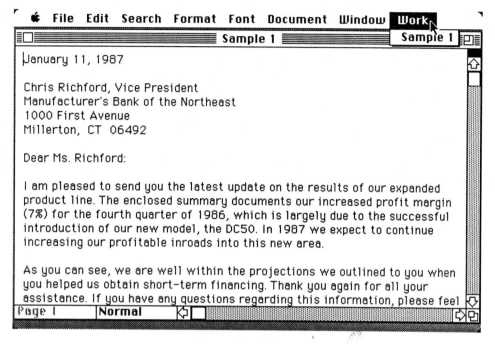

**Figure 13-5**   *The new Work menu*

# REVIEW

*1. Show ¶*

When is the Show ¶ command useful? What is the drawback to this command?

*2. Custom menus*

How do you add "small caps" to the Format menu?

# Part 4

## Advanced Word
## Features

# Chapter 14

## Outlining

There are many circumstances where outlines help you organize your thinking. Outlines can assist you in determining how important various thoughts are relative to each other. Writing an outline is also a good way to be sure you have covered all the topics that are relevant to your subject.

Of course, you can use the features of Word you have already learned to make an outline. If you set the tabs for a document at half-inch increments, you can enter text in a standard outline format. You can use Word's selection features to move groups of items around; you can even use an outline style sheet to specify a different emphasis for each level of your outline. However, Word's new outlining features allow you to do much more.

This chapter shows you how to create and modify outlines using special outlining features. With these new features you can even turn existing documents into outlines. If you are familiar with other outlining programs for the Macintosh, you may see similarities between those programs and Word. Once you've learned how to outline with Word, you will find many situations in your daily work where outlines are very useful.

# LESSON 65    Introduction to Word's Outlining Features

Every document in Word can also be viewed as an outline. Up till now, you have used the document view exclusively; since you haven't used any of Word's outlining features, you haven't needed to see your document in outline view.

It is important to understand that outlines are not separate documents in Word. Most outline programs create files that can only be used as outlines. Word, on the other hand, lets you create an outline, then fill in its parts with text. When you want to see the text, you use document view; when you want to see the outline, you use outline view. Outline view is just a different, more streamlined way to look at your document.

The outline view and the document view are used for different purposes. Editing and formatting are done in document view, as you have seen. Outline view is used to review and change the structure of your text, just as you might decide to switch the position of two major ideas after writing an outline on paper.

In Word's outline view, when you move a heading, all the text under that heading moves, too. To achieve this result in document view, you would have to select a huge amount of text, delete it to the scrap, move to the new location, and insert the text there. In outline view, you just move the heading, and the associated text moves with it.

If you have a complicated and detailed outline, you may have dozens of subheads under a main heading. When you are working with this kind of outline, you can get lost in the lower-level headings and miss the overall picture. Word lets you *collapse* an outline so that lower-level headings are invisible. For example, suppose your outline looks like Figure 14-1. Collapsing the subheads under the first-level head has the result shown in Figure 14-2.

When you are viewing the structure of a large outline, you will often find it useful to look at only the first- and second-level

```
Contract preparation
        Use standard contract as basis
        Add union work clause
                Local 112 for installing
                Local 112 and 427 for maintenance
        Add outdoor setting clause
Contract signing
        Phillips at National Generators
        Martinez and Washington at fair
Site preparation
        Verify space requirements
        Erect shelters
        Cable to main stations
        4 500' spans
        Check with Martinez for exact locations
```

*Figure 14-1*  *Sample outline*

---

```
Contract preparation
Contract signing
        Phillips at National Generators
        Martinez and Washington at fair
Site preparation
        Verify space requirements
        Erect shelters
        Cable to main stations
        4 500' spans
        Check with Martinez for exact locations
```

---

**Figure 14-2**   *Collapsed heading*

headings, collapsing the outline so that all headings below the second level are hidden. Of course, you can always expand the outline again to show all head levels.

There is a price for the convenience of using the outline view: you cannot select text across paragraph boundaries. Because of this limitation, you are usually restricted to editing a single paragraph. (In outlines, each heading is a separate paragraph.)

Moving between document view and outline view is very easy. The Outlining command in the Document menu switches between document view and outline view.

You can tell which view you are in by looking in the lower-left corner of the screen. In document view, the page looks normal. In outline view, the top portion of the window looks like Figure 14-3.

Outlines can have both headings and *body text* (body text is like regular text). Each heading has a level, starting with level 1. Body text does not have a level. As you make an outline, Word

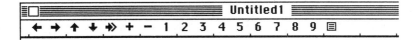

**Figure 14-3**   *The outline ruler*

remembers the level of headings by saving a paragraph style with each one. These styles are "level 1", "level 2", and so on. Body text is formatted as "Normal". As long as you enter your outline in outline view, you do not have to add these styles; Word does it for you.

Because outlines are just like regular documents, Word treats them very similarly. You can print an outline with the Print command in the File menu, and you can save it with the Save command in the File menu. In fact, you will find that handling outlines is almost identical to handling regular text files.

# LESSON 66   Creating an Outline

You can enter the text for a new outline in either document or outline view. It is usually better to enter and edit outlines in outline view.

When you want to create a new outline, be sure that you use a new document. Switch from document view to outline view by choosing the Outline command in the Document menu. Your screen will look like Figure 14-4.

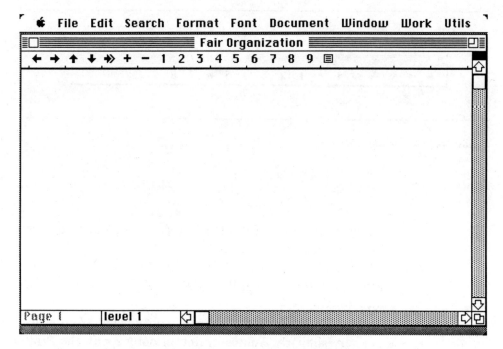

***Figure 14-4***   *Outline mode*

Figure 14-5 shows the outline you will work with in this chapter. You can begin entering it by typing in the first heading, **Contract preparation**, and pressing RETURN. Word assumes that you want to start at level 1 (the level indicator is shown in the style box near the lower-left corner of the window).

Next you want to enter the line, **Use standard contract as basis**. However, this is a level-2 entry, not a level 1. To tell Word that this line is level 2, click the → in the outline bar. Word indents the line, and the level indicator reflects the level you have chosen. Type in the line and press RETURN. Continue with the next line, "Add union work clause," and then click → again to tell Word that the next line will be level 3. If you have an extended keyboard with arrow keys, you can press the → key instead of clicking the arrow in the outline bar.

After you add the two level-3 lines, you want to go back to level 2. To do so, click ←. You can see how → and ← move the levels up and down. Finish entering all the text and save the file as Fair Organization with the Save command.

So far, you have only entered headings. Many outlines will contain body text as well, such as paragraphs under headings or a title. For this example, use body text to add a title to the outline. To do this, move to the top of the outline, press RETURN twice to add some space, and type **Millerton Art Fair** on the first line. To tell Word that this is body text, click the double-right arrow, between the ↓ and the +, as shown in Figure 14-6.

You can insert topics in the middle of an outline by moving to the beginning of a line, typing in new characters, and pressing

---

```
Contract preparation
        Use standard contract as basis
        Add union work clause
                Local 112 for installing
                Local 112 and 427 for maintenance
        Add outdoor setting clause
Contract signing
        Phillips at National Generators
        Martinez and Washington at fair
Site preparation
        Verify space requirements
        Erect shelters
        Cable to main stations
        4 500' spans
        Check with Martinez for exact locations
```

---

**Figure 14-5**  *Sample outline*

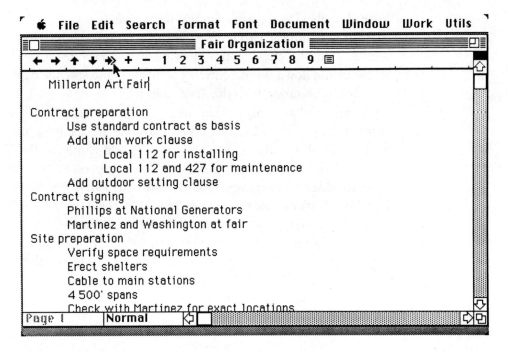

**Figure 14-6**   *New title*

RETURN. You can change the level of a heading by selecting any part of the heading and clicking → or ←. You can change a heading into body text by selecting any part of the heading and clicking the double-right arrow.

It is important to remember to use → and ← to shift headings. You cannot use the TAB key to do this; Word will not recognize it.

# LESSON 67   Collapsing and Expanding

A detailed outline can be very hard to follow, especially if it includes body text. When outlining a complex business report, for example, you can quickly lose track of the outline among all the text.

To avoid this problem, you will often want to see only higher-level portions of an outline. Word allows you to hide lower-level heads and body text with its Collapse feature. To collapse all of the headings below a particular one, simply select that heading (or any part of it) and click the minus sign on the outline bar. To restore these headings, click the plus sign on the outline bar.

For example, select the first level-1 heading, "Contract preparation", as shown in Figure 14-7. Click the minus sign in the outline bar to hide the subordinate headings. When you collapse a heading, Word puts a gray bar where the collapsed material is to remind you that there is more under that heading, as shown in Figure 14-8. You can also press MINUS on the keypad. You can expand a heading by clicking on the plus sign in the outline bar or pressing the + key on the keypad.

Expanding a heading shows only the level immediately below it. For example, if you collapse a level-1 heading and some of the level-2 heads below it have subheads, expanding the level-1 heading will not expand the level-2 heads at the same time. If you have collapsed different levels of headings and you want to expand them all at once, use the * on the keypad or click on the box with three lines at the right side of the outline bar. This will expand all the headings.

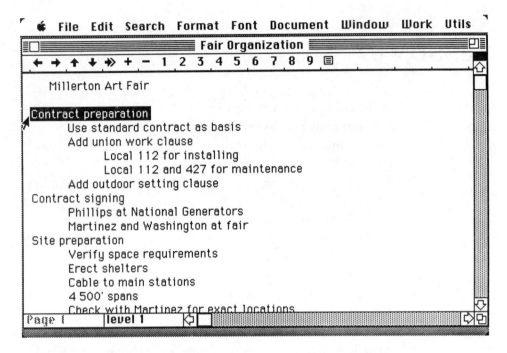

**Figure 14-7**   *Selecting the level-1 heading*

Word treats body text differently than it does subheads when you use the Collapse feature. If you collapse a heading that has body text under it, Word puts a gray mark where the text was.

Note that the minus and plus on the outline bar collapse and expand the lowest level of heading under the selected paragraph. Thus, if you have a three-level outline and have selected a top-level heading, clicking the minus on the outline bar will hide the third-level entries only.

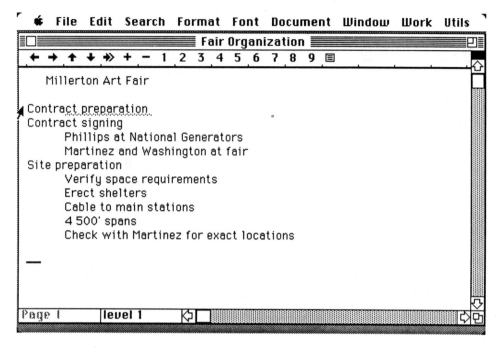

**Figure 14-8**   *Collapsed headings on screen*

It is likely that you will want to view your outline as a whole from various levels. To do this, click on the numbers in the outline bar. For example, clicking on the 2 in the outline bar collapses everything except level-1 and level-2 headings. Collapsing lower-level headings is useful when you are analyzing whether points in your outline are properly arranged and have equal weight.

# LESSON 68 Rearranging Your Outline

If you could write an outline correctly the first time you tried, there would not be much use for Word's special outlining commands. Because outlines are used to organize your thoughts, you need to rearrange headings as you decide to change their position or importance. The outline edit mode makes these adjustments especially easy.

If you are moving a heading, it is likely that you also want to move all the ideas associated with it. Word lets you do this. In outline edit mode, deleting and sending a heading to the scrap includes all subheads and body text under that heading, so moving whole ideas is easy.

For example, suppose that you want to move "Add union work clause" and its related subheads and text to follow "Add outdoor setting clause". To quickly select each subhead, double-click in the selection bar next to "Add union work clause", as shown in Figure 14-9. Now give the Cut command to cut this to the Clipboard.

"Add outdoor setting clause" is now selected. Move the insertion point so that it precedes the next heading, "Contract signing", and give the Paste command. The result is shown in Figure 14-10.

This feature is especially useful if you have a lot of body text. Instead of scrolling through many screens of text, you can simply select all the subordinate headings under the heading by double-clicking in the selection bar.

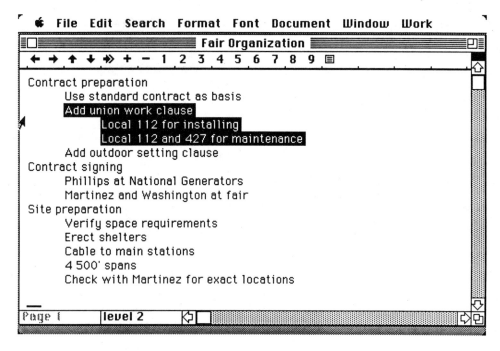

**Figure 14-9**  *Selecting the heading*

# LESSON 69   Numbering Your Outline

Up to this point, all the outlines discussed have been simple outlines without numbers and letters. If you create an outline with numbered headings, you cannot move one of these

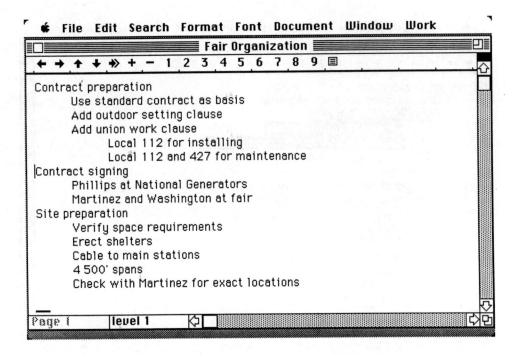

**Figure 14-10**   *Moving the selection*

headings somewhere else in the outline without affecting the numbering. Word gives you a simple way of numbering and renumbering outlines.

Word will, in fact, number anything, not just outlines. You can select a section of text in document view and have it numbered. This procedure is described in detail in the Word reference manual. This section shows you how Word numbers and renumbers outlines; numbering regular text is very similar.

All numbering is done with the Renumber command in the Document menu. Word can number in *cascading numeral* format: 1, 1.1, 1.2, 1.2.1, and so on. If you are numbering an outline, Word will not number body text.

To see how the Renumber command works, select the outline, then give the Renumber command, as shown in Figure 14-11. Select Numbers 1.1...and click OK. The outline is now numbered as shown in Figure 14-12.

If you want to use a different form of numbering, you have to indicate what form you want. In the Format box in the Renumber dialog box, enter the format using the types shown in Table 14-1. If you want to have different types of numbers for different headings, put a punctuation mark between the types for the different levels.

For example, standard outline style is to have uppercase Roman numerals for level-1 heads, uppercase letters for level-2

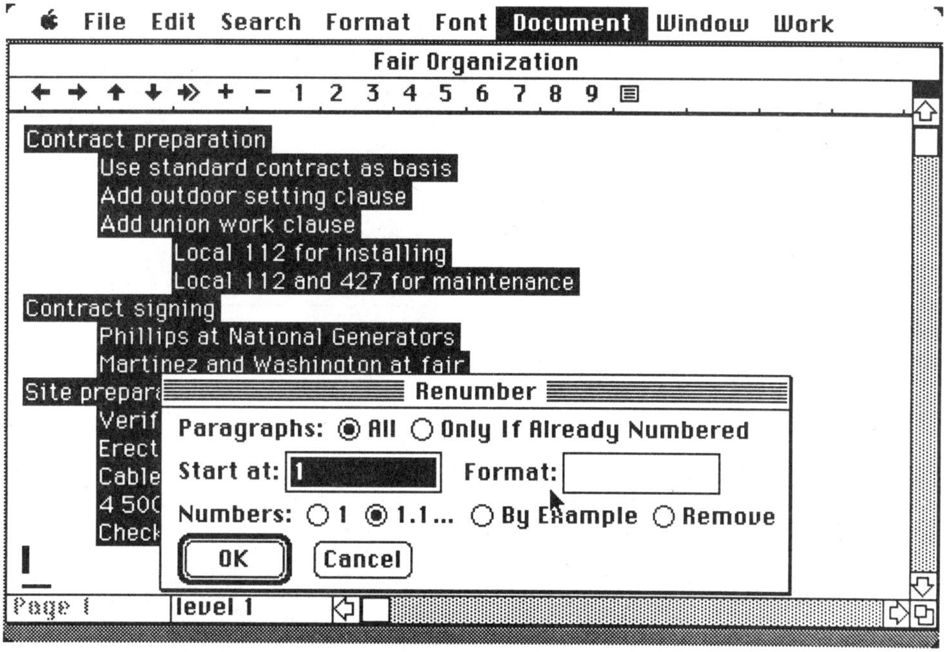

*Figure 14-11*   *The Renumber command*

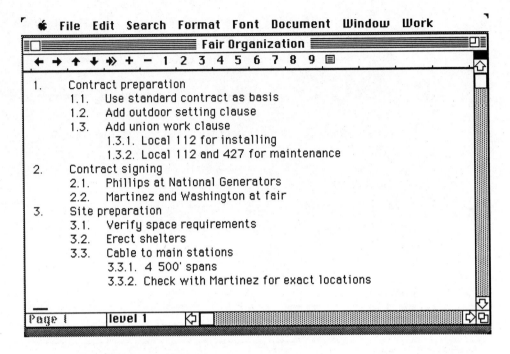

**Figure 14-12**   *Outline with numbers*

**Table 14-1**   *Format Symbols for the Renumber Command*

| Type of numeral | Symbol |
| --- | --- |
| Arabic | 1 |
| Uppercase Roman | I |
| Lowercase Roman | i |
| Uppercase letter | A |
| Lowercase letter | a |

heads, Arabic numbers for level-3 heads, and lowercase letters for level-4 heads. Each of these would have a period ( . ) after it. The format for this would be "I.A.1.a.". You can use any of the punctuation marks shown in Table 14-2 between the levels.

If you use the Renumber command to renumber a regular document, Word adds a tab between the number and text. Thus, you should be sure that you have set up your document with proper tab settings before you renumber. For example, you may want to use hanging indents, which would make the numbers stand out.

Word also renumbers your documents if you move headings around. For example, if you move the "Add union work clause" heading and give the Renumber command, Word will correctly renumber that heading and all the subsequent heads.

**Table 14-2**  *Punctuation Marks for Separating Symbols in the Renumber Command*

| | |
|---|---|
| , | comma |
| - | hyphen |
| / | slash |
| ; | semicolon |
| : | colon |
| ( ) | left and right parenthesis |
| { } | left and right brace |
| [ ] | left and right bracket |

# REVIEW

1. *Outline view*

   How do you switch between outline view and document view?

2. *Collapsing and expanding*

   What do you use to collapse and expand text?

3. *Numbering*

   How do you get Word to number your outline?

# Chapter 15

## Generating a Table
## Of Contents

Not only are tables of contents and indexes time-consuming and tedious to prepare, but they must be updated whenever you add to or rearrange your document. Very few word processing packages automatically compile tables of contents or indexes. Those that do usually restrict you to a preset style of printout that may not meet your needs.

With Word, on the other hand, you can easily create entries for the table of contents or index, and you have great flexibility in styling your printout. In addition, you can generate a new table of contents or index whenever you choose. These features make Word one of the most popular programs for business and academic use.

This chapter shows you how to create a table of contents; Chapter 16 explains how to assemble an index. Specifying the text for either one is similar, so read this chapter even if you only want to generate indexes.

# LESSON 70   Hidden Text

To create a table of contents, you must tell Word what you want in the table. You do this by flagging the headings you want included with a special marker that is formatted on the screen as hidden text.

Hidden text is similar to other text that has a character format applied to it. You can use the Character command in the Format menu to make text bold; you can also use the command to make text hidden. To make a section of text hidden, simply select it and give the Character command with the hidden option, or use COMMAND-SHIFT-X.

Once you mark something as hidden, you cannot see it on the screen (as you might have guessed). For example, select the word "Vice" in the Sample 1 file as shown in Figure 15-1. Format it as hidden, and your screen looks like Figure 15-2.

Word gives you two ways of seeing your hidden text after you have formatted it. To see all the hidden text in a document, give the Preferences command in the Edit menu and set the Show Hidden Text option. You will see the hidden text with a dotted underline, as in Figure 15-3.

Do not get into the habit of showing hidden text on the screen. Should you print or repaginate a document that has hidden text showing, Word would include that text in its calculations for the ends of pages and so on. Then, were you to generate a table of contents or an index, Word would enter incorrect page numbers.

If you want to see hidden text, you can open up a second window and use the Preferences command in that window to do so. This lets you see the document both with and without the hidden text. Be careful, though, not to repaginate the document when this second window is the selected window, or Word will include the hidden text in its page calculation. You will get used to typing hidden text fairly quickly, and most of the time you won't need to see it.

**   File   Edit   Search   Format   Font   Document   Window   Work**

**Sample 1**

January 11, 1987

Chris Richford, Vice President
Manufacturer's Bank of the Northeast
1000 First Avenue
Millerton, CT 06492

Dear Ms. Richford:

I am pleased to send you the latest update on the results of our expanded product line. The enclosed summary documents our increased profit margin (7%) for the fourth quarter of 1986, which is largely due to the successful introduction of our new model, the DC50. In 1987 we expect to continue increasing our profitable inroads into this new area.

As you can see, we are well within the projections we outlined to you when you helped us obtain short-term financing. Thank you again for all your assistance. If you have any questions regarding this information, please feel

Page 1      Normal

*Figure 15-1   Selecting "Vice"*

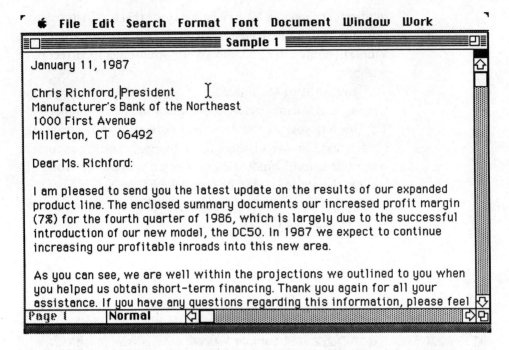

*Figure 15-2*  *Making text hidden*

# LESSON 71  Introduction to Tables Of Contents

Before you start using Word to generate tables of contents for your documents, you should consider the purpose and structure of a table of contents. Generally, a table of contents appears at the beginning of a document. It tells the reader what is presented in the document, and in what order. A document that is only one or two pages long generally does not need a table of contents.

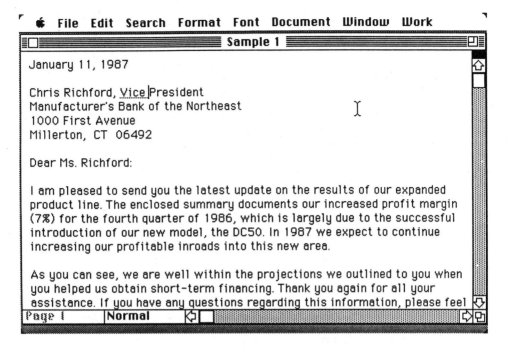

**Figure 15-3**    *Seeing hidden text*

A table of contents can be a simple list of where each section of the document begins, or it can be a detailed roadmap of the document. For example, the table of contents of most books contains only the chapter names and beginning page numbers. This keeps the table of contents short (it usually fits on one page), and gives the reader a feel for the general categories and progression of subjects.

Some tables of contents are meant to show almost the entire contents of a document. These are much longer than simple tables of contents and are often hard to browse through. Of course, someone looking for a particular subject will be more likely to find it in a detailed table of contents. However, many authors prefer to create an index for detailed listings and keep the table of contents brief.

The format of a table of contents is also important. If you list two or more levels of headings in a table of contents, Word's paragraph and character formatting will make the table of contents significantly easier to read. Compare this unformatted table of contents in Figure 15-4 to the formatted one in Figure 15-5.

Compiling a table of contents for a document is quite easy. There are basically two steps:

1. Using hidden text, type **.c.** in front of every entry that you want in the table of contents. This marks the entry for Word. There is no limit on the number of entries you can have in your table of contents.

2. Give the Table of Contents command in the Document menu. Word creates a table of contents in a new section at the beginning of your document.

---

| | |
|---|---|
| Installing | 1 |
| Unpacking | 2 |
| Checking the crates | 2 |
| In case of damage | 3 |
| Removing the main unit | 4 |
| Other units | 8 |
| Connecting to equipment | 10 |
| Adding fuel | 10 |
| Testing | 13 |
| Starting for the first time | 14 |

---

**Figure 15-4**   *Unformatted table of contents*

**Figure 15-5**   *Formatted table of contents*

There are rules and suggestions for both steps, but you do not need to do much more for Word to create a full table of contents.

If you use Word's outlining feature (discussed in Chapter 14), you can generate a table of contents even faster. The Table of Contents command has an option for automatically including all outline headings into the table of contents. You can even specify the levels of headings that you want in the table of contents. This option is discussed later in this chapter.

# LESSON 72   Marking Entries

When you give the Table of Contents command, Word scans your document for the hidden text ".c." code and identifies it as indicating an entry. The entry itself can be either hidden or regular text. Word assumes that the first character after the ".c." is the first character of the entry.

Word ends the entry when it sees a semicolon, a paragraph mark, or a division mark. Because most tables of contents contain headings from the document, and most headings are paragraphs, you can generally just add the hidden ".c." at the beginning of lines you want included in the table.

Assume that you want to add the heading shown in Figure 15-6 to the table of contents. Move the selection to the first character. Press COMMAND-SHIFT-X to turn on hidden formatting, type **.c.**, and press COMMAND-SHIFT-SPACEBAR to turn off hidden formatting. The line looks the same, but Word's marker has been added. You can see that you added it by using the Preferences command.

If the text you want in the table of contents is not a heading, and does not end with a paragraph mark, you can still specify it easily. To indicate the end of your desired entry, add a semicolon. Of course, you will want this semicolon to be hidden so that it does not appear in your text.

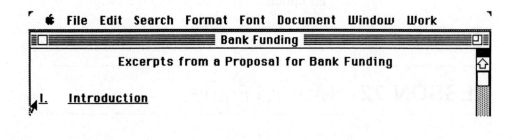

***Figure 15-6***    *Entry for table of contents*

Assume that you want the words "National Generators" from the first sentence of the first paragraph to be an entry (Figure 15-7). Move the selection to the first letter, press COMMAND-SHIFT-X to turn on hidden formatting, type **.c.**, and press COMMAND-SHIFT-SPACEBAR to turn off hidden formatting. Now move to the space after "Generators", press COMMAND-SHIFT-X to turn on hidden formatting, type the semicolon (;), and press COMMAND-SHIFT-SPACEBAR again to turn off hidden formatting once more.

So far, you have only learned how to put level-1 entries into a table of contents. As you saw earlier, however, it is often desirable to have more than one level in your table of contents. To tell Word that an entry is level 2, follow the .c with the level number. Thus, to make the previous example a level-2 head, you would insert the hidden text ".c2." To make it a level-3 head, you would insert this hidden text: ".c3." You can specify level-1 heads as either ".c." or ".c1."

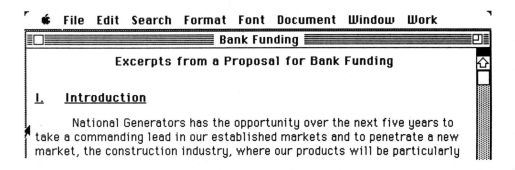

*Figure 15-7*   *First sentence*

Unfortunately, when you are specifying entries there are many special cases. If your heading contains a semicolon, you have to tell Word exactly what text you want included. Any entry that has a semicolon must have quotation marks at the beginning and end of the entry. Of course, these quotation marks should be formatted as hidden characters or they will show up in your document. For example, suppose you wanted to make the heading shown in Figure 15-8 an entry. At the beginning of the line, give the Character command and turn on hidden formatting. Type **.c."** and press COMMAND-SHIFT-SPACEBAR to turn off hidden formatting. At the end of the line, turn on hidden formatting. Type **"** and turn off hidden formatting again.

If your entry contains quotation marks, the situation is even trickier. First, you must surround the entire entry with quotation marks, just as if it contained a semicolon or a colon. Next, you must precede any quotation mark in the entry by another quotation mark. Again, use hidden formatting for all of these special quotation marks. For instance, if your desired entry is the one on the first line of Figure 15-9, you must put the text from the second line at the beginning of the line, a hidden quotation mark before the first real quotation mark, a hidden quotation mark before the second real quotation mark, and a hidden quotation mark at the end of the line. Needless to say, this can be a bit tedious.

---

The Future; More Growth

---

**Figure 15-8**   *Sample entry*

# LESSON 73  Making the Table of Contents

Once you have entered all the hidden marks for Word, you can create a table of contents with the Table of Contents command. Briefly, this command will do the following:

1. Repaginate your document (remember to set the Show Hidden Text option of the Preferences command to not show).

2. Search through your document from the beginning for marked entries.

3. Collect copies of those marked entries and their associated page numbers. (Word uses the page number of the first visible text after the heading.)

4. Create a new section at the beginning of your document containing the entries.

The Table of Contents command has many interesting features that are described in this lesson and later in the chapter. Even if you skip these descriptions, you can quickly generate a simple table of contents just by giving the Table of Contents

Finding the "Best" Solution: Optimization

.c."

*Figure 15-9*  *Another sample entry*

command and printing your document. With a bit more planning and work, however, you can create more complex tables of
contents and figure lists.

You can give the Table of Contents command at any time. If
you change your document by adding, deleting, or moving text,
you should give the command before you print your document
so that the table of contents reflects the most current revision. If
you have already created a table of contents, Word replaces the
old copy with the new one after verifying that you want this
done.

When you give the Table of Contents command, you will see
the dialog box in Figure 15-10. Choose ".C. Paragraphs" and
"Show Page Numbers," then click the Start button. Word
creates a new section at the beginning of your document containing the table of contents. Your table of contents will be
similar to the one in Figure 15-11.

Word puts the table of contents at the beginning of your
document in its own section so that it doesn't affect the numbering of the pages in the main part. Unless you have a specific
reason to move it, it is best to leave the table of contents there.

Once you have this text at the beginning of your document,
you can format it any way you want. (In general, you will want to
use Word's default formatting styles.) You can use normal character, paragraph, and section formatting on the table. Note,
however, that if you remake the table of contents, your formatting changes are lost. Items you might want to change are the
spacing, margins, and page numbering.

Word automatically uses the built-in styles "toc1", "toc2",
and so on for the entries in the table of contents. You can change
the way these default styles look by changing the style definitions, as explained in Chapter 10.

If you are making a table of contents from an outline, simply
select "Outline" in the Table of Contents command. Word
automatically assigns the same built-in styles for the entries in
the table of contents as it does for the ".C." outlines.

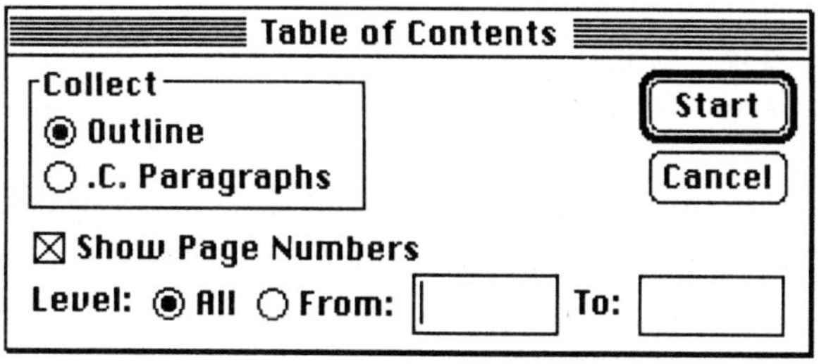

**Figure 15-10**   *Table of Contents command*

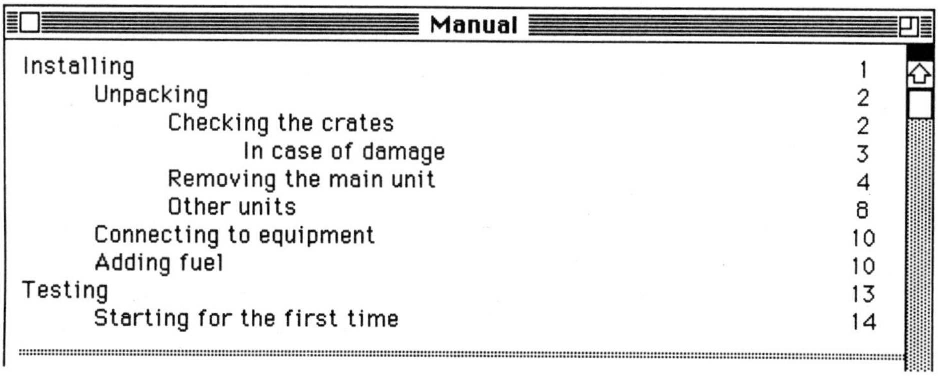

**Figure 15-11**   *Sample table of contents*

# LESSON 74 Advanced Use of Tables Of Contents

Microsoft made Word's features flexible so that you would be able to do more than just create a table of contents. This section describes how you can use these features to make advanced documents.

Word knows where previous tables of contents are in your document. When it recreates a table of contents, Word only erases the table of contents entries.

It is common to add text at the top of your table of contents, such as the title "Table of Contents." You can also format the division marker for the table of contents after the first time Word creates it; Word won't change it after that.

Many reports have numerous figures and tables. It is often useful to list these elements and let the reader know what pages they appear on. In the same way that you create tables of contents, you can also create other lists.

For example, assume that you have a figure listing such as the one in Figure 15-12. In front of the listing, add the hidden text ".c9." (instead of ".c."). Do the same in front of each figure, following the rules for special characters. Next, give the Table of Contents command. In the Level option, specify "From" to be "9". When you execute the command, Word creates a new list consisting of the entries that were marked with ".c9."

Level-9 entries for figure lists would normally appear in your regular table of contents. To prevent this, when you create your regular table of contents specify "From" to be "1" and "To" to be "8."

You can use this technique to create lists of figures, tables, charts, and so on. All other aspects of creating tables of contents are identical to those for creating other lists.

Figure 7. Power indicator at full.

**Figure 15-12**   *Figure entry*

# REVIEW

1. *Marking*

   How do you mark an entry to be included in the table of contents?

2. *Special characters*

   What are the special characters that affect marking entries? How do you handle them?

3. *Formatting the table of contents*

   How can you format your table of contents?

# Chapter 16

## Indexes and Annotations

**LESSON 75**  Creating an Index
**LESSON 76**  Annotations

Chapter 15 described using hidden text, marking your document, and using the Table of Contents command to create a table of contents. This chapter expands on those ideas to show you how you can create indexes and use hidden text to annotate your documents.

## LESSON 75  Creating an Index

The steps used to make an index are almost identical to those used for a table of contents, and the results are also similar. Almost everything you learned in Chapter 15 applies here.

To mark an entry for the index, use ".i." instead of ".c.". The same rules apply for ending the entry: use either a semicolon, a paragraph mark, or a division mark. If you are marking a visible part of your text, you will probably use many hidden semicolons. The rules for special characters apply here as well.

Subentries are created slightly differently. Because there is a predetermined order to an index, you must specify a main entry when you specify a subentry. Separate the two with a colon. For example, to include an index entry for "new models" under "Generators" you would type the following:

.i.Generators:new models

Word allows up to five levels of entries; however, indexes rarely have more than three levels, and most have only two.

As you become proficient at determining what a reader needs in an index, you will find that the words and concepts that you want to refer to on a page may not be stated specifically. Thus, many of your index entries will consist entirely of hidden text. For instance, imagine that you are discussing religion and you also want a reference to "theology", although that word does not appear in the text. You can enter ".i.theology" in hidden text to make the entry.

The dialog box for the Index command appears below.

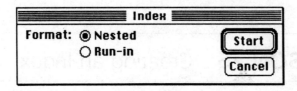

You generally will use only the Nested option.

When you execute the Index command, Word creates a new section and places the sorted index entries in it. You can format the output any way you want, just as before. Remember, though, that any formatting will be lost if you create the index again. Word uses styles "index 1," "index 2," and so on.

It is common practice to have multi-column indexes. Recall from Chapter 9 that Word can make columns easily with the Section command. Since most index entries are short, a two-column index usually looks fine. Be careful to check that none of your page numbers wrap around in a confusing fashion, however.

There are many other changes that you might want to make to standardize the appearance of your index. Remember to make these changes only after you are sure that the index is in final form. Possible changes include

- Adding a title to the page.

- Using leader characters.

- Italicizing see references.

You can use special characters in the ".i." mark to make the page number come out in a special form. For instance, ".ib." will cause the page number to come out in bold. This might be useful if you have many index instances for one word, but one of them is the most useful (for example, the one that defines the word). Table 16-1 lists the special characters you can use.

The range and text options make creating complex indexes much easier. To use the range characters (the left and right parentheses), simply put ".i(." at the first occurrence of the topic and ".i.)." at the last. For example, to make a range for the entry "Durability," the first entry should be

.i(.Durability;

The last entry should be

.i).Durability;

The result will be

Durability  21-26

To use the text option, put the pound sign (#) and your text at the end of the entry and place a semicolon at the end. This is especially useful for see references. For instance, an entry such as

.i.Gasoline#(See Fuel);

will produce the following index entry:

Gasoline  (See Fuel)

*Table 16-1*  *Index Entry Characters*

| Entry | Result |
| --- | --- |
| .ii. | Italic page number |
| .ib. | Bold page number |
| .i(. | First page in a range |
| .i). | Last page in a range |
| .i.entry#text | Replace page number with text |

# LESSON 76   Annotations

Hidden text can be used for more than the Table of Contents and Index commands. You can use hidden text to leave yourself easy-to-find notes and markers in your text. Since hidden text is stored just as regular text is, you can add it, move it, and edit it in a similar fashion.

When you are writing a long report, there are often times when you do not have complete information. You may want to write the text around the unknown data instead of waiting until you receive the data to add the sentence or paragraph that goes with it. A convenient method for doing this is to write what you can, then select all the text that is uncertain, and then hide it. If you find the missing data before the final draft of the report, simply select the hidden text, format as visible, and add the new information.

A nice feature is that the Find command will find strings in hidden text even if the text is not displayed. You can leave notes such as "Update this when the new sales figures come out" and later search for "sales figures". You may have special marks you want to put in your documents that only have meaning to you: making them hidden and finding them with the Find command is a convenient way to do this.

Sometimes you may want to create an annotated version of a document so that some people see the document without the notes and others see it with the notes. If you are not using hidden text for other purposes (such as making an index), you can create entire paragraphs of hidden text that comment on the visible text. When you print only the visible text, the notes are left out. Using the Preferences command and printing the document again gives you a copy on which the annotations appear.

It is usually a good idea to format the annotations in a style different from that used in the rest of the document.

This form of annotation can be taken one step further using style sheets. Assume that an important proposal has three classes of readers: outside clients, in-house managers, and auditors. The outside clients are to see only the basic proposal. The in-house managers are to see the basic proposal plus some comments relating to its implementation. The auditors are to see the basic proposal and comments on cost, but not the notes addressed to the in-house managers.

Clearly, you can't simply use hidden text for the notes since you want the managers and auditors to see different things. However, using a style sheet you can specify two character styles: MA for the managers' text and AU for the auditors' text. In the gallery, initially format both styles as visible. As you write the document, select individual notes and assign the appropriate style to each.

When you are ready to print the clients' copies, go to the gallery and change the formatting of MA and AU to hidden; then print. Next, go to the gallery and change the format of MA to visible; then print the managers' copies. Finally, go to the gallery and format MA as hidden and AU as visible; now print the auditors' copies.

You can use this method of annotating to include or exclude any number of styles. You can, of course, print out a master copy with all text visible. You can also print out documents with a combination of comments visible.

This method of annotating reports requires that each annotation is done as a paragraph. You can then format the paragraphs with different margins. For example, the comments for the auditors could be indented .5 inch, while the comments for the managers could be indented 1 inch. Or you could add other character formats to the styles, such as boldface for the comments to the auditors.

An interesting twist is using annotations that come from different people. If four people have to comment on one document, each can add comments formatted in a different style. Then you can use the gallery as before, but this time to hide or show notes written by various people.

# REVIEW

*1. Marking*

How do you mark an entry to be included in the index?

*2. Capitalization*

What choices does Word give you concerning capitalization in the index?

*3. Annotation*

What are some of the uses of hidden text annotation?

# Chapter 17

## Spelling Correction
## And Hyphenation

Because most people are not perfect spellers, Word has included an easy-to-use spelling checker that works closely with the other parts of Word. You can use the program at any time, and you do not need to exit from Word to do so.

Word also includes a hyphenation program. Justified text looks significantly better if all of the long words in the text have optional hyphens. Of course, inserting these yourself is tedious. The hyphenation program frees you from the task of putting optional hyphens in every word and gives you control over the way hyphens are used in your document.

# LESSON 77   Introduction to Spelling Correction

The second most useful program for writers is a spelling checker (the first, of course, is a word processor). Even if your spelling is flawless, it is likely that your proofreading is not; and a single spelling mistake in a report or memo can have a very negative effect.

The idea behind spelling checkers is fairly simple. When you run a spelling checker, it reads your document file and makes a sorted list of all the words you used. The program then compares this list against a list of all the English words it knows and tells you which words it does not recognize. You then change the words either through the program or with your word processor.

Of course, even a good spelling checker is not perfect, since you will probably use words that it does not know and it will think you have misspelled them. For example, most dictionaries that come with spelling programs do not include proper names, so a program may think that you misspelled something if, for example, it sees the word "Jones" in your text. Also, spelling checkers cannot spot words that are used incorrectly in context, as in "I son the race."

The dictionary in Word's spelling checker is quite complete. This makes it less likely that Word will not recognize a correctly spelled word. The dictionary takes up a fair amount of space, however, so you may need a separate disk for it unless you are using a hard disk.

If Word thinks you have misspelled a word in your document, it can offer help by checking through its dictionary for a few guesses at what you intended. For example, if you have the misspelled word "postion" in your document, Word will have many guesses, including *portion, position,* and *posting.*

The spelling correcter uses two types of dictionaries when it corrects a document. It searches these invisibly so that you need not keep track of the names.

- The *main* dictionary contains all common words. You cannot add words to this dictionary.

- *User* dictionaries are for words that are used in groups of documents. You can tell the speller to check one or more user dictionaries before you proof your document. It is likely that you will have one user dictionary just for words that are only used in your field. Words that are perfectly acceptable but are not in the standard dictionary also can be included in a user dictionary.

Word lists the unrecognized words one at a time. For each word, you have the following choices:

- Add the word to one of the dictionaries.

- Correct the word in your document by typing in the correct spelling or by selecting one of Word's guesses.

- Ignore the word, indicating that you know it is not recognized, but you don't care.

The spelling checker is easy to use. If you are creating a large document, you may want to check the spelling after you have entered all the text (but before you edit) and again just before you print the text. If you create a table of contents or index, you should run the spelling checker after doing so; any mistakes made in hidden text will then be found.

# LESSON 78   Using the Spelling Command

When you are ready to check the spelling of a document, give the Spelling command in the Document menu. Word displays the dialog box shown in Figure 17-1.

The "Ignore Words in All Caps" option tells Word not to bother with words that are all capital letters. Since words in all caps are usually acronyms, it is highly unlikely they will be in the standard dictionary. However, it is easy to mistype these words, so it is a good idea to include the correct versions in your user dictionary and have Word check them. If Word finds words that

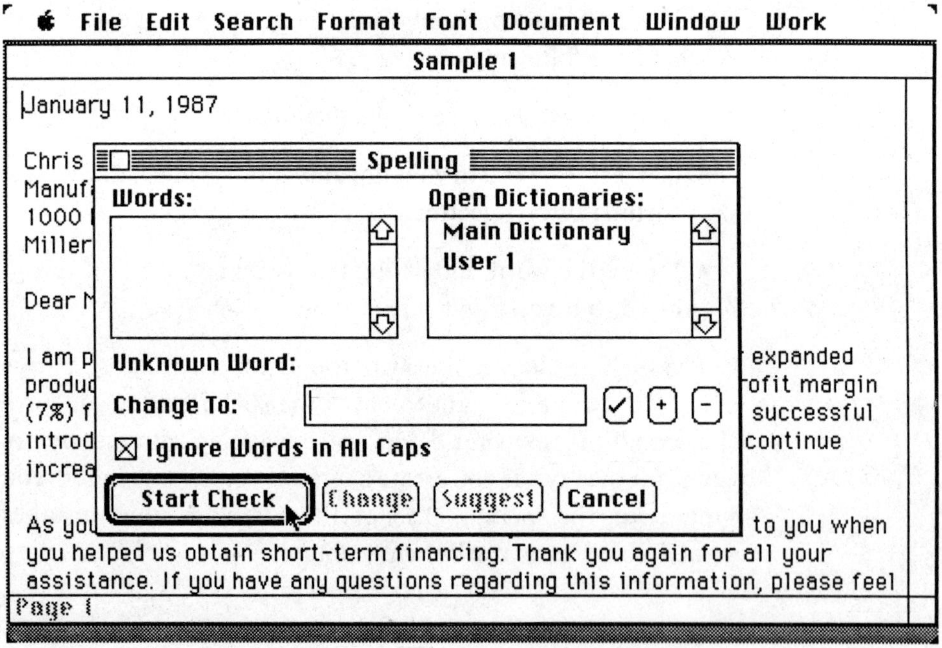

*Figure 17-1*   *The Spelling command*

it does not recognize, it changes the dialog box, as shown in Figure 17-2.

The + button tells Word this is an acceptable word that you want added to one of the dictionaries. When you select it, Word puts the word into the user dictionary you have chosen. Click the Continue Check button.

"No Change" indicates that you want to leave the word as it stands but you do not want to add it to a dictionary. If you correct this document again later, you will see all the ignored words again.

If you know the correct spelling for the word, you can simply type it in and click "Change." If you are not sure, click the Suggest button and Word will give you a list of its best guesses in the left list. You can select from this list with the mouse.

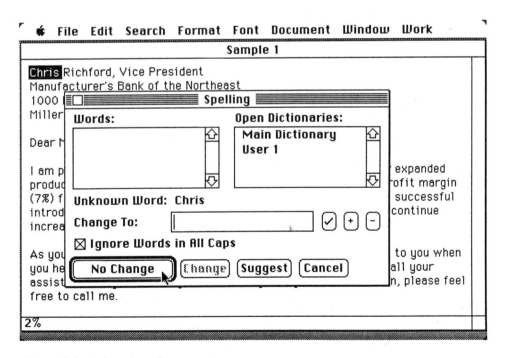

*Figure 17-2*  *Unknown spelling*

# LESSON 79   Hyphenation

You may think that there is only one kind of hyphen; however, Word has three: normal, nonbreaking, and nonrequired hyphens. Each time you hyphenate a word, you can indicate the kind of hyphen you want so that wordwrap will not produce an effect you do not want.

A normal hyphen is one that is always printed. For example, the word "fast-moving" contains a normal hyphen, since you always want the hyphen to appear in the printed text.

A *nonbreaking* hyphen is like a normal hyphen, except that Word will never break the hyphenated word if it occurs at the end of a line. For instance, if you use a normal hyphen, you may end up with a paragraph that looks like this:

> There are many different spreadsheets that perform "what-
> if" calculations.

Since there was a normal hyphen between "what" and "if", Word broke the line there. In many cases, this is all right, but in this case it looks a bit clumsy. If you want to prevent Word from possibly breaking a word at its hyphen, you use a nonbreaking hyphen, which you enter by holding down the COMMAND key and the tilde ($\sim$). The result of using a nonbreaking hyphen is the following:

> There are many different spreadsheets that perform
> "what-if" calculations.

If a paragraph contains many long words, wordwrap will make the paragraph look a bit sparse. For instance:

> His telecommunications discussion was
> significantly sidetracked as he started
> expostulating about interplanetary associations of
> antediluvian civilizations.

To make the lines more even, you will need to hyphenate some of the words. However, the Word program cannot guess where to hyphenate words that do not contain hyphens. If you want Word to hyphenate a word, you have to enter a nonrequired hyphen. You usually do this only when you notice that a particular set of lines is broken unevenly.

A nonrequired hyphen is not used until it is needed. You can include nonrequired hyphens anywhere in a word. To enter a nonrequired hyphen, use COMMAND-HYPHEN (hold down the COMMAND key and press the HYPHEN key). You do not see these hyphens unless they appear because of wordwrap. If you use nonrequired hyphens in the previous example, the result is

> His telecommunications discussion was significant-
> ly sidetracked as he started expostulating about
> interplanetary associations of antediluvian civili-
> zations.

Word can help you hyphenate by automatically putting optional hyphens in every word that is at the end of a line and that might be split. The Hyphenate command in the Document menu will let you decide where the hyphen goes in each word or will hyphenate without confirmation.

The Hyphenate command will hyphenate your whole document if you are at the beginning. If you want to hyphenate only part of the document, select that part before giving the command. The window is shown in Figure 17-3. It is unlikely that you will want to have Word confirm hyphenation for each word, especially in a long document. If you do choose to have Word confirm each hyphenation, click on "Start Hyphenation" and Word will change the display as though you had selected Printer Display in the Preferences command. For each word, the program shows you where it thinks the hyphen should go and asks you to enter a response, as shown in Figure 17-4. Click "Change" to confirm the choice or "No Change" to change the position.

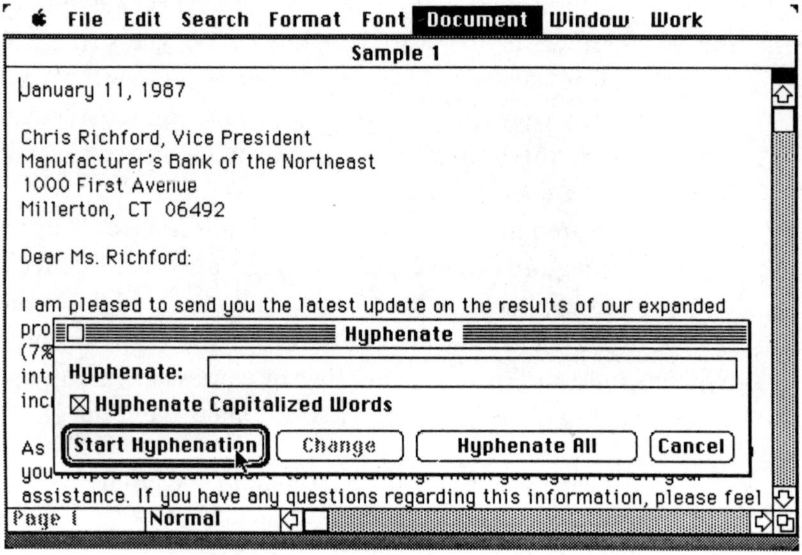

**Figure 17-3**   *The Hyphenate command*

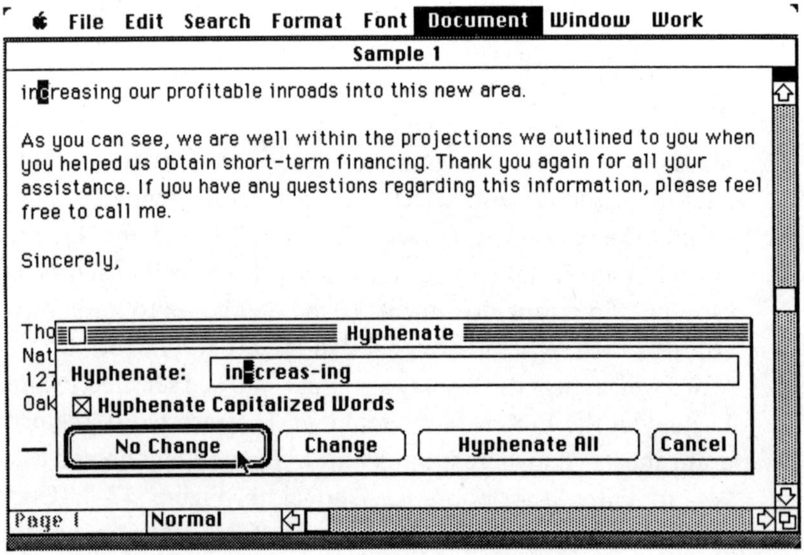

**Figure 17-4**   *Suggested hyphen*

# REVIEW

1. *Spelling*

   Describe how Word decides what is misspelled.

2. *Hyphenating*

   Which keys do you use to specify normal, nonbreaking, and nonrequired hyphens?

# Chapter 18

## Sorting

There are often times when you want to sort a list inside one of your documents. If the list is only five or ten lines long, it is fairly easy to sort by hand, but sorting long lists by hand is extremely inconvenient. Word's Sort command in the Document menu makes sorting any list easy.

Word can sort both text and numbers. This distinction may seem trivial, but most sorting programs cannot sort text in a way useful to people because computers don't store characters the ways humans do.

Computers think in terms of numbers, not of characters such as letters, punctuation, numerals, and so on. Early computer scientists got around this problem by assigning an internal value to each letter. Most computers use a specific system called

ASCII to relate characters to internal numbers. Roughly, the ASCII sorting order is

1. Most punctuation marks

2. Numerals (0, 1, 2, . . . 9)

3. More punctuation marks

4. Uppercase letters (A, B, C, . . . Z)

5. Lowercase letters (a, b, c, . . . z)

6. More punctuation marks.

This order, dating back to the 60s, presents some problems, most of which Word overcomes

The first problem is that sorting numerals is very different than sorting numbers. Look at the following list:

23
142
5

Of course, you would sort it numerically as "5, 23, 142." However, in ASCII code, 1 comes before 2, and 2 before 5. Thus, an unintelligent sorter (the kind most word processing programs use) would sort the list as

142
23
5

Fortunately, however, Word can sort numerals as numbers,

rather than as ASCII characters.

A second problem is that upper- and lowercase letters are normally separated in the sorting sequence; all words that start with uppercase letters are sorted before all words that start with lowercase letters. This list, for example,

```
terrapin
Shakedown
blues
American
Workingman's
```

would be sorted as

```
American
Shakedown
Workingman's
blues
terrapin
```

Most of the time you will want your lists sorted in alphabetical order, regardless of case. Word sorts upper- and lowercase words together.

A third, minor, problem is that not all punctuation comes before all numerals in the ASCII system. Some characters, such as the equal sign, fall between the numerals and the letters; others, such as the circumflex, fall between the upper- and lowercase letters; and some, such as the vertical bar, follow the lowercase letters. In general, avoid sorting lists that include punctuation as the first character. Figure 18-1 shows the ASCII sorting sequence.

```
space
! " # $ % & ' ( ) * + , - . /
0 1 2 3 4 5 6 7 8 9
: ; < = > ? @
A B C D E F G H I J K L M N O P Q R S T U V W X Y Z
[ \ ] ^ _ `
a b c d e f g h i j k l m n o p q r s t u v w x y z
{ | } ~
```

**Figure 18-1**   *The ASCII sorting sequence*

# LESSON 80   Sorting Text

The most frequent use for Word's sorter is sorting lists that are formatted as individual paragraphs. Usually, you will want to sort based on entire lines and you will want to sort text.

The Sort command is easy to use. First, select the range of paragraphs you want to sort (Word will only sort paragraphs, not lines separated by NEWLINE). For this example use the following list:

```
terrapin
Shakedown
blues
American
Workingman's
```

Give the Sort command and Word sorts the list.

```
American
blues
Shakedown
terrapin
Workingman's
```

You can tell Word whether you want to sort from A to Z (*ascending*) or from Z to A (*descending*). To choose descending, hold down the SHIFT key when giving the Sort command. This produces the following list:

```
Workingman's
terrapin
Shakedown
blues
American
```

In addition to sorting lists, you can sort text that runs many lines; Word simply sorts full paragraphs in this case.

# LESSON 81   Sorting Numbers

You can use the Sort command to sort numbers in their correct sequence. For example, the following list:

```
509
22.7
448
100
1000.
17
```

would be sorted as

```
17
22.7
100
448
509
1000.
```

You can, of course, sort numbers in either ascending or descending order.

# LESSON 82   Sorting in Tables

So far, you have only learned how to sort based on the first character in a paragraph. While this is usually what you want, there are some circumstances where you might want to sort a table by a column other than the first one. For instance, you may want to sort the following table on the "Amount" column:

| Who | Last paid | Amount |
|---|---|---|
| Robin Morgan | 2/18/87 | 1732.50 |
| William Bradley | 1/27/87 | 7100.00 |
| Cathy Ng | 2/7/87 | 332.00 |

Word lets you sort a table by any column if you select just that column. To do this, use the column selection methods discussed in Chapter 8 (hold down the OPTION key while selecting). After selecting the column, give the Sort command. For example, if you select the numbers in the "Amount" column, sorting will produce:

| Who | Last paid | Amount |
|---|---|---|
| Cathy Ng | 2/7/87 | 332.00 |
| Robin Morgan | 2/18/87 | 1732.50 |
| William Bradley | 1/27/87 | 7100.00 |

# REVIEW

1. *Numeric and alphanumeric*

   Describe the difference between numeric and alphanumeric sorting.

2. *Case*

   How does Word handle case in sorting?

# Chapter 19

## Desktop Publishing with Word

In the last few years, many businesses have shown an intense interest in the field of desktop publishing. Much of this interest was generated by the Macintosh and the Apple LaserWriter. Although Word is not a desktop publishing program, it has many features that make it function like one.

During the early 1980s most people thought of computers as useful machines for word processing. In most cases, the end result of this word processing was pages printed by their printers. Because the print quality of early printers was poor, the output of most word processors made it obvious that the original had been created on a computer. To make things worse, even the fastest printers were slow and expensive.

By the mid-1980s there was more demand for word processors

to produce material that didn't look computer-generated. Fortunately, printer technology had improved, and word processors (such as Microsoft Word for the IBM PC and the Macintosh) were able to do a better job. However, there were still problems:

- Even though letter-quality printers had become faster and less expensive, their output looked like that of a typewriter. People wanted output that looked typeset.

- Word processing programs were geared toward people who were writing simple business reports and memos. The programs were not versatile enough to produce newsletters and brochures.

- Although a few computers were becoming faster and more efficient (most notably, the Macintosh), the most common computers were slow and could not run advanced word processing programs efficiently.

# LESSON 83   The Beginning of Desktop Publishing

In early 1985 Apple started stressing a new concept in computer use: desktop publishing. Though many users had dreamed of getting typeset-quality results from their computers, until now the microcomputer industry had offered little to these users.

People wanted desktop publishing capabilities for many reasons. For small jobs, like four-page newsletters and foldover brochures, typesetting is expensive and inconvenient. For larger jobs, such as reports or advertisements, typesetting can hold things up since small changes often cause long delays. Being able to produce these types of documents yourself would give you more freedom and fewer headaches.

Apple's new desktop publishing marketing strategy was based on two things: the Macintosh's ability to quickly display accurate graphics on the screen, and the Apple LaserWriter's high resolution. Without this combination, simple desktop publishing would not be possible. In order to know what a document looks like before it is printed, a good graphics display is necessary. To make the output look similar to typesetting requires a good laser printer.

The Macintosh had already established itself as the computer of choice for many designers. Its high-resolution screen and easy-to-use software also made it attractive to many writers. Many of these people already were responsible for producing high-quality output. However, they usually did it by taking printed output (or, if they were lucky, a diskette) to a typesetting shop.

With the LaserWriter, designers and writers who wanted good-looking type could produce it in their companies. In contrast to large machines that used smelly chemicals to produce type, the LaserWriter was a relatively small, clean machine that could sit on a desk. Apple coined the term "desktop publishing" based on this capability.

# LESSON 84   Desktop Publishing Software

Soon after Apple began their desktop publishing marketing push, many software companies announced Macintosh products for the market. Most of the early desktop publishing products were *page layout* programs. Page layout programs, such as PageMaker from Aldus and MacPublisher from Boston

Software Publishers, enable you to set up your document page by page. As you enter text, you see all the page formatting, including where lines are broken in columns.

Microsoft does not market Word as a desktop publishing program, but you will find that it has many of the best features of other programs. For example, with the Page Preview command, you can see exactly what your pages will look like. In fact, Word is much better at standard word processing tasks (such as editing) than are desktop publishing programs. Some of Word's most notable features for desktop publishing are

- *Advanced use of the Apple LaserWriter* Like most word processing software, Word can produce excellent-looking documents on the LaserWriter. Beyond that, however, you can use Word to give LaserWriter commands that produce graphics and special text effects. To do this, you need to use the LaserWriter paragraph style described in the Word manual. You also need to know about *PostScript,* the language inside the LaserWriter.

- *Incorporation of graphics in text* As described in Chapter 5, Word lets you include graphics in your text in many ways. You can make a picture on a line by itself, or you can include text next to (or, as in Chapter 8, on top of) the picture. You can put a variety of borders around the pictures and around parts of your text.

- *Precise page layout* Unlike other word processing programs, Word lets you define exactly where each element of your document appears on the page. Not only can you place headers and footers exactly where you want, you can specify the spacing between lines and between paragraphs. This lets you expand and contract the paragraphs to fill up the space to the precise limits. Word also gives you much greater freedom to move the margins to fit the text in a well-designed manner.

- *Previewing printed output* The Page Preview command lets you see exactly how your document will look when it is printed, accurate to 1/72 of an inch (the resolution of the Macintosh screen). Thus, if you put text on top of a graphic, you can preview the placement. Most desktop publishing programs let you see what your page will look like constantly during the editing process, so these programs have an advantage over Word. However, most other Macintosh desktop publishing programs run much slower than Word, often because they spend so much time calculating exactly what will appear on the screen.

- *Style sheets* Even though the concept of style sheets has been around for many years, most desktop publishing packages do not incorporate them. However, Word offers this convenient feature. For example, if you are putting together a long report with many levels of headings, Word's style sheets will enable you to format each heading correctly. Word's style sheets also allow you to easily remember the style conventions used between documents.

# LESSON 85   Some Desktop Publishing Techniques

Although this book covers most of Word's capabilities, you will discover many useful tricks as you use Word. This section shows you some techniques that are related specifically to desktop publishing.

If you are creating a newsletter or a report, you often will want certain information to appear as headings within your document. For instance, it is likely that you will want to have a

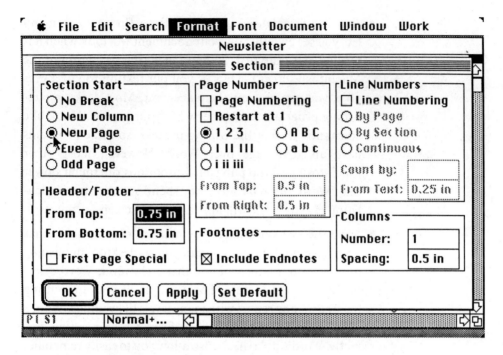

*Figure 19-1*   *Formatting the heading*

page-wide headline on the front page of a newsletter, even if the newsletter itself has more than one column.

To make a page-wide headline, enter the headline text and put a section marker between the headline and the rest of the text. Select some text in the headline section and give the Section command. Select New Page and 1 column, as shown in Figure 19-1. Click the OK button and format your headline as you want.

Now format the body text. Select some text in the main

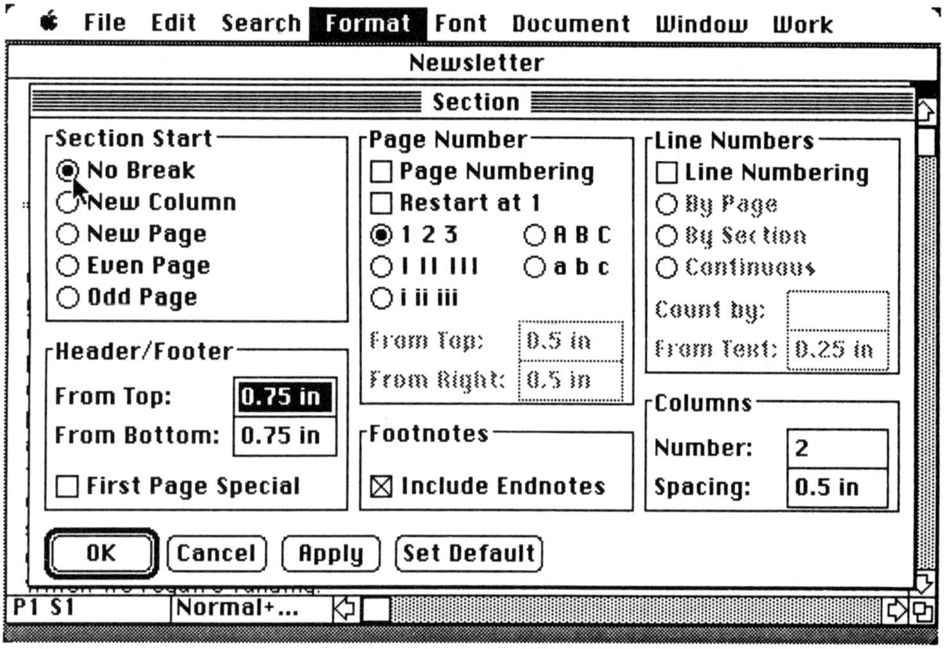

**☰ File Edit Search Format Font Document Window Work**

**Newsletter**

**Section**

┌─**Section Start**─────────┐ ┌─**Page Number**─────┐ ┌─**Line Numbers**────┐
● No Break ☐ Page Numbering ☐ Line Numbering
○ New Column ☐ Restart at 1 ○ By Page
○ New Page ● 1 2 3    ○ A B C ○ By Section
○ Even Page ○ I II III    ○ a b c ○ Continuous
○ Odd Page ○ i ii iii

Count by: [        ]

From Top:  [0.5 in] From Text: [0.25 in]

┌─**Header/Footer**────────┐ From Right: [0.5 in]

From Top:   [0.75 in] ┌─**Footnotes**──── ┌─**Columns**─────────┐

From Bottom: [0.75 in] ⊠ Include Endnotes Number:  [2]

☐ First Page Special Spacing:  [0.5 in]

( **OK** )  ( Cancel )  ( Apply )  ( Set Default )

P1 S1     │ Normal+...

*Figure 19-2*   *Formatting the body text*

section of the newsletter and give the Section command again. This time, select No Break and multiple columns, as shown in Figure 19-2. The result is shown in Figure 19-3.

You can also use Word to create business forms. This is a very helpful feature of desktop publishing: some businesses not only have many forms, but the content of the forms changes often. Although you can use drawing programs (such as MacDraw) to create forms, rearranging them and adding sections in the middle is much easier with Word.

## National Generators NEWS   Volume 1, Issue 3

National Generators has the opportunity over the next five years to take a commanding lead in our established markets and to penetrate a new market, the construction industry, where our products will be particularly attractive. This report is intended to provide an overview of the company's business development strategies along with a description of those areas for which we require funding.

National Generators can become the premier producer of electrical generation equipment for the entertainment and exposition industries. Our portable yet sturdy generators have acquired a solid reputation in these fields. As the number of outdoor concerts, large conventions, and other events that use portable generators continues to increase each year, we will be better able than our competitors to satisfy the demand for reliable equipment.

While accelerating efforts aimed at our existing base of industrial users, we propose to enter the construction industry. We have already begun developing a small, quiet generator for this market. Research is also under way to design a larger, more efficient generator for heavy construction projects that can replace several smaller ones.

### II.   Market Analysis

National Generators currently has a 42% share of the markets we now serve. Our nearest competitor, Regional Outdoor Electricity, has 34%, with the rest divided among other manufacturers. We believe that our superior products will ensure that we will increase our share of sales to the entertainment and exposition industries. Some of our competitors will be unable to match our new technology, and we will pick up their business.

*Figure 19-3*   *The heading over the newsletter*

If your forms use long fill-in boxes or square check boxes, you can create these by making empty paragraphs and using box borders. You can place them on the same line as other text by using side-by-side paragraph formatting.

For example, you can create the form in Figure 19-4 as follows:

1. Enter the regular text (name, address, and so on) in separate paragraphs. Select all these paragraphs and set their right margins to 2 inches.

2. Create a blank paragraph and give the Paragraph command. Set the left margin to 2.25 inches and select a single box border, as shown in Figure 19-5.

3. Make a copy of this paragraph between each of the text paragraphs, as shown in Figure 19-6.

4. Select the first pair of text and box, give the Paragraph command, and select Side-by-Side. Repeat this for each pair of text and box. You can view the result with the Page Preview command or by printing out the form.

Some of your forms may require grids; for instance, a grid would be needed if you want the person to only fill in a specific number of characters and to separate the letters. Figure 19-7 shows a variation on the form shown in Figure 19-4.

To create this grid, before copying the box, select the box paragraph and give the Paragraph command. Use the vertical

```
Name
Address
City, State, Zip
Occupation
```

**Figure 19-4**   *Sample form*

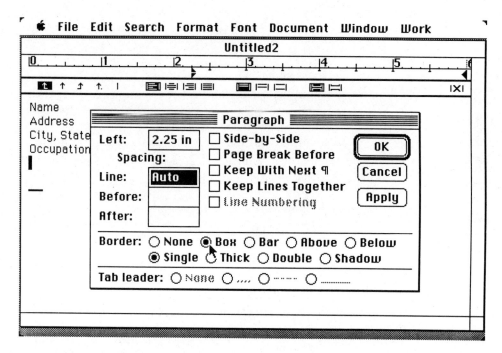

*Figure 19-5*   *Paragraph format for boxes*

bar icon on the ruler (next to the tab styles) to place vertical bars at even spacing along the box. For example, Figure 19-8 shows placing the vertical bars every 3/16 of an inch for the grid.

## REVIEW

*1.  Desktop publishing features*

List some of Word's desktop publishing features.

*2.  Fill-in boxes*

How do you make a fill-in box appear next to its associated text?

```
  ┌─────────────────────────────────────────────────────────────────────┐
  │  🍎  File   Edit   Search   Format   Font   Document   Window   Work │
  ├─────────────────────────────────────────────────────────────────────┤
  │ ▢│▤▤▤▤▤▤▤▤▤▤▤▤▤▤▤▤▤▤▤ Untitled2 ▤▤▤▤▤▤▤▤▤▤▤▤▤▤▤▤▤│◰ │
  │ Name                                                              △  │
  │                            ┌──────────────────────────────────┐     │
  │ Address                    └──────────────────────────────────┘     │
  │                            ┌──────────────────────────────────┐     │
  │ City, State, Zip           └──────────────────────────────────┘     │
  │                            ┌──────────────────────────────────┐     │
  │ Occupation                 └──────────────────────────────────┘     │
  │                            ┌──────────────────────────────────┐     │
  │                            └──────────────────────────────────┘     │
  │  ──                                                                  │
  │                                                                      │
  │                                                                      │
  │                                                                   ▽  │
  │ Page 1    │ Normal+... │ ◁▢▬▬▬▬▬▬▬▬▬▬▬▬▬▬▬▬▬▬▬▬▬▬▬▷◰│
  └─────────────────────────────────────────────────────────────────────┘
```

**Figure 19-6**   *The boxes between the text paragraphs*

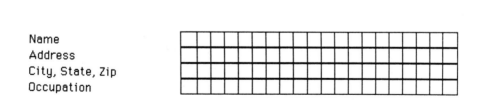

Name
Address
City, State, Zip
Occupation

**Figure 19-7**   *Sample form with grid*

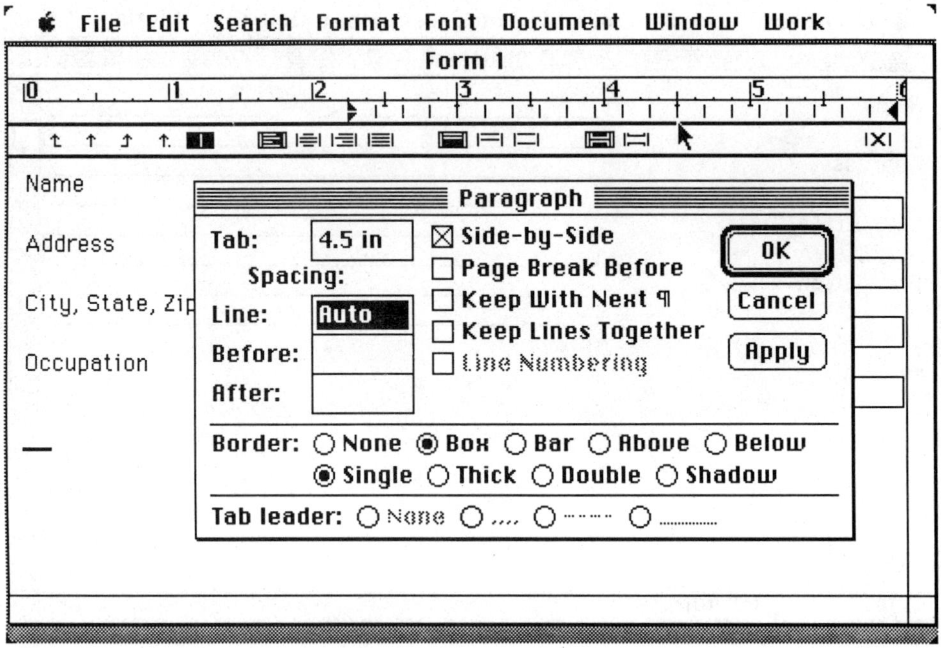

**É   File   Edit   Search   Format   Font   Document   Window   Work**

**Form 1**

|0 . . . . . |1 . . . . . |2 . . . . . |3 . . . . . |4 . . . . . |5 . . . . . |

↰ ↑ ↱ ↰ ■   ▤▤▤▤   ▤▢▢   ▤▤   ▶   |X|

Name

Address

City, State, Zip

Occupation

—

```
╔══════════════ Paragraph ══════════════╗
║ Tab:    [ 4.5 in ]   ⊠ Side-by-Side        ( OK )    ║
║     Spacing:         ☐ Page Break Before             ║
║ Line:   [ Auto ]     ☐ Keep With Next ¶   ( Cancel ) ║
║                      ☐ Keep Lines Together           ║
║ Before: [      ]     ☐ Line Numbering     ( Apply )  ║
║ After:  [      ]                                     ║
║                                                      ║
║ Border: ○ None ● Box ○ Bar ○ Above ○ Below           ║
║         ● Single ○ Thick ○ Double ○ Shadow           ║
║ Tab leader:  ○ None  ○ ....  ○ ------  ○ ..........   ║
╚══════════════════════════════════════════════════════╝
```

***Figure 19-8***   *Making the grid*

# Part 5

## Appendixes

# Appendix A

## Editing Command Summary

The tables in this appendix summarize the editing commands covered in Part 1 of this book. You can use them as a quick reference guide when you are entering or editing text.

Table A-1 shows the keys that you use when entering text with Word. Table A-2 lists the ways you can select text with the mouse. Table A-3 lists other Word commands used to edit text. Table A-4 shows the insertion point movement and delete keys, and Table A-5 shows the additional choices for the extended keyboard.

**Table A-1**   *Text Entry Keys*

| Key | Meaning |
| --- | --- |
| ENTER | New paragraph |
| SHIFT-ENTER | New line but continue paragraph; this is also called NEWLINE |
| COMMAND-ENTER | New division |
| COMMAND-SHIFT-ENTER | New page but continue division |
| TAB | Go to next tab stop |
| HYPHEN | Normal hyphen |
| OPTION-HYPHEN | Nonbreaking hyphen:  Word will never split a line here |
| COMMAND-HYPHEN | Nonrequired hyphen:  Word will only split a line here to wrap words |
| OPTION-SPACEBAR | Nonbreaking space:  Word will never split a line here |

**Table A-2**   *Selecting Text With the Mouse*

| Where Pointing | Click | Selection |
| --- | --- | --- |
| Character | Single | Set insertion point |
| Character | Double | Word |
| Character | COMMAND-Click | Sentence |
| Selection bar | Single | Line |
| Selection bar | Double | Paragraph |
| Selection bar | COMMAND-Click | Entire document |

**Table A-3**   *Other Editing Commands*

| Command | Mouse or Key Equivalent of Word Command | Action |
|---------|------------------------------------------|--------|
| Change | COMMAND-H | Replaces with new text |
| Copy | COMMAND-C | Copies to Clipboard |
| Cut | COMMAND-X | Deletes to Clipboard |
| Find | COMMAND-F | Searches for text |
| Go To | COMMAND-G | Moves to specific page |
| Paste | COMMAND-V | Inserts from Clipboard |
| Undo | COMMAND-Z | Reverses last edit |

**Table A-4**   *Insertion Point Movement and Delete Keys*

| Key | Action |
|-----|--------|
| COMMAND-OPTION-L | Move character right |
| COMMAND-OPTION-K | Move character left |
| COMMAND-OPTION-O | Move line up |
| COMMAND-OPTION-, | Move line down |
| COMMAND-OPTION-; | Move word right |
| COMMAND-OPTION-J | Move word left |
| COMMAND-OPTION-Y | Move paragraph up |
| COMMAND-OPTION-B | Move paragraph down |
| COMMAND-OPTION-P | Move screen up |
| COMMAND-OPTION-. | Move screen down |
| COMMAND-OPTION-[ | Scroll line up (don't move) |
| COMMAND-OPTION-/ | Scroll line down (don't move) |
| COMMAND-OPTION-Z | Jump to last insertion place |
| COMMAND-OPTION-F | Delete character to the right |
| COMMAND-OPTION-G | Delete word to the right |
| COMMAND-OPTION-BACKSPACE | Delete word to the left |

**Table A-5**   *Insertion Point Movement With the Extended Keyboard*

NUMERIC indicates the number on the numeric keypad.

| Key | Action |
| --- | --- |
| → | Move character right |
| ← | Move character left |
| ↑ | Move line up |
| ↓ | Move line down |
| NUMERIC-1 | Move to end of line |
| NUMERIC-2 | Move line down |
| NUMERIC-3 | Move page down |
| NUMERIC-4 | Move character left |
| NUMERIC-5 | No action |
| NUMERIC-6 | Move character right |
| NUMERIC-7 | Move to beginning of line |
| NUMERIC-8 | Move line up |
| NUMERIC-9 | Move page up |
| COMMAND-NUMERIC-1 | Move to end of sentence |
| COMMAND-NUMERIC-2 | Move paragraph up |
| COMMAND-NUMERIC-3 | Move to end of document |
| COMMAND-NUMERIC-4 | Move word left |
| COMMAND-NUMERIC-5 | No action |
| COMMAND-NUMERIC-6 | Move word right |
| COMMAND-NUMERIC-7 | Move to beginning of sentence |
| COMMAND-NUMERIC-8 | Move paragraph down |
| COMMAND-NUMERIC-9 | Move to beginning of document |

# Appendix B

## Formatting Command Summary

The tables in this appendix summarize the COMMAND-key combinations for formatting characters and paragraphs covered in Part 2 of this book. Use these as a quick reference guide when entering or reformatting text with Word. The character and paragraph formatting commands are covered in Tables B-1 and B-2, respectively.

**Table B-1**   *Character Formats*

| Format | Key Combination |
|---|---|
| Normal | COMMAND-SHIFT-SPACEBAR |
| Italic | COMMAND-SHIFT-I |
| Bold | COMMAND-SHIFT-B |
| Underline | COMMAND-SHIFT-U |
| Word underline | COMMAND-SHIFT-] |
| Double underline | COMMAND-SHIFT-[ |
| Dotted underline | COMMAND-SHIFT-\ |
| Small caps | COMMAND-SHIFT-H |
| All caps | COMMAND-SHIFT-K |
| Strikethrough | COMMAND-SHIFT-/ |
| Shadow | COMMAND-SHIFT-W |
| Outline | COMMAND-SHIFT-D |
| Subscript | COMMAND-SHIFT-− |
| Superscript | COMMAND-SHIFT-+ |
| Increase font size | COMMAND-SHIFT-→ |
| Decrease font size | COMMAND-SHIFT-← |

**Table B-2**   *Paragraph Formats*

| Format | Key Combination |
|---|---|
| Left-aligned | COMMAND-SHIFT-L |
| Right-aligned | COMMAND-SHIFT-R |
| Center-aligned | COMMAND-SHIFT-C |
| Justified | COMMAND-SHIFT-J |
| Open spacing | COMMAND-SHIFT-O |
| Indent first line .5" | COMMAND-SHIFT-F |
| Nest paragraph .5" | COMMAND-SHIFT-N |
| Un-nest paragraph | COMMAND-SHIFT-M |
| Hanging indent | COMMAND-SHIFT-T |
| Clear characteristics | COMMAND-SHIFT-P |
| Side-by-side | COMMAND-SHIFT-G |
| Double space | COMMAND-SHIFT-Y |

# Appendix C

## Mouse Keyclicks
## Summary

The purpose of the Macintosh mouse is to make interacting with software easier. However, use of the mouse is not foolproof, and it can be intimidating to users who are accustomed to a keyboard. Fortunately, Word uses the mouse in a very consistent fashion, and there are only a few rules to learn about it.

When you first use the mouse, you may find it hard to aim the pointer accurately. You may select some text or execute a command accidentally. However, you will probably find that learning to use the mouse is much like learning to use a car with a standard shift: at first it may seem clumsy, but with practice, it will become second nature.

## POINTING WITH THE MOUSE

Using a mouse is attractive to many people because you can point at something without making anything happen. You do not need to worry about accidentally pointing at something, since pointing never causes an action; only pressing the button does.

As you experimented with Word, you may have noticed that the pointer changed shapes as you moved it around the screen. Sometimes this happens simply by moving the pointer to an area; other times it will happen when you press a button and then delay in releasing it.

Table C-1 shows the shapes the mouse pointer takes when you simply move the mouse. Figure C-1 shows the different parts of the screen and the shape of the mouse pointer in each area.

You can change the way that the mouse and keyboard respond by using the Control Panel desk accessory. When you select the Control Panel, you are presented with the dialog box shown in Figure C-2.

**Table C-1**   *Pointer Shapes*

| Shape | Area | Action When Button Is Pressed |
| --- | --- | --- |
| I | Text window | Selects text or sets insertion point |
| ▶ | Menu area, title bar, or scroll bars | Chooses a command or changes the window |
| ◢ | Selection bar | Selects a group of text |

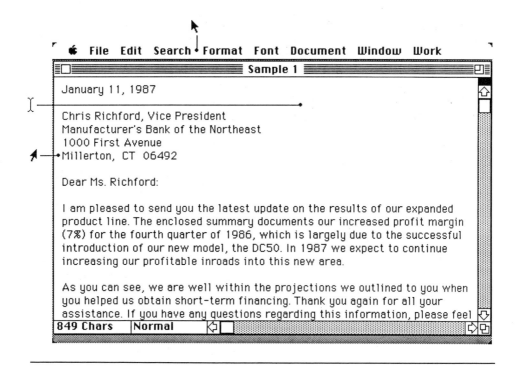

***Figure C-1***   *Areas of the screen and their pointer shapes*

The Mouse Tracking selection (the box with the picture of the mouse moving) allows you to change the amount that the pointer moves when you move your mouse quickly. Setting this to Mouse causes Word to move the pointer more when you move the mouse quickly, which makes moving around the screen easier. If you set this to Tablet, you will have to move the mouse farther on your desktop.

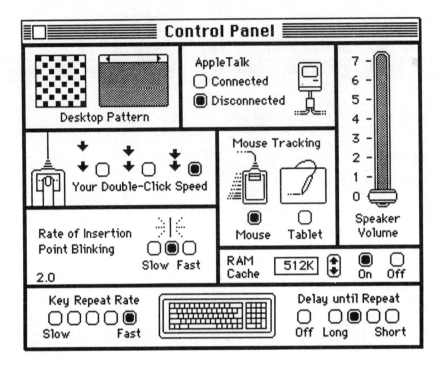

**Figure C-2**   *The Control Panel window*

The Double-Click Speed selection (the box with the picture of the finger on the mouse button and the double arrows) tells the Macintosh at what speed you want to double-click. The far right button indicates that you double-click fairly quickly; the far left button indicates that you double-click slowly. Using the far right button is safer, because you may accidentally click an object twice and cause the double-click action.

You may also want to change the Key Repeat Rate and Delay Until Repeat settings if you use the COMMAND sequences to move the insertion point. Setting Key Repeat Rate to fast and Delay Until Repeat to short makes moving around faster and easier.

# Appendix D

## Word Commands

This appendix covers all Word commands available from the menu bar. Figure D-1 shows all of Word's menus. Figures D-2 through D-6 show the dialog boxes that can be accessed from these menus. Table D-1 lists Word's commands in alphabetical order by action. Table D-2 lists the same commands arranged by key name.

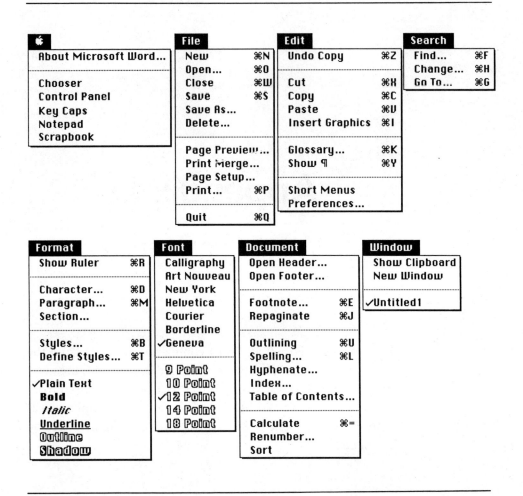

**Figure D-1**   *Word's menu*

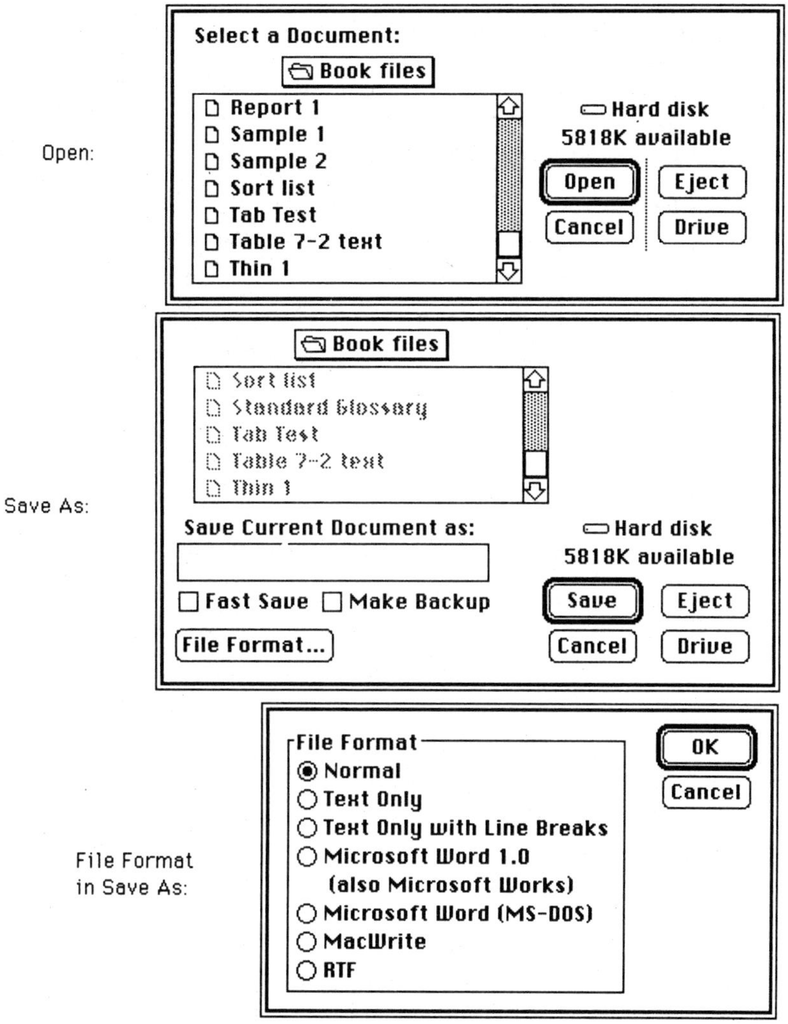

Open:

**Select a Document:**

📁 Book files

| | |
|---|---|
| 📄 Report 1 | |
| 📄 Sample 1 | |
| 📄 Sample 2 | |
| 📄 Sort list | |
| 📄 Tab Test | |
| 📄 Table 7-2 text | |
| 📄 Thin 1 | |

💾 **Hard disk**
5818K available

[ Open ]   [ Eject ]
[ Cancel ]   [ Drive ]

Save As:

📁 Book files

📄 Sort list
📄 Standard Glossary
📄 Tab Test
📄 Table 7-2 text
📄 Thin 1

**Save Current Document as:**

💾 **Hard disk**
5818K available

☐ Fast Save   ☐ Make Backup   [ Save ]   [ Eject ]

[ File Format... ]   [ Cancel ]   [ Drive ]

File Format
in Save As:

┌─ **File Format** ─────────────┐
● Normal
○ Text Only
○ Text Only with Line Breaks
○ Microsoft Word 1.0
   (also Microsoft Works)
○ Microsoft Word (MS-DOS)
○ MacWrite
○ RTF

[ OK ]
[ Cancel ]

*Figure D-2*   *The dialog boxes for the File menu*

Page Setup:

**Page Setup**

Paper: ⦿ US Letter  ◯ A4 Letter       [ OK ]
       ◯ US Legal  ◯ International Fanfold

Orientation:  ⦿ Tall  ◯ Wide       [ Cancel ]

Paper Width: [ 8.5 in ]  Height: [ 11 in ]     [ Set Default ]

Margins:  Top: [ 1 in ]  Left: [ 1.25 in ]  ☒ Facing Pages

      Bottom: [ 1 in ]  Right: [ 1.25 in ]  Gutter: [ ]

Default Tab Stops: [ 0.5 in ]  ☒ Widow Control

Footnotes at: ⦿ Bottom of Page  ◯ Beneath Text  ◯ Endnotes

☒ Restart Numbering  Start Footnote Numbers at: [ 1 ]

Start Page Numbers at: [ 1 ]    Line Numbers at: [ 1 ]

Next File: [ ]

Print Merge:

**Print Merge**

Merge Records: ⦿ All  ◯ From: [ ]  To: [ ]

[ Print ]  [ New Document ]  [ Cancel ]

Print:

**Print**

Printer: ImageWriter         [ OK ]

Pages: ⦿ All  ◯ Selection  ◯ From: [ ]  To: [ ]  [ Cancel ]

Copies: [ 1 ]  Paper Feed: ⦿ Automatic  ◯ Manual

☐ Print Hidden Text  ☐ Tall Adjusted

Quality: ◯ Best  ⦿ Faster  ◯ Draft

***Figure D-2***  *The dialog boxes for the File menu (continued)*

Glossary:

Preferences:

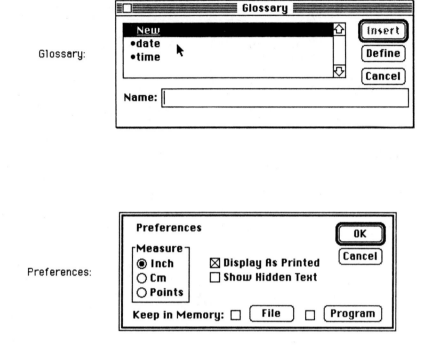

**Figure D-3**   *The dialog boxes for the Edit menu*

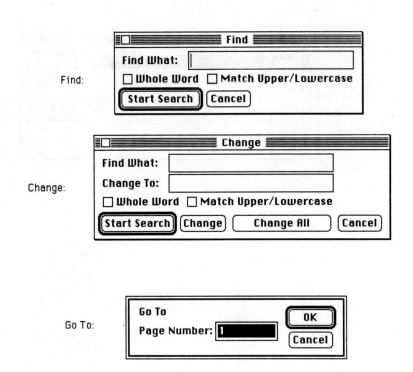

Find:

Change:

Go To:

*Figure D-4*   *The dialog boxes for the Search menu*

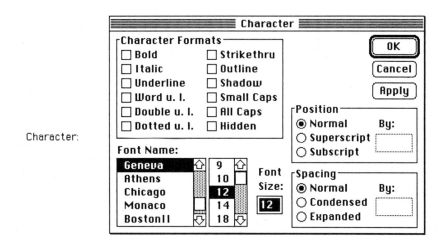

Character:

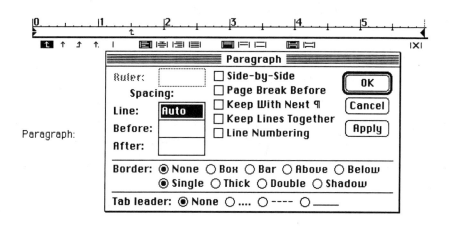

Paragraph:

***Figure D-5***   *The dialog boxes for the Format menu*

Section:

Styles:

Define Styles:

```
┌──────────────────────── Section ────────────────────────┐
│ ┌─Section Start─┐ ┌─Page Number─────┐ ┌─Line Numbers──┐ │
│ │ ○ No Break    │ │ ☒ Page Numbering│ │ ☐ Line Numbering││
│ │ ○ New Column  │ │ ☐ Restart at 1  │ │ ◉ By Page     │ │
│ │ ◉ New Page    │ │ ◉ 1 2 3   ○ A B C│ │ ○ By Section  │ │
│ │ ○ Even Page   │ │ ○ I II III ○ a b c│ │ ○ Continuous  │ │
│ │ ○ Odd Page    │ │ ○ i ii iii      │ │                 │ │
│ └───────────────┘ │                 │ │ Count by:  1  │ │
│ ┌─Header/Footer─┐ │ From Top:  0.5 in│ │ From Text: Auto│ │
│ │ From Top:  0.5 in│ From Right: 0.5 in│ ┌─Columns───────┐│
│ │ From Bottom: 0.5 in└─────────────────┘ │ Number:    1  ││
│ │               │ ┌─Footnotes──────┐ │ Spacing:      ││
│ │ ☐ First Page Special│ ☐ Include Endnotes│ └───────────────┘│
│ └───────────────┘ └─────────────────┘                    │
│   (OK)  (Cancel)  (Apply)  (Set Default)                 │
└──────────────────────────────────────────────────────────┘
```

```
┌───────────────── Styles ─────────────────┐
│ •Normal                          ⬆ │ (OK)    │
│                                    │ (Cancel)│
│                                  ⬇ │ (Apply) │
│ Font: Geneva 12 Point, Flush left          │
└────────────────────────────────────────────┘
```

```
┌──────────── Define Styles: Untitled ────────────┐
│ New Style                          ⬆ │ ( OK )   │
│ ✓•Normal                            │ (Cancel) │
│                                     │ (Apply)  │
│                                     │          │
│                                   ⬇ │ (Set Default)│
│ Style: │                            │ (Define) │
│ Normal +                                        │
│ Next Style: │        │ Based on: Normal         │
└──────────────────────────────────────────────────┘
```

***Figure D-5***   *The dialog boxes for the Format menu (continued)*

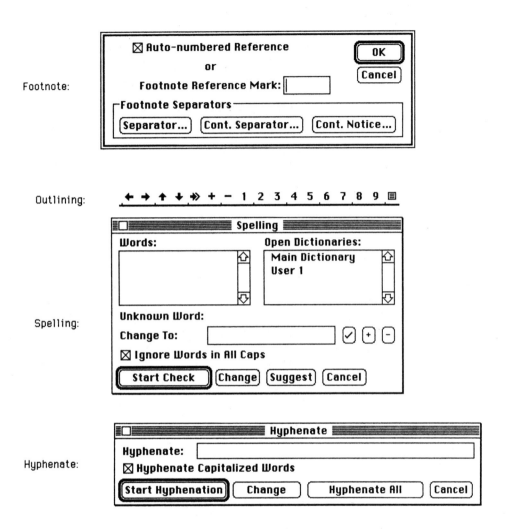

Footnote:

Outlining:

Spelling:

Hyphenate:

**Figure D-6**   *The dialog boxes for the Document menu*

Index:

Index

Format:  ⦿ Nested
         ○ Run-in

Start

Cancel

Table of contents:

Table of Contents

Collect
⦿ Outline
○ .C. Paragraphs

Start

Cancel

☒ Show Page Numbers

Level: ⦿ All ○ From: [ ]   To: [ ]

Renumber:

Renumber

Paragraphs: ⦿ All ○ Only If Already Numbered

Start at: [ ]   Format: [ ]

Numbers: ⦿ 1 ○ 1.1... ○ By Example ○ Remove

OK   Cancel

**Figure D-6**   *The dialog boxes for the Document menu* (*continued*)

***Table D-1***    *Alphabetical Command List by Action*

| Command | Key(s) |
|---|---|
| Add menu | COMMAND-OPTION-+ |
| Add paragraph ahead | COMMAND-OPTION-RETURN |
| Again | COMMAND-A |
| All caps | COMMAND-SHIFT-K |
| Bold | COMMAND-SHIFT-B |
| Calculate | COMMAND-= |
| Cancel | COMMAND-. |
| Centered | COMMAND-SHIFT-C |
| Change | COMMAND-H |
| Character | COMMAND-D |
| Clear Character | COMMAND-SHIFT-SPACEBAR |
| Clear paragraph | COMMAND-SHIFT-P |
| Close | COMMAND-W |
| Copy | COMMAND-C |
| Copy looks | COMMAND-OPTION-V |
| Copy text as picture | COMMAND-OPTION-D |
| Cut | COMMAND-X |
| Decrease font size | COMMAND-SHIFT-- |
| Define Styles | COMMAND-T |
| Delete character right | COMMAND-OPTION-F |
| Delete word left | COMMAND-OPTION-BACKSPACE |
| Delete word right | COMMAND-OPTION-G |
| Dotted underline | COMMAND-SHIFT-\ |
| Double space | COMMAND-SHIFT-V |
| Double underline | COMMAND-SHIFT-[ |
| Dyadic copy | COMMAND-OPTION-C |
| Dyadic move | COMMAND-OPTION-X |
| Expand Glossary | COMMAND-BACKSPACE |
| Find again | COMMAND-OPTION-A |
| Find | COMMAND-F |
| First line indent | COMMAND-SHIFT-F |
| Font change | COMMAND-SHIFT-E |
| Footnote | COMMAND-E |
| Formula | COMMAND-O |
| Formula | COMMAND-OPTION-\ |

***Table D-1***   *Alphabetical Command List by Action (continued)*

| Command | Key(s) |
|---|---|
| Glossary | COMMAND-K |
| Goto | COMMAND-G |
| Graphic character | COMMAND-OPTION-Q |
| Hanging indent | COMMAND-SHIFT-T |
| Help | COMMAND-? |
| Increase font size | COMMAND-SHIFT-→ |
| Insert Graphics | COMMAND-I |
| Italic | COMMAND-SHIFT-I |
| Jump to last insert | COMMAND-OPTION-Z |
| Justified | COMMAND-SHIFT-J |
| Keyboard menus | OPTION-TAB |
| Left aligned | COMMAND-SHIFT-L |
| More | COMMAND-OPTION-' |
| Move character left | ← |
| Move character left | COMMAND-OPTION-K |
| Move character left | NUMERIC-4 |
| Move character right | → |
| Move character left | NUMERIC-6 |
| Move character right | COMMAND-OPTION-L |
| Move line down | ↓ |
| Move line down | COMMAND-OPTION-, |
| Move line down | NUMERIC-2 |
| Move line up | ↑ |
| Move line up | COMMAND-OPTION-O |
| Move line up | COMMAND-NUMERIC-8 |
| Move page down | NUMERIC-3 |
| Move page up | NUMERIC-9 |
| Move paragraph down | COMMAND-NUMERIC-8 |
| Move paragraph down | COMMAND-OPTION-B |
| Move paragraph up | COMMAND-NUMERIC-2 |
| Move paragraph up | COMMAND-OPTION-Y |
| Move screen down | COMMAND-OPTION-. |
| Move screen up | COMMAND-OPTION-P |
| Move to document beginning | COMMAND-NUMERIC-9 |
| Move to document end | COMMAND-NUMERIC-3 |

***Table D-1***   *Alphabetical Command List by Action* (*continued*)

| Command | Key(s) |
|---|---|
| Move to line begin | NUMERIC-7 |
| Move to line end | NUMERIC-1 |
| Move to sentence begin | COMMAND-NUMERIC-7 |
| Move to sentence end | COMMAND-NUMERIC-1 |
| Move word left | COMMAND-NUMERIC-4 |
| Move word left | COMMAND-OPTION-J |
| Move word right | COMMAND-NUMERIC-6 |
| Move word right | COMMAND-OPTION-; |
| Nest paragraph | COMMAND-SHIFT-N |
| New | COMMAND-N |
| New Division | COMMAND-ENTER |
| New page | SHIFT-ENTER |
| New paragraph | RETURN |
| Newline | SHIFT-RETURN |
| Next window | COMMAND-OPTION-W |
| No action | COMMAND-NUMERIC-5 |
| No action | NUMERIC-5 |
| Nonbreaking hyphen | COMMAND-' |
| Nonbreaking space | OPTION-SPACEBAR |
| Nonrequired hyphen | COMMAND-− |
| Open | COMMAND-O |
| Open spacing | COMMAND-SHIFT-O |
| Outline | COMMAND-SHIFT-D |
| Outline prefix | COMMAND-OPTION-T |
| Outlining | COMMAND-U |
| Paragraph | COMMAND-M |
| Paste | COMMAND-V |
| Print | COMMAND-P |
| Quit | COMMAND-Q |
| Remove menu | COMMAND-OPTION-− |
| Repaginate | COMMAND-J |
| Right aligned | COMMAND-SHIFT-R |
| Save | COMMAND-S |
| Scan looks | COMMAND-OPTION-R |
| Scroll up | COMMAND-OPTION-[ |

**Table D-1** *Alphabetical Command List by Action (continued)*

| Command | Key(s) |
| --- | --- |
| Select whole document | COMMAND-OPTION-M |
| Shadow | COMMAND-SHIFT-W |
| Show Paragraph | COMMAND-Y |
| Show Ruler | COMMAND-R |
| Side-by-Side | COMMAND-SHIFT-G |
| Small caps | COMMAND-SHIFT-H |
| Spell | COMMAND-L |
| Split Window | COMMAND-OPTION-S |
| Strikethrough | COMMAND-SHIFT-/ |
| Style name | COMMAND-SHIFT-S |
| Styles | COMMAND-B |
| Subscript | COMMAND-SHIFT-- |
| Superscript | COMMAND-SHIFT-+ |
| Symbol font | COMMAND-SHIFT-Q |
| Underline | COMMAND-SHIFT-U |
| Undo | COMMAND-Z |
| Unnest paragraph | COMMAND-SHIFT-M |
| Vanish | COMMAND-SHIFT-X |
| Word underline | COMMAND-SHIFT-] |
| Zoom | COMMAND-OPTION-] |

**Table D-2**  *Alphabetical Command List by Key Name*

| Key(s) | Command |
| --- | --- |
| COMMAND-A | Again |
| COMMAND-B | Styles |
| COMMAND-C | Copy |
| COMMAND-D | Character |
| COMMAND-E | Footnote |
| COMMAND-F | Find |
| COMMAND-G | Goto |
| COMMAND-H | Change |
| COMMAND-I | Insert Graphics |
| COMMAND-J | Repaginate |
| COMMAND-K | Glossary |
| COMMAND-L | Spell |
| COMMAND-M | Paragraph |
| COMMAND-N | New |
| COMMAND-O | Open |
| COMMAND-P | Print |
| COMMAND-Q | Quit |
| COMMAND-R | Show Ruler |
| COMMAND-S | Save |
| COMMAND-T | Define Styles |
| COMMAND-U | Outlining |
| COMMAND-V | Paste |
| COMMAND-W | Close |
| COMMAND-X | Cut |
| COMMAND-Y | Show Paragraph |
| COMMAND-Z | Undo |
| COMMAND-- | Nonrequired hyphen |
| COMMAND-. | Cancel |
| COMMAND-0 | Formula |
| COMMAND-= | Calculate |
| COMMAND-? | Help |
| COMMAND-' | Nonbreaking hyphen |
| COMMAND-BACKSPACE | Expand Glossary |
| COMMAND-ENTER | New Division |
| COMMAND-SHIFT-B | Bold |

**Table D-2**   *Alphabetical Command List by Key Name (continued)*

| Key(s) | Command |
| --- | --- |
| COMMAND-SHIFT-C | Centered |
| COMMAND-SHIFT-D | Outline |
| COMMAND-SHIFT-E | Font change |
| COMMAND-SHIFT-F | First line indent |
| COMMAND-SHIFT-G | Side-by-Side |
| COMMAND-SHIFT-H | Small caps |
| COMMAND-SHIFT-I | Italic |
| COMMAND-SHIFT-J | Justified |
| COMMAND-SHIFT-K | All caps |
| COMMAND-SHIFT-L | Left aligned |
| COMMAND-SHIFT-M | Unnest paragraph |
| COMMAND-SHIFT-N | Nest paragraph |
| COMMAND-SHIFT-O | Open spacing |
| COMMAND-SHIFT-P | Clear paragraph |
| COMMAND-SHIFT-Q | Symbol font |
| COMMAND-SHIFT-R | Right aligned |
| COMMAND-SHIFT-S | Style name |
| COMMAND-SHIFT-T | Hanging indent |
| COMMAND-SHIFT-U | Underline |
| COMMAND-SHIFT-W | Shadow |
| COMMAND-SHIFT-X | Vanish |
| COMMAND-SHIFT-Y | Double space |
| COMMAND-SHIFT-+ | Superscript |
| COMMAND-SHIFT-− | Subscript |
| COMMAND-SHIFT-/ | Strikethrough |
| COMMAND-SHIFT-← | Decrease font size |
| COMMAND-SHIFT-→ | Increase font size |
| COMMAND-SHIFT-[ | Double underline |
| COMMAND-SHIFT-\ | Dotted underline |
| COMMAND-SHIFT-] | Word underline |
| COMMAND-SHIFT-SPACEBAR | Clear character |
| COMMAND-OPTION-A | Find again |
| COMMAND-OPTION-B | Move paragraph down |
| COMMAND-OPTION-C | Dyadic copy |
| COMMAND-OPTION-D | Copy text as picture |
| COMMAND-OPTION-F | Delete character right |

**Table D-2**  *Alphabetical Command List by Key Name* (*continued*)

| Key(s) | Command |
|---|---|
| COMMAND-OPTION-G | Delete word right |
| COMMAND-OPTION-J | Move word left |
| COMMAND-OPTION-K | Move character left |
| COMMAND-OPTION-L | Move character right |
| COMMAND-OPTION-M | Select whole document |
| COMMAND-OPTION-O | Move line up |
| COMMAND-OPTION-P | Move screen up |
| COMMAND-OPTION-Q | Graphic character |
| COMMAND-OPTION-R | Scan looks |
| COMMAND-OPTION-S | Split Window |
| COMMAND-OPTION-T | Outline prefix |
| COMMAND-OPTION-V | Copy looks |
| COMMAND-OPTION-W | Next window |
| COMMAND-OPTION-X | Dyadic move |
| COMMAND-OPTION-Y | Move paragraph up |
| COMMAND-OPTION-Z | Jump to last insert |
| COMMAND-OPTION-' | More |
| COMMAND-OPTION-+ | Add menu |
| COMMAND-OPTION-, | Move line down |
| COMMAND-OPTION-− | Remove menu |
| COMMAND-OPTION-. | Move screen down |
| COMMAND-OPTION-/ | Scroll down |
| COMMAND-OPTION-; | Move word right |
| COMMAND-OPTION-[ | Scroll up |
| COMMAND-OPTION- \ | Formula |
| COMMAND-OPTION-] | Zoom |
| COMMAND-OPTION-BACKSPACE | Delete word left |
| COMMAND-OPTION-RETURN | Add paragraph ahead |
| NUMERIC-1 | Move to end of line |
| NUMERIC-2 | Move line down |
| NUMERIC-3 | Move page down |
| NUMERIC-4 | Move character left |
| NUMERIC-5 | No action |
| NUMERIC-6 | Move character right |
| NUMERIC-7 | Move to beginning of line |
| NUMERIC-8 | Move line up |

**Table D-2**   *Alphabetical Command List by Key Name* (*continued*)

| Key(s) | Command |
| --- | --- |
| NUMERIC-9 | Move page up |
| COMMAND-NUMERIC-1 | Move to end of sentence |
| COMMAND-NUMERIC-2 | Move paragraph up |
| COMMAND-NUMERIC-3 | Move to end of document |
| COMMAND-NUMERIC-4 | Move word left |
| COMMAND-NUMERIC-5 | No action |
| COMMAND-NUMERIC-6 | Move word right |
| COMMAND-NUMERIC-7 | Move to beginning of sentence |
| COMMAND-NUMERIC-8 | Move paragraph down |
| COMMAND-NUMERIC-9 | Move to beginning of document |
| OPTION-SPACEBAR | Nonbreaking space |
| OPTION-TAB | Keyboard menus |
| RETURN | New paragraph |
| SHIFT-ENTER | New page |
| SHIFT-RETURN | Newline |
| ↓ | Move line down |
| ← | Move character left |
| → | Move character right |
| ↑ | Move line up |

# Appendix E

## Using Other Programs That Work With Word

Since Word works with text and text files, many other Macintosh programs that read or write text files can be used with Word. However, it is important to remember that these programs often only work with unformatted Word files. That is, most programs cannot read your Word files unless you specify "Text Only" in the Save As command. Other programs can only read text that Word stores in the Clipboard or Scrapbook.

Saving files without formatting means you lose all of Word's formatting when you read the file again. Thus, it is likely that you will not want to use many of the available programs if they force you to lose the capability to format your text. You can overcome this problem by saving two copies of the file (one formatted, the other unformatted) with different file names. However, if the applications program changes the unformatted file (such as a spelling checker correcting mistakes), your formatted file will not contain the changes.

You can still use Word to edit text files created with other programs and to include these files with your formatted Word documents. For instance, most spreadsheet programs allow you to save their results in the Clipboard, which can then be read by Word and included with Word documents.

The programs listed in this chapter are examples of the many programs available for the Macintosh that can either work with formatted Word files or produce files that you can read and edit with Word. Even more programs can work with unformatted Word files, but they are not listed here because you will probably not produce many documents without formatting.

If you want to find out more about the software listed here or about other programs that work with Word, you should read software reviews in computer magazines. Many magazines specialize in the Macintosh, such as *Mac User* and *Mac World,* as well as the newsletters of many owners' groups.

## USING A KEYBOARD ENHANCER

Although Word is meant to be a mouse-oriented editor, it provides many commands that you give from the keyboard with COMMAND-key combinations and the function keys. However, you may want to perform different functions with these keys, or many functions with only one keystroke. To do this, you need a keyboard enhancer.

Software keyboard enhancers such as Tempo are useful for turning one keystroke into many. For instance, if you often select the current paragraph and make it centered, underlined, and bold, you can use an enhancer to redefine a key (for instance, OPTION-X) to represent the sequence COMMAND-C COMMAND-B COMMAND-U. This makes formatting your documents much easier. An enhancer can also be used to insert an entire name and address with a single keystroke (similar to the glossary).

## USING OTHER TEXT PROGRAMS

Many of the currently available text programs that work with MacWrite will probably be updated to work with Word in the future. For example, it is likely that you will see packages that perform such tasks as analyzing what you have written and making suggestions about how to improve your text, finding common grammatical mistakes, incorrect punctuation, and so on.

Think Tank and More from Living Videotext (1000 Elwell Court, Suite 232, Palo Alto, California 94303) is an outline-writing aid that helps you organize your thoughts. One of the hardest tasks in writing an outline is ensuring that ideas on the same level of the outline are actually parallel. Think Tank lets you easily form an outline and then look at parts of it. You can, for example, examine just the top-level headings to make sure that they are all of equal importance.

Think Tank makes forming an outline easier, since you can use the mouse to indicate how each idea you enter relates to the one above it. You can save your outlines in the Clipboard and then use the Paste command.

If you need to keep your documents secure from other users, there will probably be many programs that will scramble the contents so only you can read them. This process is called *encryption*. Data security is becoming an important issue as more people do more of their writing on computers, since it is easy to steal information from a computer by taking its disks.

Many people feel ill-at-ease about writing, so there are a number of companies that sell standard form letters on disk. Although the quality of these letters varies, they are sometimes good beginning points for your own writing. Many of these programs are written for MacWrite, but you can read the files with Word.

Many other programs can write text into the Clipboard that

you may want to use. Many of the data filing and data base management systems can write records to the Clipboard. Microsoft File can write records to a file that can be used as a datafile by the Print Merge command. Spreadsheet applications like Microsoft Multiplan can also write files that Word can read.

## MATHEMATICAL FORMULAS

If you want to include formulas in your Word documents, you can use Word's formula feature. However, most people find it arcane and hard to use. Instead, there are many programs available that let you easily describe formulas on the screen and save them to the Clipboard.

These programs often let you make complex equations in a simple way. Some even include nonmathematical symbols, such as those used in quantum physics and chemistry. One popular program is called MacEqn, from Software for Recognition Technologies (110 University Park, Rochester, NY 14620).

# Appendix F

## Microsoft Word
## On Other Computers

Word can be run on many different computers. Most of Word's features are the same from computer to computer, and most computers running Word will respond to commands as specified in this book, although the way in which you give Word commands may differ.

### IBM PERSONAL COMPUTER

Microsoft Word was first introduced for the IBM PC in 1983. Word has become one of the more popular word processing programs used on the PC due to its numerous features and excellent use of the PC's keyboard.

The IBM PC version of Word can be used with the Microsoft mouse, which can be added easily to a PC. The mouse has two buttons; they function similarly to single- and double-clicking on the Macintosh mouse. Dragging is often accomplished by pressing both buttons and moving the mouse.

The commands in the IBM PC version of Word are very similar to those in the Macintosh version. Since the PC does not have a standard user interface like the Mac (such as consistent methods for scrolling, closing windows, etc.), Word users on the PC have to learn how to perform these editing functions by themselves.

## XENIX COMPUTERS

Microsoft markets a version of the UNIX operating system called XENIX. It runs on many types of microcomputers and has many features that normal UNIX systems don't have (such as easy-to-use menus for commands).

Some manufacturers who sell XENIX systems also sell Microsoft Word. Word on XENIX is similar to Word on MS-DOS. However, the screen may look different because XENIX systems can use terminals made by many different manufacturers. Many of these systems do not support the graphics capabilities of Word, so the screen display is similar to the IBM PC's monochrome display.

Word also runs on the AT&T 3B series of computers under UNIX System V.

# Appendix G

## Answers to the
## Review Questions

**Getting Started**

*1.* If the file exists, double-click on the icon for the Timeclock file. If the file does not exist, double-click the Word icon, enter your text, and save the file with the name "Timeclock."

*2.* With the mouse, point to the "t" in "the;" then drag the pointer to the "u" in "you."

*3.* Point at any letter in the sentence and double-click; then drag down the Edit menu to the Cut command.

*4.* In a business letter you would probably use NEWLINE in the opening and closing addresses. (Use the SHIFT-RETURN combination to make a new line without ending the paragraph.)

5. Use COMMAND-SPACEBAR to make a nonbreaking space. In the sentence, the spaces after "Ms." and "1" should be non-breaking, since a line break at either point could cause the reader's eye to stop abruptly.

## Chapter 1

1. To load Orders, first point at File in the menu bar and drag down to Open. Then scroll through the list box until you find "Orders" and double-click it.

2. With the I-beam in the text, clicking places the insertion point, double-clicking selects the word, and clicking with the COMMAND key selects the sentence. With the pointer in the selection bar, clicking selects the line, double-clicking selects the paragraph, and clicking with the COMMAND key selects the entire document. You can also drag the mouse (while holding down either button) to make a selection of variable length.

3. To get to the top of a document, drag the scroll box to the top of the scroll bar. To get to the bottom, drag it to the bottom of the scroll bar. To get to the middle, drag it halfway down the scroll bar.

4. Only *b* and *c* can be undone, since the Undo command only reverses an editing change, not a change in the position of the selection indicator.

5. Before giving the Print command, be sure that your printer is turned on, that it has paper in it, and that the printer is connected to your Macintosh.

**Chapter 2**

*1.* You can display the Clipboard with the Show Clipboard command. The Cut and Copy commands are the only commands that put text in the Clipboard.

*2.* Select the first three words, including the comma and the space after the comma. Delete the selection with the Cut command, move the insertion point to the "h" in "she," press the BACKSPACE key, and then type a capital S. Now move the insertion point to the left of the period and give the Paste command. Use the BACKSPACE key to remove the space and comma, and then move to the "v" in "Over;" remove the "O" and type a space and a lowercase o.

Alternatively, you can select the first three words, including the comma and the space after the comma. Press COMMAND-OPTION-X, move the insertion point to the left of the period, and press RETURN. Finish the changes as above.

*3.* Make a line of ten dashes, select them, and use the Copy command to put them in the Clipboard. Move the insertion point to the left of the end-of-file mark, press the RETURN key, and give the Paste command; then press the BACKSPACE key. Press the RETURN key again, paste the text, press the BACKSPACE key twice, and continue until you have completed the design.

**Chapter 3**

*1.* Use the Find command, and click the Find Next button twice. Use the Find command with the phrase, but select the case choice so Word will look specifically for the capital "F."

2. Before you give the Replace command, be sure that you do not select the "Match Upper/Lowercase" option in case the word "Buy-out" appears at the beginning of a sentence. This will ensure that if "Buy-out" is capitalized, "Takeover" will also be capitalized where appropriate.

3. You may have included nonrequired hyphens in the word since it is long. Try searching with various combinations of nonrequired hyphens. Or you might use "fun*y".

## Chapter 4

1. Simply open each window, re-size it, and drag it by its title bar.

2. *a* and *d*

3. If you were writing a report that compared the information in two other reports, you would use one window for the new text and a window for each of the reports being compared.

## Chapter 5

1. MacWrite files can be read directly into Word with the Open command. Text from other programs must be read through the Clipboard unless the program can write text-only files.

2. As characters

## Chapter 6

1. The easiest way to differentiate similar names is to add a letter (or letters) to one.
   *a.* mw, mwi ("i" for italics)
   *b.* tnyt, nyt ("t" for "The")
   *c.* aicer, aeder (use the word ending)

2. To see all the entries, give the Glossary command and scroll through the box. Delete an entry by selecting it and giving the Cut command.

3. The file Standard Glossary is loaded by Word when you start.

## Chapter 7

1. *a.* section
   *b.* paragraph
   *c.* character

2. *a.* underlining or italics
   *b.* boldface, underlining, or all caps
   *c.* superscript

3. Select the word, press COMMAND-SHIFT-B, press COMMAND-SHIFT-U, and then press COMMAND-SHIFT-SPACEBAR.

4. Select any character in "in conjunction", press COMMAND-OPTION-V, select "sometimes," and press RETURN.

5. Press OPTION-U, then **U**.

## Chapter 8

1. *b*, *d*, and *e*

2. *a.* Rectangular, 1.2 inches from the left margin, no first-line indentation
   *b.* Narrow, centered text
   *c.* Outdented paragraph with first line against the left margin, with ragged right margin; first line hangs over 1 inch.

3. You can separate the first line from the rest of the text with a

paragraph mark (not a NEWLINE). Select both paragraphs and format them with a 1.5-inch indent from each margin. Center the first line and justify the rest of the text.

4. Triple spacing is useful if you are going to edit the text on paper and you expect to be adding a lot of text, or if someone else may be adding numerous comments.

5. 12 lines. Justifying simply adds spaces to each line in a left-aligned paragraph to make the right margin even — it never changes the line length.

6. No, since this is done automatically by Word. Only use the Keep option if you want to be sure that the paragraph is not broken at all.

7. *a.* Decimal
   *b.* Left, center, or right
   *c.* Right or decimal

8. Press the OPTION key while you select.

## Chapter 9

*1.* *a* and *d*

2. Give the Section command and set "Number" to 2 and "Spacing" to .5 in. Use left-aligned formatting, and use non-required hyphens when possible. Also, you may want to put footnotes at the end of the text instead of at the bottom of the page.

3. Give the Open Heading command, enter (**page**, and a space. Then click the Page icon and enter). Next select the text, give the Paragraph command, and choose center alignment. Then close the window.

4. It ends the current page and starts a new page.

5. With Page Setup command

6. You can either use COMMAND-ENTER, or you can create a new section.

## Chapter 10

1. Style sheets allow you to format consistently and to make global changes to the format of a document easily.

2. The new style could be bold, centered, with 24 points below. You also could use a larger font, and could place a box around the paragraph.

## Chapter 11

1. The Typewriter driver

2. Printer Setup, Page Setup, and Print. With the Paper Feed choice of the Print command.

## Chapter 12

1. You create a main document with merge commands and field names, and create a datafile with a header of the field names followed by data records. You then use the Print Merge command.

2. OPTION-\ and OPTION-SHIFT-\

3. *a.* ≪IF policy-type = home≫ ≪ELSE≫ We also have a home policy. . . ≪ENDIF≫
   *b.* ≪IF policy-type = car≫ We have new car plans. . . ≪ENDIF≫

4. You must put quotation marks around any field's commas.

5. *a.* INCLUDE
   *b.* ASK
   *c.* IF

## Chapter 13

*1.* When you want to see if you have ended lines with a paragraph mark or NEWLINE. It is slower because it displays many more characters, such as the dots between the words.

*2.* Press COMMAND-OPTION-+, give the Character command, select small caps, and click OK.

## Chapter 14

*1.* With the Outline command

*2.* With the + and − on the outline ruler, or the + and − keys on the extended keypad

*3.* With the Renumber command

## Chapter 15

*1.* Precede the entry with ".c."

*2.* If the entry contains a semicolon, the entire entry must be in quotes. If the entry contains a quote, that quote must be preceded by an additional quote.

*3.* You can format the table of contents in the same way that you format normal text. You can also change the style sheet for the document.

### Chapter 16

*1.* Precede the entry with ".i."

*2.* Word will follow your capitalization exactly.

*3.* Hidden text can be used to leave notes for yourself or other people.

### Chapter 17

*1.* If a word does not appear in Word's dictionary or in the user dictionary, Word reports it as misspelled.

*2.* Use - for a normal hyphen, COMMAND-~ for a nonbreaking hyphen, and COMMAND-HYPHEN for a nonrequired hyphen.

### Chapter 18

*1.* Numeric sorting follows the rules of math, whereas alphanumeric sorting follows the ASCII sequence.

*2.* Word ignores the case of letters, mixing upper- and lowercase words.

### Chapter 19

*1.* Advanced LaserWriter capabilities, graphics and text, precise page layout, exact viewing of printed output, and style sheets

*2.* Use the side-by-side paragraph formatting.

# Trademarks

The following names are trademarked products of the corresponding companies.

| | |
|---|---|
| MacDraw™ | Apple Computer, Inc. |
| MacEqn™ | Software for Recognition Technologies |
| Macintosh | Apple Computer, Inc. |
| MacPaint™ | Apple Computer, Inc. |
| MacPublisher™ | Boston Software Publishers |
| MacWrite™ | Apple Computer, Inc. |
| Microsoft® | Microsoft Corporation |
| More | Living Videotext |
| PageMaker® | Aldus Corporation |
| PostScript™ | Adobe Systems, Inc. |
| ThinkTank™ | Living Videotext |

# Index

*The manuscript for this book was prepared and submitted to Osborne/McGraw-Hill in electronic form.*

*The acquisitions editor for this project was Jeff Pepper. The technical reviewer was Michael Fischer. Lyn Cordell was the project editor.*

*Text type is Times Roman. Display type is Univers.*

*Cover art is by Bay Graphics Design Associates. Cover supplier is Phoenix Color Corporation. This book was printed and bound by R. R. Donnelley & Sons Company, Crawfordsville, Indiana.*

Available at fine bookstores and computer stores everywhere.

## The Advanced Guide to Microsoft® Works
*by Donald J. Scellato*

This guide addresses the needs of experienced users by offering advanced methods for implementing Microsoft® Works. With a Macintosh™ computer and this dynamic new software, you can integrate all five functions—word processing, database, spreadsheet, graphics, and communications—for a variety of business and classroom uses. Donald Scellato, author of numerous computer books, provides detailed descriptions of intricate procedures for trouble-shooting glitches, transferring data between Microsoft® Works and other software, fine-tuning printers, and merging special hardware input from the mouse, numeric keypad, and printers. You'll also learn how to incorporate data from Microsoft® Works with Excel™ Microsoft's powerful, graphics-oriented spreadsheet software.

**$18.95 p**
0-07-881240-2, 250 pp., 7³⁄₈ x 9¹⁄₄

## Planning Big With MacProject™
*by James Halcomb*

Recently named "Mr. Planner" by *InfoWorld*, James Halcomb, a recognized authority on project management, shows Macintosh™ users how to win big in *Planning Big With MacProject™* With Halcomb's expertise and Apple's new project management software, you'll head up a project that's even more profitable than you imagined. *Planning Big With MacProject™* illustrates a five-step process that can be used by all business professionals to launch a successful venture. You'll learn how to devise the perfect plan; determine the tasks needed to reach the objective; identify, sequence, and display milestones, describe and logically interconnect tasks; and estimate completion time, resources, and costs. All business professionals can prosper from the creative ideas in *Planning Big With MacProject™*

**$16.95 p**
0-07-881219-4, 250 pp., 7³⁄₈ x 9¹⁄₄

## Multiplan™ Made Easy
### MACINTOSH™ Edition
*by Walter A. Ettlin*

Now there's a version of the Multiplan™ program tailored for your Macintosh™ computer—and the result is all business. Realize the potential of this remarkable duo with the practical instructions and skill-building exercises in this all-in-one tutorial. It covers everything from basic Mac commands and icons, to formatting worksheets, entering data, building formulas, and utilizing basic and advanced mathematical functions.

**$15.95 p**
0-07-881153-8, 200 pp., 7³⁄₈ x 9¹⁄₄

## Running Your Business With Excel™
*by Amanda C. Hixson*

Business professionals can get optimal performance from Excel™ with this guide to advanced level use of Microsoft's integrated package for the Macintosh.™ Amanda Hixson, computer book author and reviewer for *InfoWorld*, shows experienced Excel users how to master all of the capabilities of this software—spreadsheet, graphics, and data base. Advanced techniques are thoroughly explained and illustrated with practical business examples. Array calculation, charting, linking worksheets, manipulating the database, and designing macros are some of the sophisticated processes that help you in *Running Your Business With Excel™*

**$16.95 p**
0-07-881206-2, 250 pp., 7³⁄₈ x 9¹⁄₄

## Business Problem Solving With Excel™
*by James F. Molloy, William Fletcher, and Dennis P. Curtin*

*Business Problem Solving With Excel™* the first in a series of three books written by well-known authors William Fletcher and Dennis Curtin, provides detailed descriptions of analytical business tools implemented with Microsoft's Excel™ Step-by-step, you'll learn to use this super spreadsheet on your Macintosh™ to calculate breakeven points, control inventory, determine prices and discounts, analyze costs of business loans and supplier discounts, and manage gross margins. Packed with clever solutions for greater productivity, *Business Problem Solving With Excel™* is your companion in profitable business management.

**$17.95 p**
0-07-881224-0, 225 pp., 7³⁄₈ x 9¹⁄₄

## Planning and Budgeting With Excel™
*by Jeffrey R. Alves, William Fletcher, and Dennis P. Curtin*

*Planning and Budgeting With Excel™* follows *Business Problem Solving With Excel™* as the second in a series of three books written by industry notables Fletcher and Curtin. This guide for business managers presents detailed descriptions of three important financial tools—a 12-month cash budget, a pro forma income statement, and a pro forma balance sheet. Follow detailed instructions and you'll learn how to set up all three projects and customize them for your own business. Then you'll investigate a series of "what if" questions to determine the influence of various marketing and financial conditions. Even if you've never used Excel before, planning and budgeting have never been easier or more effective.

**$17.95 p**
0-07-881225-9, 225 pp., 7³⁄₈ x 9¹⁄₄

## Preparing Your Business Plan With Excel™

by William R. Osgood, William Fletcher, and Dennis P. Curtin

*Preparing Your Business Plan With Excel™* follows *Business Problem Solving With Excel™* and *Planning and Budgeting With Excel™* as the third and final title in the series of books written by Fletcher, Curtin, *et al.* For businesses large and small, this book carefully explains the development of an essential and successful plan using the Excel™ super-spreadsheet on the Macintosh.™ You'll examine the elements and format of the business plan as well as its financial aspects: sources and applications, a capital-equipment list, breakeven analysis, a pro forma budget, historical financial statements, and supporting documents. Both beginning and experienced Excel users can learn to plan and achieve vital financial goals with *Preparing Your Business Plan With Excel.*™

**$17.95p**
*0-07-881226-7, 225 pp., 7⅜ x 9¼*

## The Complete Book of Excel™ Macros

by Louis Benjamin, Don Nicholas, and the Consultants of Lighthouse Publishing Services, Ltd.

For business applications, Excel,™ Microsoft's new super spreadsheet for the Macintosh,™ features powerful macro capabilities that enable you to save valuable time by activating a series of computing steps with just one keystroke. In *The Complete Book of Excel™ Macros*, you'll find macros that can be implemented immediately to format worksheets, generate formulas, control data entry and manipulation, and for handling file security, database management, graphics display, and printing routines. In addition, appendixes provide commonly used macro command phrases that can be combined into sophisticated systems.

**$16.95p**
*0-07-881214-3, 176 pp., 6⅜ x 9¼*

## AppleWriter™ II Made Easy

by Leah Freiwald

This step-by-step tutorial teaches you how to use AppleWriter™II, the best-selling, powerful word processing system for your Apple® IIe and IIc computer. Written to include AppleWriter II, version 2.0, *AppleWriter™ II Made Easy* provides you with hands-on experience you need to produce business letters, sales reports, memos, and much more. Application exercises show you how to use specific features of AppleWriter II to develop glossaries and handle mail merge. Complete explanations of system commands, helpful screen displays, and convenient appendixes guide you smoothly through the program and make this book the perfect complement to your AppleWriter II package.

**$16.95p**
*0-07-881166-X, 210 pp., 7⅜ x 9¼*

## Apple® IIGS™ Technical Reference

by Michael Fischer

Osborne announces the book on Apple's hot new computer, the *Apple® IIGS™ Technical Reference.* Michael Fischer, the same author who wrote the acclaimed *65816/65802 Assembly Language Programming*, now looks inside the Apple IIGS and gives serious programmers detailed information on all aspects of its architecture. All three operating modes are clearly explained so you can write software that runs on 8-, 16-, or 32-bit systems. Fischer's insights on software and firmware, the Apple IIGS' powerful toolbox. Programming with color graphics, sound, desk accessories, AppleTalk,™ and other enhancements are thoroughly covered. The *Apple® IIGS™ Technical Reference* shows you how to upgrade from your Apple®II, design elegant software, and wholly understand the inner workings of Apple's incredible IIGS.

**$19.95p**
*0-07-881009-4, 350 pp., 6⅜ x 9¼*

## Apple® II User's Guide For Apple® II Plus and Apple® IIe, Third Edition

by Lon Poole, Martin McNiff and Steven Cook

The all-time best-selling *Apple® II User's Guide*, with more than 500,000 copies in print, is now available in a third edition. Apple expert Lon Poole has revised the text to show you how to use the enhanced Apple®IIe, as well as the Apple II, Apple II Plus, Apple IIe, and all peripherals. You'll also find complete instructions for using the ProDOS® and DOS 3.3 operating systems. With Poole's easy-to-follow tutorials in BASIC programming, you'll learn how to utilize all the sound and graphics capabilities of your Apple, including the double high-resolution feature of the enhanced Apple IIe. As a handy reference for years of computing with your Apple, the *Apple® II User's Guide* is an undisputed classic.

**$18.95p**
*0-07-881176-7, 512 pp., 6⅞ x 9¼*

## DisplayWrite 4™ Made Easy

by Gail Todd

Upgrading from DisplayWrite 3™ to DisplayWrite 4™? Here's the book that provides a thorough introduction to IBM's word processing software. Handle new menus, screens, and options with ease as Todd leads you from basic steps to more sophisticated procedures. The famous "Made Easy" format offers hands-on exercises and plenty of examples so you can quickly learn to produce letters and reports. All of DisplayWrite 4's new features are covered, including printing interfaces; the voice add-on; Paper Clip, the cursor control that lets you take up where you left off; and Notepad, a convenience that enables you to insert notes into documents. Todd, the author of numerous user guides and manuals, has the know-how to get you up and running fast.

**$19.95p**
*0-07-881270-4, 420 pp., 7³⁄₈ x 9¹⁄₄*

## Advanced Microsoft® Word
*by Mark Brownstein*

Incorporate the powerful new features of Word 3.0 in your work while using *Advanced Microsoft® Word* to take command of this software's sophisticated capabilities. Brownstein shows experienced users how to produce professional-looking reports, letters, and documents with the assistance of a built-in outline processor and features for automatic preparation of tables of contents and numbered sections. For your desktop publishing projects, you'll also discover how to download type fonts for several laser printers. Outlines, style sheets, five-function math, enhanced column formats, and window manipulation are among the many additional topics that are explored. Throughout the text various options, techniques, and tricks for getting the most from Word are presented with clear examples in a tightly organized format. Includes coverage of Word 2.0.

**$17.95p**
*0-07-881010-8, 400 pp., 7³⁄₈ x 9¹⁄₄*

## Using dBASE III® PLUS™
*by Edward Jones*

Osborne's top-selling title, *Using dBASE III,®* by Edward Jones, has now been updated to include Ashton-Tate's new upgrade, dBASE III® PLUS.™ With Jones' expertise you'll be in full command of all the new features of this powerful database software. Learn to design, create, and display a dBASE III PLUS database, devise entry forms with the dBASE III PLUS screen painter, generate reports, use Query files, and plug into dBASE III PLUS networking. In addition, you'll find out how to install dBASE III PLUS on a hard disk, conduct data searches, and manipulate assistant pull-down menus. *Using dBASE III® PLUS™* is

a thorough and practical handbook for both beginning and experienced dBASE III users.

**$18.95**
*0-07-881252-6, 350 pp., 7³⁄₈ x 9¹⁄₄*

## Advanced WordPerfect®: Programming and Techniques, Second Edition
*by Eric Alderman and Lawrence J. Magid*

*"Highly recommended...even I learned some new tricks and I'm a pretty old dog."*
RICHARD P. WILKES, Editor of The WordPerfectionist, National Newsletter for the WordPerfect Support Group.

*"This is it folks. The WordPerfect book you have been waiting for. I can't imagine a WordPerfect user who couldn't benefit by using this book...I can recommend purchase without reservation..."*
ANN KIMBER, President of the Seattle WordPerfect User Group.

*"...This one is worth every penny of what turns out to be nearly the lowest-priced WordPerfect book I've seen."* RICHARD SHROUT, Librarian, Member of the WordPerfect Support Group.

Make this popular IBM® PC-compatible software work above and beyond the usual word processing procedures with *Advanced WordPerfect,®* now in its second edition. Revised to cover the newly released version 4.2, *Advanced WordPerfect®* shows you how to use macros to perform office automation tasks, control mail-merge operations, produce columnar reports, handle paragraph numbering and outlining, and create indexes. Ambitious WordPerfect users will also learn how to apply WordPerfect's mathematical capabilities and how to integrate WordPerfect with other products, such as Lotus® 1-2-3,® dBASE III,® SideKick,® and ProKey.™ Two well-known columnists, Alderman and Magid have written the *best* WordPerfect book available. Read it and find out why.

**$18.95p**
*0-07-881271-2, 350 pp., 7³⁄₈ x 9¹⁄₄*
*AVAILABLE: 2/87*

For a complimentary catalog of all our current publications contact: Osborne/McGraw-Hill, 2600 Tenth Street, Berkeley, CA 94710

Phone inquiries may be made using our toll-free number. Call 800-227-0900 or 800-772-2531 (in California). TWX 910-366-7277.

Prices subject to change without notice.